Investment Management Certificate

Unit 1 – The Investment Environment

Practice & Revision Kit

Syllabus version 20

Contents

ISBN 9781 5097 4381 0

© BPP Learning Media Ltd – November 2022

Printed in the United Kingdom

Investment Management Certificate

Unit 1 – The Investment Environment

Question Bank

Unit 1 – The Investment Environment		Page Number	
		Questions	Answers
Chapter 1	Financial Markets and Institutions	3	11
Chapter 2	Ethics and Investment Professionalism	15	21
Chapter 3	The Regulation of Financial Markets and Institutions	25	49
Chapter 4	Legal Concepts	63	67
Chapter 5	Client Advice	69	75
Chapter 6	Taxation in the UK	77	85

1 Financial Markets and Institutions

Questions

The following information relates to Questions 1 to 5.

An economic target of the UK Government is price stability. To achieve this, the Government has set the target for inflation at 2%. If the annual rate of inflation falls below 1% or goes above 3%, then the Governor of the Bank of England must write an open letter to the Chancellor of the Bank of England.

1   **Interest rates in the UK are set following a meeting of the:**

     A   Debt Management Office

     B   Treasury

     C   Financial Policy Committee

     D   Monetary Policy Committee

2   **The control of interest rates as a means of managing the economy may best be described as a key element of:**

     A   Fiscal policy

     B   Monetary policy

     C   Industrial policy

     D   Keynesian policy

3   **Faced with a 'double dip' recession, the Government announces that it intends to stimulate the economy by pursuing an expansionary fiscal policy. Which of the following would it be least likely to pursue?**

     A   Increasing government expenditure

     B   Increasing the amount it collects in taxation with no change in spending

     C   Borrowing more money so as to implement a road building policy

     D   Maintaining current government spending plans while not reducing taxation

4   **The UK Government must borrow each year to cover the amount by which its expenditure exceeds its income. This amount is known as the:**

     A   National debt

     B   PSNCR

     C   PNBR

     D   Current account deficit

5 **The Treasury will fund the PSNCR by:**

A Borrowing from the Bank of England

B Borrowing from the Federal Reserve

C Issuing government shares

D Issuing gilts

---

6 **Which of the following is/are correct with regard to proxies?**

I A proxy has the right to speak in a general meeting

II A proxy may vote on a show of hands

III A proxy may vote on a poll

A III only

B I and II

C II and III

D I, II and III

---

7 **Which of the following conditions is/are correct for a 'premium' Stock Exchange listing?**

I The expected market value of shares must be at least £30m

II Accounts must have been approved by an auditor for at least the last five years

III At least 10% of the shares must, at the time of admission, be held by the public

A I only

B I and II

C II and III

D I and III

---

8 **How long after the half-year must interim results be produced for a listed company?**

A One month

B Six months

C Two months

D Four months

---

9 **The Disclosure Guidance and Transparency Rules (DTR) impose various requirements. Which of the following is not such a requirement?**

A Require directors of listed companies to report transactions in shares of the company

B Impose obligations on listed companies to keep shareholders informed of price-sensitive information

C Impose disclosure requirements in cases where there is suspicion of money laundering or terrorist financing

D Impose notification requirements on major shareholders of listed companies

10 **When an individual acquires a material interest in a company, the company should be notified of this within:**

   A   One business day

   B   Two business days

   C   Three business days

   D   Four business days

11 **How many days' notice is usually required for a General Meeting of a company where a special resolution is to be passed?**

   A   7 calendar days

   B   14 calendar days

   C   21 calendar days

   D   28 calendar days

12 **How many shareholders must be present at an Annual General Meeting (AGM) to pass a valid resolution?**

   A   2 persons personally present or their proxies

   B   5 persons personally present or their proxies

   C   10 persons personally present or their proxies

   D   20 persons personally present or their proxies

13 **A shareholder who owns 17½% of the shares of ABC plc, a listed company, sells part of his shareholding, leaving a holding after the sale of 16½%. What disclosure obligations does the shareholder have?**

   A   Disclose the sale to the company concerned within two business days

   B   Disclose the sale to the company concerned by noon the next day

   C   Disclose the sale to the market via a Regulated Information Service within two business days

   D   Disclose the sale to the market via a Regulated Information Service by noon the next day

14 **Which of the following entities is responsible for considering applications by a company for its shares to be listed?**

   A   The London Stock Exchange

   B   The Department for Business, Energy & Industrial Strategy

   C   Financial Conduct Authority

   D   Her Majesty's Treasury

15 **How is price-sensitive information required to be disseminated by listed companies?**

   A   Through the press

   B   Through the analysts of securities houses

   C   Through a Regulated Information Service

   D   Through the Annual Report

The following information relates to Questions 16 and 17.

Shearer plc is a medium-sized company which intends to have a listing on the Alternative Investment Market (AIM). It is hoping to raise £1,500,000 by issuing ordinary share capital. Because the company is not very well known, it is not expected to be a very liquid stock when traded but will be held by a small number of qualified investors.

16   Given that the company intends to list on AIM, what is the least market value of the shares that the company could have offered?

    A   £200,000

    B   £700,000

    C   £7,000,000

    D   No minimum

17   The AIM listing proves to be successful. However, two years later the company has a dispute with their Nominated Adviser (NOMAD) and the NOMAD ceases to work for the company. What action will be taken regarding the company as a result, if they fail to appoint a replacement NOMAD within 30 days?

    A   The firm's listing will be suspended

    B   No action will be taken

    C   The firm will be fined

    D   The NOMAD will be fined

18   Which one of the following is not a requirement for a company listed on the AIM?

    A   The company must have a broker

    B   The company must publish immediately price-sensitive information

    C   The company's free float must be at least 25%

    D   The company must have an LSE-approved NOMAD

19   Which entity regulates the AIM?

    A   The Financial Conduct Authority

    B   The Bank of England

    C   The London Stock Exchange

    D   The United Kingdom Listing Authority

20 **The ordinary shares of Abercombe Fookes plc, a company listed on the London Stock Exchange, have been traded in high volumes in recent weeks. You have been asked to check if all the required disclosures have been made where individual shareholdings have changed.**

The shares all carry the same voting rights. Which one of the following events concerning shareholdings in Abercombe Fookes plc must be publicised in order to comply with the Disclosure and Transparency Rules (DTR)?

A   On 10 March, the shareholding of Greenhouse Holdings plc moved from 0% to 1.0%

B   On 5 April, Brian Hewlett sold shares so that his interest in the company dropped from 2.9% to 1.7%

C   On 21 April, Cranford Investment Funds bought more shares, moving their holding from 5.9% to 6.1%

D   On 4 May, Streetford Capital reduced their shareholding from 6.8% to 6.1%

21 **The inability to sell an asset quickly at a fair price is associated with:**

A   Trade failure risk

B   Liquidity risk

C   Exchange rate risk

D   Financial risk

22 **Which of the following is not a potential benefit of high-frequency trading?**

A   Lower transaction costs

B   Reduced financial exclusion

C   More efficient market pricing

D   Improved liquidity

23 **A shareholder has considered the documentation relating to a forthcoming company meeting and wishes to appoint another person to vote against a particular resolution. The shareholder should appoint:**

A   A general proxy

B   A two-way proxy

C   An agency proxy

D   An attorney proxy

24 **A Eurobond is:**

A   Denominated in a currency not native to where it is issued

B   Sold only to European investors

C   Sold in the currency of the issuer's own country and internationally tradeable

D   Alternatively known as a Matilda bond

25 **Which of the following is least likely to mitigate or reduce the agency problem?**

A   Separation of ownership and control

B   Separation of roles in the organisation

C   Remuneration of managers that is related to economic value added

D   Executive share option plans

26 **Which entity has stated its single mission as being: 'to promote the good of the people of the United Kingdom by maintaining monetary and financial stability'?**

A   Her Majesty's Treasury

B   Financial Conduct Authority

C   Bank of England

D   Prudential Regulation Authority

27 **Corradex plc has declared its first dividend. On which day of the week will the ex-dividend date fall?**

A   Tuesday

B   Wednesday

C   Thursday

D   Friday

28 **Which of the following is a requirement for a company to be eligible for the LSE's High Growth Segment (HGS)?**

A   Prior membership of the AIM

B   Compound annual growth in revenue of 30% over three years

C   Incorporation in the UK

D   Minimum free float of 10% at initial public offering

29 **Which of the following is not an admission criteria for a listing on the AQSE Growth Market?**

A   Have at least 36 months of audited accounts

B   Have at least 10% free float

C   Demonstrate appropriate levels of corporate governance, including having at least one independent non-executive director

D   Appoint and retain a corporate adviser at all times

30 **Which of the following is the best description of the reporting requirements of a company in accordance with Section 172 of the Companies Act?**

A Section 172 of the Companies Act requires a director to act in the way they consider most appropriate to enhance shareholder value

B Section 172 of the Companies Act requires a director to act in the way they consider, in good faith, would be most likely to promote the success of the company for the benefit of its members as a whole

C Section 172 of the Companies Act requires a director to act in the way they consider appropriate to most likely enhance the success of the board of directors and their stewardship responsibilities

D Section 172 of the Companies Act requires a director to establish effective audit, risk and internal controls and to oversee the procedures for managing the risks the company faces

31 **Which one of the following statements best described the issue known as 'groupthink'?**

A Groupthink can be described as good corporate governance that promotes diversity within the board

B Groupthink is a theoretical concept that suggests that board directors may have individual skill and ideas, and these can be considered by the group before a final decision is made

C Groupthink suggests that a board of directors may make the final decision, however they will consult with other stakeholders, such as the employees, before the decision is reached

D Groupthink can be described as behaviour that minimises conflicts and results in consensus decision making

32 **Which of the following statements regarding board diversity are correct?**

I The Hampton-Alexander review recommended that all FTSE 100 boards have at least one director from an ethnic background

II The Hampton-Alexander review set a voluntary target of 33% women representation on FTSE 350 company boards

III The Parker review recommended that all FTSE 100 boards have at least one director from an ethnic background

IV The Parker review set a voluntary target of 33% women representation on FTSE 350 company boards

A I and III

B II and III

C II and IV

D I and IV

Answers

1   **D**   The Monetary Policy Committee (MPC) of the Bank of England was given responsibility for setting interest rates in the UK. In many economies, emphasis is placed on controlling inflation by using interest rates, and in the UK, this is carried out by the Monetary Policy Committee (MPC)

2   **B**   Monetary policy is the area of government economic policy making that is concerned with changes in the amount of money in circulation. The key tools used are the control of money supply and the setting of interest rates

3   **B**   Increasing the level of taxation would take money out of the economy and if the Government does not increase its level of spending to replace the reduced spending the effect would be contractionary

4   **B**   PSNCR (Public Sector Net Cash Requirement) is the term used by the UK Government to describe this borrowing requirement

5   **D**   The PSNCR is the Government's borrowing requirement which is funded by issuing UK government bonds, known as gilts

6   **D**   Following Companies Act 2006 changes, proxies may exercise all the powers the member would have if they were present in person. Any member entitled to attend and vote at a company meeting may appoint another person (the proxy) to attend and vote on their behalf. A proxy has the right to vote on a show of hands and also in a poll. A proxy is valid for the general meeting and any adjournment, and can take one of two forms, being a general proxy, appointing a person to vote as they think fit, bearing in mind what is said at the meeting, and secondly, a special proxy, appointing a person to vote for or against a particular resolution, sometimes referred to as a 'two-way proxy'

7   **D**   The company must provide three years (not five) of audited accounts to the UKLA along with other documentation at least 48 hours prior to the hearing to decide the listing application. The expected aggregate market value of all the securities to be listed must be at least £30m for shares (and at least £200,000 for debt securities). 10% of the listed securities must be held by the public

8   **C**   Interim results must be produced within two months of the end of the half-year

9   **C**   Listed companies are subject to the FCA's disclosure guidance and transparency rules (DTR). These deal with reporting transactions in a company's securities (including derivatives) by 'persons discharging managerial responsibilities' (PDMRs), which includes directors. PDMRs and their connected persons must notify the listed company concerned within four business days of a transaction. The DTRs do not impose anti-money laundering disclosures

10   **B**   A material interest is an investor who has a 3% or more holding in the company (aggregated with those investments of connected parties, eg spouses, infant child but not siblings). Once the investor reaches 3% and every time the investor changes the holding by going through a percentage point, eg 6.7% to 7.1%, the investor must inform the company by the end of the second business day following the day of trade, ie T + 2

11 **B** Any meeting of a company other than an annual general meeting (AGM) is called a general meeting. General meetings must be called by giving not less than 14 calendar days' notice. A special resolution involves a voting majority of 75% or more and would be required for certain major decisions, such as changing the company's name or undertaking a share buyback

12 **A** In general, a 'quorum' is achieved when two members (or their proxies) are present

13 **A** This relates to the major interests disclosure requirements under the Disclosure and Transparency Rules (DTR)

14 **C** The UK Listing Authority is a function of the Financial Conduct Authority (FCA), which is the 'competent authority'

15 **C** Disclosures are made through a Regulated Information Service (RIS), also known as a primary information provider (PIP)

16 **D** If going for full listing, the minimum expected market value would be £700,000 of shares. However, since the company is to be AIM-listed, there is no minimum value

17 **A** The NOMAD is retained to advise the directors once an AIM listing is granted. Should the company lose its NOMAD, it must appoint a new one within 30 days or the company will have its listing suspended

18 **C** Full listed companies, and not AIM-listed companies, must have 25% free float

19 **C** Although the UKLA (part of the FCA) regulates the Full List, the London Stock Exchange (LSE) regulates the AIM, publishing the AIM Rules and monitoring compliance with them. AIM is also known as an exchange-regulated market, as it is essentially regulated by the LSE

20 **C** The change must be publicised if the 3% threshold is crossed in either direction, and if full percentage points above 3% are crossed, again in either direction. Therefore, a movement from 5.9% to 6.1% is an example of a transaction that requires disclosure, as this is an incremental movement that moves through the 6% threshold

21 **B** Liquidity risk is the risk of not being able to sell an asset quickly with the potential for loss of value. Liquidity risk therefore tends to be higher in low volume markets and emerging markets. Any asset that cannot easily be sold quickly at a reasonable price is 'illiquid'. During the financial crisis of the late 2000s, mortgage-backed securities became illiquid when the market for them effectively seized up, and there were no ready buyers

22 **B** Reduced exclusion of individuals from financial markets and products will not stem from high-frequency trading (HFT), but the other options listed, such as lower transaction costs, improved liquidity and more efficient market pricing are all identified as benefits

23 **B** A two-way proxy (or 'special proxy') is used to appoint another person to vote in a particular way, either for or against a resolution. A proxy is valid for the general meeting and any adjournment, and can take one of two forms, one being a two-way proxy and the other being a general proxy, where a person is appointed to vote as they think fit, bearing in mind what is said at the actual meeting itself

24 **A** A Eurobond is a bond denominated in a currency that is not native to its place of issue, ie these are bonds that are denominated in a currency other than that of the country in which they are issued

25 **A** The separation of ownership and control that is characteristic of larger firms is one of the main reasons that the agency problem arises. This separation leads to the principal–agent problem, which arises because owners and managers generally have different interests. Owners want to maximise the value of the firm, while managers want to maximise their own interests such as salary and other benefits. It is unlikely that the managers' pursuit of their own interests will maximise a firm's value – hence the 'agency problem'

26 **C** This stated mission echoes the Bank of England's original Charter of 1694: "Now know ye, That we being desirous to promote the public good and benefit of our people...". The Bank of England's Monetary Policy Committee (MPC) can focus on monetary stability and the Financial Policy Committee (FPC) focuses on the Bank's objective to protect and enhance financial stability, through identifying and taking action to remove or reduce systemic risks, with a view to protecting and enhancing the resilience of the UK financial system

27 **C** The ex-dividend date (ie buying the share without the entitlement to the dividend) will always fall on a Thursday. The on register day, also known as the books closed date, falls on a Friday, as a result of shares having a settlement period of T+2, then the ex-dividend date will start on the Thursday. The last cum-div date will be on the Wednesday

28 **D** Previous AIM membership is not required. Revenue compound annual growth rate (CAGR) must be at least 20% (not 30%) over three years. The High Growth Segment (HGS) is designed to attract high growth, mid-sized UK and European companies aspiring to an official listing. An HGS company is larger than a typical AIM company and normally aspires to ultimately join the premium segment of the main market. A HGS company must be incorporated in any EEA state, be a commercial company, issuing equity shares only, have a minimum free float of 10% at initial public offering, and demonstrate historic revenue (on a compound annual growth rate basis) of 20% over three years

29 **A** Having at least 36 months of audited accounts is is not an admission criteria for a listing on the Aquis Stock Exchange (AQSE) Growth Market, as the requirement is 24 months of audited accounts. A company must have at least 10% free float, being shares in the hands of the public, demonstrate appropriate levels of corporate governance, including having at least one independent non-executive director and appoint and retain an AQSE corporate adviser at all times

30 **B** Section 172 of the Companies Act requires a director to act in the way they consider, in good faith, would be most likely to promote the success of the company for the benefit of its members as a whole. All UK-incorporated companies (other than small and medium-sized companies) will be required to publish in their strategic report a separately identifiable statement describing how the directors have had regard to fulfilling their statutory duty

31 **D** 'Groupthink' can be described as a psychological behaviour of minimising conflicts and reaching a consensus decision without critically evaluating alternative ideas, leading to unchallenged, poor quality decisions being reached. It can be argued that a diverse group of directors with different skills, backgrounds and experiences may approach problems from a greater range of perspectives and raise challenging questions. This may help to minimise the risk of 'groupthink'

32 **B** The Hampton-Alexander review set a voluntary target of 33% women representation on FTSE 350 company boards. The Parker review recommended that all FTSE 100 boards have at least one director from an ethnic background

2 Ethics and Investment Professionalism

Questions

1   The senior management of a firm aims to ensure adoption of a corporate culture throughout the firm. Which of the following is least likely to be an effective method for achieving this?

    A   Outsourcing

    B   Training

    C   Setting an example

    D   Communication

2   Jerome is told during his induction of the firm's emphasis on managerial responsibility for ethical behaviour combined with a concern for the law. This approach might best be described as being which of the following?

    A   Supervision-based

    B   Integrity-based

    C   Rules-based

    D   Enforcement-based

3   There has been much discussion in recent years of different regulatory approaches in the financial services industry, and of the central concepts on which regulation is based.

Outcomes-based regulation can be expected to have the result that:

    A   Appropriate examination passes will be required for staff in a wider range of roles

    B   Customer confidence will increase and firms will experience increased business

    C   Continuing Professional Development will be given greater prominence

    D   Relatively more of firms' income will be generated from fees compared with commissions

4   Diana Jones is an analyst working for ABC Investment Advisers. One of ABC's clients in the mergers and acquisitions department is XYZ Inc. and ABC's President is a director of XYZ. Diana has been asked to write a report on XYZ. Which one of the following courses of action is most appropriate?

    A   Do not write a report due to the directorship held by ABC's President

    B   Write a report of a purely factual nature

    C   Write a report but disclose in it the relationship between ABC and XYZ

    D   Do not write the report if it would express a favourable opinion on XYZ

5   John Maple recently left his employer to start a new business. He did not sign a non-compete agreement with his old employer and is operating in the same industry. When he leaves, he contacts his old clients to tell them of his new business, using the telephone directory to obtain their telephone numbers. Which one of the following statements regarding John's conduct is most appropriate?

A   John has breached Standard IVA – Loyalty by contacting his old clients

B   John has breached Standard VB – Communication with Clients and Prospective Clients by contacting clients using the phone book

C   John has breached both Standard IVA – Loyalty and Standard VB – Communication with Clients and Prospective Clients

D   John has not breached any Standards

6   An investment professional presents some research about a company at a client meeting. The presentation includes various data and charts. She makes no mention of the fact that the research comes from a financial newspaper. Which Standard in the CFA Code of Ethics has she most clearly breached?

A   Standard IB – Independence and Objectivity

B   Standard IC – Misrepresentation

C   Standard IIIC – Suitability

D   Standard VC – Record Retention

7   'Members and candidates must determine applicable fiduciary duty and must comply with such duty to persons and interests to whom it is owed.' In which Standard of the CFA Code of Ethics is this stated?

A   Standard IB – Independence and Objectivity

B   Standard IC – Misrepresentation

C   Standard IIIA – Loyalty, Prudence, and Care

D   Standard VB – Communication with Clients and Prospective Clients

8   When communicating information about investment performance, investment professionals may employ, as an accepted set of common standards:

A   The City Code

B   The Code of Market Conduct

C   Fact find principles

D   Global Investment Performance Standards

9   Which one of the following is *least likely* to be a breach of Standard IIB – Market Manipulation?

A   Spreading a rumour about the poor health of a company's CEO to depress its share price

B   Transacting in back-to-back buy/sell strategies in order to exploit tax loopholes

C   Distorting the price of a security by issuing a misleading statement

D   Building a dominant position in a commodity in order to influence the price of a related derivative

10   **The term 'material' in the phrase 'material non-public information' refers to information that is likely to significantly affect the market price of the issuing company's securities, or that is:**

    A   Derived by the financial analyst from direct communication with an issuing company's management

    B   Likely to preclude the financial analyst or the analyst's firm from rendering unbiased or objective advice

    C   Acquired by the financial analyst from a special or confidential relationship with the issuing company

    D   Likely to be considered important by reasonable investors in determining whether to trade a particular security

11   **Jane Doe is a junior research analyst with Howard & Sons, a brokerage and investment banking firm. Howard's mergers and acquisitions department, which handles mergers and acquisitions, has represented Britland Company in all its acquisitions for the past 20 years. Two of Howard's senior officers are directors of various Britland subsidiaries. Doe has been asked to write a research report on Britland. In the context of the Code and Standards, what is Doe's best course of action?**

    A   Doe may write the report provided the officers agree not to alter it

    B   Doe may write the report if she discloses Howard & Sons' special relationship with Britland in the report

    C   Doe may write the report but must refrain from expressing any opinions because of the special relationships between the two companies

    D   Doe should not write the report because the two Howard & Sons officers are 'constructive insiders'

12   **Neil Smith is on a business trip to Japan to meet the management of one of the firms that he covers as a research analyst. He is currently rating the company as a 'buy'. While in a meeting, he is informed by the management that they are anticipating significant delivery problems at most of their factories and that this will have a negative impact on sales. No other analyst currently knows this information. Which of the following statements is most accurate?**

    A   Neil must change his recommendation to a sell, as to not include the information would breach his fiduciary duty to his clients

    B   Neil must not change his recommendation under any circumstances as to do so would breach the Code and Standards on the use of material non-public information

    C   Neil should encourage the company to disseminate the news to the market before publishing his own updated recommendation

    D   Neil must not issue a recommendation on the stock until the extent of the delivery problem is known

13   **Which one of the following is most likely to conflict with CFA Institute Code and Standards?**

A   Analysts may change their investment recommendations without obtaining approval from their supervisor

B   Personal account transactions by analysts should not be scrutinised for confidentiality reasons

C   A portfolio manager should conduct a fact-find about a new customer before undertaking investment action on the customer's behalf

D   A portfolio manager receives gifts from clients but discloses these to his employer

14   **Burt Hoffman is a portfolio manager who has the pension plan of a company as an account. The company's directors are asking him to vote in their favour at a forthcoming stakeholders' meeting. Since the account is a large one, Burt does not wish to offend the directors and risk losing it.**

In addition, Burt puts the transactions of the account through a broker who gives Burt useful investment advice on European equities. This information is of no use in relation to the pension plan account but is useful for other accounts. The broker gives best execution and offers very low commissions.

Burt reviews the arguments for and against the directors and decides that the balance of argument is in their favour and votes for them. Which of the following statements is most appropriate?

A   Burt has violated CFA Standards by voting for the directors and by using the broker for the account's transactions

B   Burt has violated CFA Standards by voting for the directors

C   Burt has violated CFA Standards by using the broker for the account's transactions

D   Burt has not violated CFA Standards

15   **Which of the following is most appropriate with respect to Standard IA – Knowledge of the Law for an analyst who is a CFA Institute member operating overseas, where the local laws are less strict than US laws and CFA Institute Code and Standards and where local laws apply?**

A   The analyst must follow US laws in conducting his investment activities, since he is a US citizen

B   The analyst must follow local laws because they are less strict than US law and CFA Institute Code and Standards

C   The analyst must follow the appropriate international laws, since there is a conflict between the level of severity of local and US laws and regulations

D   The analyst must follow CFA Institute Code and Standards since they are stricter than the local laws

16   Matthew Brown has just completed a quantitative analysis of stock returns relative to book value for a number of stocks over the last year. Ben Evans has just overheard a conversation that a company is likely to be reporting higher earnings this year. Both now issue research reports on the basis of the above. Which one of the following statements is most appropriate?

A   Both Matthew and Ben have breached Standards

B   Neither has breached Standards

C   Ben has breached Standards

D   Matthew has breached Standards

17   Lucy Miller is an analyst for the seafood industry. She has just received a package from the Lobster Shank, a company that is not one of her existing clients, containing 100 kilos of lobster tails – a delicacy. Miller estimates that the tails are worth over £6,000. According to the CFA Institute Code and Standards Lucy should:

A   Advise her superior of the gift and split it with them

B   Accept the gift, since it is from a company rather than a client

C   Refuse the gift because the Standards of Professional Conduct prohibit analysts from receiving gifts from the companies or industries they review

D   Return the gift, as it is a large gift from a company

18   Which of the following is covered by the CFA's Standard III: Duties to Clients?

A   Misconduct

B   Knowledge of the law

C   Misrepresentation

D   Performance presentation

19   Which of the following is regarded as positive behavioural indicator, with regard to ethical and compliance-driven behaviour along with good corporate governance?

A   The application of strong internal procedures

B   Overly encouraging risk-taking and applying undue pressure

C   An unwillingness to conduct proper research into a particular product

D   An ability to rationalise unethical behaviour as the other party is acting in a similar manner

20   Which of the following would be an example of plagiarism?

I   Using excerpts from an article, along with some graphs, without referring to the original source

II   Using non-written information obtained during a client presentation, without the required permission

III   Using a report obtained from another firm, without identifying the source of the report, however a few changes have been made to the original report

A   I only

B   I and II

C   I, II and III

D   I and III

Answers

1   **A**   Outsourcing is unlikely to have a direct positive effect on the corporate culture, and might even weaken it. It is important that a strong ethical and corporate culture is led by the behaviour of management. Good corporate ethics can be enhanced by many factors typically found in companies with good corporate governance. These include independent directors, strong internal procedures and fair remuneration packages that do not overly encourage risk taking. It is also helpful to encourage employees to take some degree of personal responsibility for their actions, and not to follow instructions unquestioningly or respond to peer pressure that condones some form of unethical activity or behaviour

2   **B**   An integrity-based approach combines a concern for the law with an emphasis on managerial responsibility for ethical behaviour. The CFA Code of Ethics sets out ethical standards, including acting with integrity, competence, diligence, respect and in an ethical manner with the public, clients, prospective clients, employers, employees, colleagues in the investment profession, and other participants in the global capital markets. It also focuses on placing the integrity of the investment profession and the interests of clients above their own personal interests, and promoting the integrity and viability of the global capital markets for the ultimate benefit of society

3   **B**   Outcomes-based regulation focuses on outcomes for consumers rather than the detail of rule compliance. The use of principles and outcomes-based regulation to promote ethical and fair outcomes, and the ability to apply this framework in practice for the consumer is a central concept on which regulations are based

4   **C**   Standard VI: Conflicts of Interest – A: Disclosure of Conflicts – Disclosure of Conflicts is the relevant Standard. Members and candidates must make full and fair disclosure of all matters that could reasonably be expected to impair their independence and objectivity, or interfere with respective duties to their clients, prospective clients and employer. Members and Candidates must ensure that such disclosures are prominent

5   **D**   John can contact his old clients once he has left his old company, provided that he does not use his client lists to do so. With regard to Standard IV: Duties to employers - A Loyalty - when investment professionals plan to leave their current employers, there is scope for conflicts to arise, but they still have a duty to act in their employer's best interests until their resignation becomes effective. For example, the investment professional must be careful not to misappropriate trade secrets, misuse confidential information, solicit the employer's clients or misappropriate client lists

6   **B**   Standard I: Professionalism – C: Misrepresentation – covers plagiarism of this and other types. Members and candidates must not knowingly make any misrepresentations relating to investment analysis, recommendations, actions, or other professional activities. A misrepresentation is any untrue statement, or any other statement that is false or misleading. It may also be omission of a fact or a failure to correct a known misunderstanding

7   **C**   A fiduciary is an individual or institution that is in a position of trust: that is, they have the duty of acting for the benefit of another party in respect of matters that come within the scope of the relationship between them

8   **D**   The Global Investment Performance Standards (GIPS) have been developed by the CFA Institute as a common, accepted set of standards for the investment management industry. Although compliance is voluntary, investment professionals and their firms are encouraged to adopt the standards, and they are becoming more widely used. All performance statements must be fair, accurate and complete

9   **B**   Buying and selling securities for tax reasons, known as tax-loss harvesting, is allowed. Standard II: Integrity of capital markets – B: Market Manipulation – states that members and candidates must not engage in practices that distort prices or artificially inflate trading volume with the intent to mislead market participants. Market manipulation is often related to transactions that artificially distort prices or volumes of securities traded, or taking a dominant position in a security in order to manipulate the price of a related derivative, or the dissemination of false or misleading information in order to artificially inflate or decrease a security price

10   **D**   Standard II: Integrity of capital markets - A: Material Non-public Information – is the relevant Standard. 'Material' means that disclosure is likely to have an impact on the price of a security, or that reasonable investors would want to know the information before making an investment decision. The reliability of the source of the information is also a factor in determining whether it is material. The less reliable the source is, then the less likely it is to be material

11   **B**   Standard VI: Conflicts of Interest - A: Disclosure of Conflicts – is the relevant Standard. Members and candidates must make full and fair disclosure of all matters that could reasonably be expected to impair their independence and objectivity, or interfere with respective duties to their clients, prospective clients and employer. The Standard considers potential conflicts between investment professionals, their employer, clients and prospective clients. The emphasis is on full disclosure of conflicts, so that all the parties can evaluate the objectivity of advice or investment actions being taken

12   **C**   Standard II: Integrity of capital markets – A: Material Non-public Information – is the relevant Standard. Neil cannot trade or cause others to trade on the information unless it has been disseminated to the public. 'Non-public' means that the information has not been disseminated in the market and investors have not had a chance to react to it. In the situation that an analyst is given information by a company, it is still non-public information until it has been disseminated to other investors in the market

13   **B**   Standard IV: Duties to employers – C: Responsibilities of Supervisors – is the relevant Standard. Checks should be carried out by supervisors. Members and candidates must make reasonable efforts to ensure that anyone subject to their supervision or authority complies with applicable laws, rules, regulations, and the Code and Standards. Supervisors are responsible for their subordinates' ethical behaviour

14   **D**   Standard III: Duties to Clients - A: Loyalty, Prudence and Care – states that members 'have a duty of loyalty to their clients and must act with reasonable care and exercise prudent judgment'. They 'must act for the benefit of their clients and place their clients' interests before their employer's or their own interests'. Burt has not violated the Standards. His vote for the directors is supported by his opinion on their arguments. His choice of broker is in the interests of clients because the broker offers best execution and low commissions

15   **D**   Standard I: Professionalism – A: Knowledge of the Law – is the relevant Standard. The rule of thumb is to follow the stricter of applicable legal requirements, and the Code and Standards

16   **A**   Standard V: Investment analysis, recommendations and actions – A: Diligence and Reasonable Basis – is the relevant Standard. A longer period of analysis would be required for Matthew. Members and candidates must: exercise diligence, independence, and thoroughness in analysing investments, making investment recommendations and taking investment actions. They must also have a reasonable and adequate basis, supported by appropriate research and investigation, for any investment analysis, recommendation, or action. This applies to primary research, secondary research or third-party research. Investment professionals must make reasonable and diligent efforts to ensure that the research is sound

17   **D**   Standard I: Professionalism – B: Independence and Objectivity – suggests modest gifts and entertainment are acceptable. Every member should avoid situations that might cause, or be perceived to cause, a loss of independence or objectivity in recommending investments or taking investment actions. Gifts from clients are less of a problem than gifts from a company

18   **D**   Performance presentation is part of Standard III: Duties to Clients, as is Loyalty, Prudence and Care, Fair Dealing, Suitability and Preservation of Confidentiality. Misconduct, Knowledge of the Law, and Misrepresentation, along with Independence and Objectivity are all elements of Standard I: Professionalism

19   **A**   Good corporate ethics can be enhanced by many factors typically found in companies with good corporate governance. These include independent directors, strong internal procedures and fair remuneration packages that do not overly encourage risk-taking. However, there are many factors that can lead to unethical behaviour, including undue pressure or incentives to perform; an ability to blame others, rather than an individual accepting personal responsibility for their actions; an ability to rationalise unethical behaviour, where the other party is being unethical too; a conflicts of interest that can affect judgement; as well as a lack of rigour due to overcapacity, such as an unwillingness to conduct proper research into a product

20   **C**   All of these statements are examples of plagiarism – Standard I: Professionalism, within Misrepresentation. Using excerpts from an article, along with some graphs, without referring to the original source or obtaining permission; using non-written information obtained during a client presentation, without the required permission (as the Standard also applies to oral communications); and using a report obtained from another firm, without identifying the source of the report, even if a few changes have been made to the original report, as an individual must not represent themselves as the author of that report

3 The Regulation of Financial Markets and Institutions

Questions

1   Within MiFID, which of the following is the responsibility of the host state regulator, for activities of a branch within the host state?

A   Conduct of business

B   Authorisation

C   Client assets

D   Capital adequacy

2   Which of the following instruments does MiFID cover?

    I   Money market instruments

    II   Collective investment schemes

    III   Derivative instruments for transferring credit risk

A   I, II and III

B   I and II

C   I and III

D   II and III

The following information relates to Questions 3 to 8.

The Market in Financial Instruments Directive (MiFID) was implemented in the UK in 2007, and replaced the Investment Services Directive.

3   Which of the following trading venues is not within the scope of MiFID?

A   A multilateral trading facility (MTF)

B   The NYSE

C   Systematic internalisers

D   An organised trading facility (OTF)

4   A number of organisations are excluded from the scope of MiFID. Which of the following would not be excluded?

A   Group treasury activities

B   Operating a multilateral trading facility (MTF)

C   Insurance companies

D   Professional investors investing only for themselves

5   **The regulator's organisational and systems and controls requirements are implemented through a set of high-level rules known as:**

A   The common platform

B   The Stewardship Code

C   The trading platform

D   Principles for Businesses

6   **MiFID is a European Union directive and this means that:**

A   It may be addressed to a state, person or company and is immediately binding but only on the recipient

B   Once issued, EU member state governments are required to alter national laws to conform within a specified period

C   It has the force of law in every EU state without the need for national legislation

D   Under the principle of subsidiarity, it may be adopted if a particular member state believes it will be beneficial

7   **Throughout which group of States may member firms use domestic authorisation to passport core investment business, under the terms of MiFID?**

A   EEA

B   EU

C   EEC

D   G20

8   **Which of the following financial instruments would not be covered under the terms of MiFID?**

A   An Exchange Traded Fund (ETF) investing in US equities

B   Treasury bills

C   A contract of insurance

D   A futures contract based upon snowfall

9   **Which of the following is not part of the role of ESMA?**

A   Working with the EBA and EIOPA

B   Rule-making for the FCA and PRA

C   Continuing the work of the CESR

D   Prohibiting financial products that threaten financial stability

10   **The European Market Infrastructure Regulation (EMIR) comprises a set of standards for all of the following, except which one?**

A   Trade repositories

B   Central counterparties

C   Equities settlement systems

D   Over-the-counter derivatives

11   **For an individual with a personal pension plan, from what age is flexi-access drawdown currently available?**

    A   50 years

    B   55 years

    C   57 years

    D   65 years

12   **Which of the following are categorised as a regulated activity and require authorisation?**

    I   Arranging deals in investments

    II   Establishing a collective investment scheme

    III Sending dematerialised instructions

    A   I and II

    B   II and III

    C   I and III

    D   I, II and III

13   **Which of the following constitute a regulated activity as defined by the Financial Services and Markets Act 2000?**

    I   Provision of investment advice

    II   Fund management

    III Acting as an unremunerated trustee

    A   I and II

    B   I and III

    C   II and III

    D   I, II and III

14   **Which of the following statements is/are true in the event that a regulated activity is undertaken with an unauthorised firm?**

    I   Any contract entered into is unenforceable by the unauthorised firm

    II   Any contract entered into is unenforceable by either party

    III The maximum penalty is an unlimited fine and a two-year imprisonment sentence

    A   I and III

    B   II and III

    C   I only

    D   III only

15 **Which of the following are exempt from the requirement to be authorised to conduct regulated activities?**

     I   Members of a Recognised Investment Exchange

     II   Appointed representatives

     III   Lenders of regulated mortgages

A I and II

B II only

C II and III

D I and III

16 **The Senior Management Arrangements, Systems and Controls Sourcebook (SYSC) in the regulatory Handbook contains the Remuneration Codes. It is most correct to state that the Remuneration Codes:**

A Apply to senior management in all listed companies

B Prohibit the use of guaranteed bonuses

C State that non-financial metrics should not be used in setting the performance-related component of remuneration

D Require at least 50% of bonuses to comprise non-cash instruments

17 **The following are all specified investments under the Financial Services and Markets Act (FSMA) 2000, except:**

A ADRs

B Life assurance policies

C Deep discount bonds

D Currencies

18 **Which of the following is not one of the purposes of the two consultation papers that were issued to implement Part 4 of the Financial Services (Banking Reform) Act 2013?**

A To improve investor protection by imposing new depositary standards and enhanced transparency through new investor disclosure rules and mandatory reporting to competent authorities

B To extend the class of individuals subject to sanctions for misconduct to all of a firm's staff who pose a risk of significant harm to the firm or its customers

C To make it easier for the regulators to hold individuals accountable for breaches

D To increase and to define more clearly the responsibilities of those at the highest levels of banks' management

19   **Which of the following would generally be regarded as carrying out an investment business under FSMA 2000?**

    I   Arranging deals in investments
    II   Advising on investments in a *Financial Times* column
    III   Publishing a tip sheet

A   I and II

B   I and III

C   II and III

D   I, II and III

20   **The prudential regulation of UK fund managers will normally be the responsibility of:**

A   The Financial Conduct Authority

B   The Prudential Regulation Authority

C   The European Securities and Markets Authority

D   The Bank of England

21   **Up to what percentage may a listed company make purchases in a target company, without being required to make a mandatory offer for the target?**

A   9.9%

B   14.9%

C   29.9%

D   49.9%

22   **What is the name of the UK pensions regulator?**

A   The Pensions Regulator

B   The Office for Pension Regulation

C   The Pensions Ombudsman

D   The Occupational Pensions Board

23   **In relation to takeovers, which of the following statements is true?**

A   An offer must remain open for at least 21 days

B   An offer can be made to selected shareholders

C   Purchases in the open market during the offer period are prohibited

D   Partial offers are never permitted

24 **A listed company makes an offer of £2.00 cash per share for another company's shares and, during the offer period, buys some of the offeree's shares in the market place for £2.10. Which of the following will it be obliged to do?**

    I   Make an announcement of the purchase

    II   Increase the offer to £2.10 per share for future acceptances

    III   Increase the offer to £2.10 per share for offeree shareholders who have already accepted the offer at £2.00 a share

A I and II

B II and III

C I and III

D I, II and III

25 **How is the Panel on Takeovers and Mergers mainly funded?**

A By government subsidy

B By a levy on share transactions

C By a levy on all Stock Exchange transactions

D By contributions from all firms regulated by either the FCA and the PRA

26 **Under the Trustee Act 2000, how much of a fund should be invested into gilts and other fixed income securities?**

A There is no minimum

B At least 25%

C At least 40%

D At least 50%

27 **One of the conditions for a merger to qualify for investigation by the Competition and Markets Authority (CMA) is where the merged company has a market share of more than:**

A 10%

B 15%

C 25%

D 50%

28 **A merger may be referred to the Competition and Markets Authority (CMA) if the value of the turnover of the company being taken over exceeds:**

A £60m

B £70m

C £80m

D £90m

29 **Which of the following is incorrect with respect to the Takeover Code (the City Code)?**

A   The Code has statutory force

B   The Code applies to all public and private companies registered in the UK

C   The Code has six general principles

D   When a shareholding exceeds 30%, the shareholder must make a takeover offer

30 **Tiger plc has announced that it intends to make a bid for Antelope plc. The Competition and Markets Authority (CMA) was established under the Enterprise and Regulatory Reform Act 2013, and has the power to investigate the potential takeover to consider whether there are any competition issues. In this case:**

A   An investigation may be triggered where the combined enterprise controls at least 20% of the goods and services in the sector of the UK market

B   The combined turnover of Tiger and Antelope exceeding £70m may trigger an investigation

C   The Competition and Markets Authority (CMA) may impose fines if its requests for information are not met

D   There are no appeals against the decision of the Competition and Markets Authority (CMA)

31 **Natasha is an adviser who is preparing a newsletter for distribution to high net worth clients at seminars and other events. There will be a section in the newsletter on the Trustee Act 2000. Natasha has prepared a first draft of part of these notes.**

Which part of the notes, as set out in Options A, B, C and D, is least correct and therefore requires amendment?

A   The Trustee Act 2000 widened the investment powers of trustees, thus overriding provisions included in the trust instrument

B   The Act allows trustees to delegate functions to agents, including their powers of investment

C   Under the Act, trustees can make any investment of any kind that they could as if the funds were their own, except for investment in overseas land

D   Trustees must obtain and consider 'proper advice' when making or reviewing investments, and keep investments under review

32 **Which of the following is not one of the seven main blocks of the FCA Handbook?**

A   High Level Standards

B   Business Standards

C   Perimeter Guidance

D   Redress

33 **Which of the following is not one of the threshold conditions for authorisation that is applied specifically by the FCA?**

A   Business to be conducted in a prudent manner

B   Appropriate resources

C   Effective supervision

D   Business model

34 **Which of the following is not specifically mentioned in the FCA's 11 Principles for Businesses?**

A   Skill, care and diligence

B   Relations with regulators

C   Unreasonable charging

D   Conflicts of interest

35 **To whom do the Principles for Businesses of the FCA apply?**

A   All authorised firms

B   All member firms of Designated Professional Bodies

C   All Recognised Investment Exchange member firms

D   All customers receiving financial advice

36 **Which of the following is not one of the Principles for Businesses of the FCA?**

A   Clients' assets

B   Integrity

C   Polarisation

D   Financial prudence

37 **One of the regulators' Principles for Businesses states: 'A firm must take reasonable care to ensure the suitability of its advice and discretionary decisions for any customer who is entitled to rely upon its judgement'. The Principle is:**

A   Principle 6: Customers' interests

B   Principle 7: Communications with clients

C   Principle 8: Conflicts of interest

D   Principle 9: Customers: relationships of trust

38 **SYSC rules on apportionment of responsibilities relate to, and expand on, the Principle for Businesses entitled:**

A   Integrity

B   Skill, care and diligence

C   Management and control

D   Communication with clients

39 **Which of the following is correct regarding the Conduct Rules (COCON)?**

A All apply to senior managers only

B All apply to all certified staff

C Some apply to all certified staff and some apply to senior managers only

D Some apply to all certified staff and some apply to those in customer functions only

40 **Retail investment advisers are required to hold a Statement of Professional Standing (SPS) that is issued by:**

A The firm employing the adviser

B The Financial Conduct Authority

C The Financial Skills Partnership

D An FCA-accredited body

41 **The Conduct Rules, consisting of five rules, apply to everyone. Which one of the following is not a Conduct rule?**

A You must pay due regard to the interests of customers and treat them fairly

B You must act with due care, skill and diligence

C You must observe proper standards of market conduct

D You must disclose appropriately any information of which the FCA or PRA would reasonably expect notice

42 **The following are all Conduct Rules included in the Code of Conduct for Staff sourcebook (COCON). Which one of these rules is a first-tier Individual Conduct Rule?**

A You must observe proper standards of market conduct

B You must disclose appropriately any information of which the FCA or PRA would reasonably expect notice

C You must take reasonable steps to ensure that the business of the firm for which you are responsible is controlled effectively

D You must take reasonable steps to ensure that any delegation of your responsibilities is to an appropriate person and that you oversee the discharge of the delegated responsibility effectively

43 **Amanda is a retail investment adviser. She is assessing how close she is to meeting FCA requirements for Continuing Professional Development (CPD). In the year so far, she has carried out 28 hours of unstructured CPD and 16 hours of structured CPD. Which of the following further CPD hours must Amanda complete to meet the annual requirement?**

A None, as she has already met the annual requirement

B 5 hours of structured CPD

C 5 hours of CPD which may be either structured or unstructured

D 12 hours of CPD of which 5 hours must be structured

BPP
LEARNING
MEDIA

44 **Which of the following is not one of the recognition requirements applying to an investment exchange?**

A There must be complaints investigation and resolution arrangements

B The exchange must be authorised to conduct regulated activities

C The exchange must have financial resources sufficient for the proper performance of its functions

D The exchange must have rules covering default by an exchange member

45 **What is the main rationale for enabling the FCA to make product intervention rules that are temporary?**

A To limit the FCA's powers to shorter-term interventions

B To avoid imminent possible detriment to consumers

C As a low-cost solution that avoids costly consultations

D To deal with a systemic financial crisis

46 **When a discretionary manager buys and sells investments more than would be reasonably expected, given the client's agreed investment strategy, the rule that is specifically being breached is the rule related to:**

A Best execution

B Suitability

C Churning

D Inducements

47 **Appropriateness needs to be established:**

A Before every transaction

B For every class of investments and services at the outset of the business relationship

C For non-advised sales in respect of complex instruments

D At the start of every business relationship

48 **Which of the following would be a *per se* professional client?**

I   An entity requiring authorisation or regulation to operate in the financial markets

II In relation to MiFID business, an undertaking with a balance sheet total of €25m, net turnover of €30m, and €1m own funds

III A non-MiFID business with share capital of £5m

A I, II and III

B I and II

C I and III

D II and III

49 **Research provided to an investment firm will not be regarded as an inducement if it is either directly paid for by the firm out of its own resources or if it is received in return for payments from a special research payment account (RPA), which is funded by charges to clients, not by third parties. Operating such an RPA will require new policies, systems and controls, as well as additional disclosures. Which of the following policies are required?**

      I   Regular assessment of the quality of the research purchased, based on robust quality criteria and its ability to contribute to better investment decisions

      II   Detailed policies for assessing quality and the benefit to client portfolios, and for the fair allocation of costs to clients

      III Appropriate controls and senior management oversight of assessment of the need for third party research, and the allocation of the budget to ensure that it is managed and used in the best interests of clients

      IV Reporting to clients both in advance and on at least an annual basis

A I and II

B I and III

C II, III and IV

D I, II, III and IV

50 **A customer has asked you for clarification of the client money rules.**

You explain that the main purpose of the rules is:

A To protect customers against the effect of investments falling sharply in price

B To ensure that the highest level of interest on deposits accrues to customers

C To protect and segregate customer assets from those of the firm in case the firm gets into financial difficulties

D To protect the firm against claims of loss from customers

51 **The Retail Distribution Review (RDR) resulted in professionalism requirements for retail investment advisers. The aims were to improve the clarity with which firms describe their services to consumers; address the potential for adviser remuneration to distort consumer outcomes; and increase the professional standards of advisers. The RDR adviser charging regime does not apply to:**

A Product providers who advise clients directly

B Advisers using pre-scripted questions to advise on stakeholder products

C Advisers giving independent advice on a full range of retail investment products

D Advisers giving advice on the products of a restricted range of product providers

52 **You are seeking to give investment advice on an independent basis, and you are expanding your awareness of the range of 'retail investment products'. Which of the following does not fall within the definition of retail investment products?**

A A self-invested personal pension plan

B A stakeholder pension plan

C Shares in an open-ended investment company

D A deposit in a building society share account

53 **P & Q Investments have prepared a research report on a small pharmaceutical company. They are planning to make the report available to their clients.**

Under which of the following circumstances is the firm allowed to deal ahead of releasing the research report?

    I   In anticipation of client orders
    II   When acting as a market maker
    III   When executing an unsolicited client trade

A I and II

B I and III

C II and III

D I, II and III

54 **Gemma is considering an investment in an authorised UCITS fund but says that she would like to see a short document helping her to understand the nature and risks of the fund, to help with her decision to invest. Gemma should:**

A Obtain a key investor information document, which the fund manager must prepare

B Ask whether the fund makes available a key investor information document, which is optional for the fund manager to prepare

C Obtain a prospectus, which the fund manager must prepare

D Ask whether the fund makes available a prospectus, which is optional for the fund manager to prepare

55 **January 2021 is Adam's earliest possible opportunity to take an uncrystallised funds pension lump sum (UFPLS). Which of the following is true?**

A 100% of the payment Adam receives will be taxable

B Adam reaches the age of 75 years in January 2021

C Adam's pension plan is a defined benefit plan

D Adam will be able to take further UFPLS payments

56 **Nazmi Kaya is a retail client of your firm. Nazmi requests in writing that he be treated as an elective professional client with respect to share purchases. Nazmi has worked for a major bank for nine months carrying out daily transactions in equity dealing, and has a portfolio worth £450,000.**

Which of the following best describes your firm's appropriate treatment of the client?

A As a retail client, because Nazmi does not satisfy the quantitative test for MiFID business

B As a retail client, because Nazmi does not satisfy the qualitative test

C As a *per se* professional client

D As an elective professional client

57 **An FCA-regulated firm. Jeffreys & Sumter, issues an investment advertisement which invites readers to apply for units in a unit trust. A tear-off slip is provided.**

Which of the following criteria is the advertisement not required to meet?

A Be approved by the Financial Conduct Authority

B Be fair and not misleading

C Include details of charges or expenses

D Be tailored to the likely level of sophistication of the reader

58 **An FCA-regulated firm, Fellowes Bryson Smythe, issues a financial promotion that is not a direct offer promotion.**

The firm must do all of the following, except which one?

A Apply appropriate expertise

B Ensure that the advertisement is clear, fair and not misleading

C Ensure that the advertisement identifies it as the issuer

D Ensure that the advertisement identifies it as regulated by the Financial Conduct Authority

59 **Which of the following is not exempt from financial promotions rules under FSMA 2000?**

A Communications with certified high net worth individuals

B Promotions issued by a firm's appointed representatives

C Communications with certified sophisticated investors

D Generic advertising

60 **Following a complaint, a firm concludes that Stephen, an investment adviser, should not have made a cold (unsolicited) call to Mr Singh.**

This could be because:

A The call was made following two unsuccessful attempts to call Mr Singh on the same day

B Stephen did not state the firm he worked for during the call

C The call was about a package product

D Mr Singh already has an established client relationship with the firm

61 **Harry Blunt, a retail investment adviser (RIA), is not required to supply a suitability letter to his client. This is because:**

A The client has been introduced to the RIA by another client

B The RIA is acting on a fee basis

C The business is conducted on an 'execution only' basis

D The RIA is regulated by the Financial Conduct Authority

62 **Rimcastle Investments is not required to assess appropriateness in respect of part of its business. This is because the firm is executing client orders in:**

A Units in a collective investment scheme

B Derivatives

C Warrants

D Unlisted shares

63 **Barry has recently started a stakeholder pension plan. Barry is allowed a 'cooling-off' or cancellation period of:**

A 30 calendar days

B 21 calendar days

C 14 business days

D 7 business days

64 **The following statements concern rules governing investment research activities. Which of the statements is incorrect?**

A Financial analysts can take positions in securities contrary to their current recommendations only in exceptional circumstances and with senior permission

B Analysts must refrain from dealing on the information contained in research until the clients have been provided with time to consider it

C Research analysts must not promise issuers favourable research coverage

D The issuer should be permitted to review unpublished research on their company at any time

65 **Oakley & Sunderland makes a research recommendation. The firm must make disclosures in relation to all of the following, except:**

A All relationships and circumstances that may reasonably be expected to impair the objectivity of the recommendation

B Whether employees involved have remuneration tied to investment banking transactions

C Shareholding held by the issuer of over 3% of the share capital of the recommending firm

D The names of those individuals involved in preparing the research

66 **Which of the following is true of the rule on inducements?**

A The rule only applies to retail clients

B Payments must be made by or on behalf of the client

C Third-party payments are allowed if immaterial and disclosed in the conflicts of interest policy

D Third-party payments are permitted if the client consents

67   Which of the following is not associated with the safe custody rules?

A   Internal system evaluation method

B   Internal custody record check

C   Prudent segregation

D   Physical asset reconciliation

68   Which of the following is not one of the types of client bank account that a firm may operate?

A   Designated client fund account

B   Client suspense account

C   Designated client bank account

D   General client bank account

69   An investor in an authorised fund requests that the fund manager send them all reports about the progress of the fund that are required by the regulator. Which reports should they receive?

A   A short report half-yearly and annually, and a long report half-yearly and annually

B   A short report after the half-year end, and a long report annually

C   A short report quarterly, and a long report half-yearly and annually

D   A short report half-yearly and annually

70   Which of the following does not describe one of the 'pillars' of the FCA's supervision model?

A   Analysis of issues and products

B   Event-driven work

C   The firm systematic framework

D   Dual regulation

71   Red Bush Investments is given Part 4A permission to offer investment advice but a period of 13 months passes during which it carries out no business in this field at all. It is also authorised deal on its own account which it continues to do during this period. The FCA becomes concerned that it should protect potential clients from receiving inappropriate advice. What would be the regulator's most likely action?

A   Cancel the firm's Part 4A permission

B   Remove authorisation

C   Vary the firm's permission

D   Fine the firm

72   A professional client who is a large company (£8m annual turnover) has lost £80,000 (in respect to a derivatives transaction) owing to the negligence of an FCA-authorised firm that has now become insolvent. The client would be eligible to make a maximum claim from the Financial Services Compensation Scheme (FSCS) of:

A   £150,000

B   £85,000

C   £75,000

D   Nil

73   How often must an authorised firm inform the regulator of all complaints received?

A   Annually

B   Six-monthly

C   Monthly

D   Daily

74   Which of the following can the Financial Ombudsman Service (FOS) do?

    I   Require that a firm involved complies with a money award
    II   Make an award to cover costs of a complainant
    III   Make a money award of £125,000

A   I and II

B   II and III

C   I and III

D   I, II and III

75   If the outcome of an investigation by the Financial Ombudsman Service (FOS) is accepted by the complainant, then it is:

A   At the discretion of the firm to comply

B   Implemented by the FCA

C   Binding on the firm

D   Binding on the customer

76   If a complaint has not been resolved within eight weeks, which of the following must be given to a complainant?

A   Information about the Financial Ombudsman Service

B   Information about the Financial Conduct Authority

C   Information about the Financial Services Compensation Scheme

D   Information about the Retail Distribution Review

77 **To whom should an eligible complainant take their complaint about an authorised firm to first?**

A The Financial Conduct Authority

B The Financial Ombudsman Service

C The authorised firm

D The Complaints Commissioner

78 **The FCA may not exercise its power to make temporary product intervention rules (TPIRs):**

A If it has not conducted a public consultation

B In respect of complex or niche products

C Which last for 24 months

D Until it has consulted the PRA

79 **Under which Act is money laundering an offence?**

A Proceeds of Crime Act 2002

B Companies Act 2006

C Financial Services and Markets Act 2000

D Money Laundering Regulation 2019

80 **Which of the following will generally not be an insider?**

A A company director

B A market maker

C Someone who receives information from an insider

D A fund manager

81 **Which of the following is responsible for insider dealing legislation?**

A The Financial Conduct Authority

B The Department of Business, Energy & Industrial Strategy

C Her Majesty's Treasury

D The London Stock Exchange

82 **Which of the following statements about insider dealing is incorrect?**

A It only relates to unpublished, price-sensitive information

B Legislation covers unit trusts

C It is prosecuted by the FCA

D It cannot be prosecuted if information is passed on in the proper course of duties

83   **A market maker acting in good faith will not be prosecuted for insider dealing because there is:**

   A   A special defence for market makers

   B   A general defence for market makers

   C   Defence covering bid facilitation

   D   Defence covering stabilisation

84   **An investment firm should undertake enhanced due diligence before taking undertaking investment business in a case where the client:**

   A   Has close business relationships with other clients of the firm

   B   Is based overseas

   C   Is new to the investment firm

   D   Is a senior public official in a country other than the UK

85   **Under the EU benchmark regulation you may be a benchmark administrator if you provide indices that are used in:**

   I   Financial instruments traded on an EU trading venue
   II   Mortgage contracts
   III   Investment funds

   A   I and II

   B   II and III

   C   I and III

   D   I, II and III

86   **The Packaged Retail and Insurance-based Investment Products (PRIIPs) Regulation has applied since 1 January 2018. It requires persons who advise a retail investor on a PRIIP or sells a PRIIP to a retail investor to provide the investor with a KID before any transaction is concluded. For which of the following do the PRIIP rules not apply:**

   A   UK corporate bond OEIC

   B   Deposit account

   C   Discretionary managed investment portfolio

   D   FTSE 100 option contract

87   **The FCA Product intervention and Product governance sourcebook (PROD) contains rules and guidance on the obligations of manufacturers and distributors when creating or distributing financial instruments. Which of the following is not a phase of the product governance cycle?**

   A   Monitoring and review

   B   Collect and analyse

   C   Design and approval

   D   Launch and promotion

88 **The FCA has created a process for recognising industry codes for certain unregulated financial markets and activities. Which of the following is not a FCA recognised industry code?**

A FX Global Code

B UK Money Market Code

C Global Commodities Market Code

D Standard of Lending Practice for business customers

89 **Markets in Financial Instruments Regulation (MiFIR) is regulation related to MiFID II but there is no requirement to implement it into national law. Which one of the following statements best reflects MiFIR?**

A MiFIR does not cover any of the assets covered in MiFID II

B MiFIR covers exactly the same assets as MiFID II

C MiFIR covers less assets than MiFID II

D MiFIR covers more assets than MiFID II

90 **Two of the following were introduced under UCITS V. Which two were they?**

I   The list of products that could be included in a fund were widened

II   The rules on the responsibilities of depositaries were enhanced

III The need for higher qualifications for fund managers was introduced

IV   Remuneration policies for UCITS fund managers were introduced

A II and IV

B II and III

C I and III

D I and IV

91 **How many principles are there in the GDPR (General Data Protection Regulation)?**

A Ten

B Six

C Seven

D Eight

92 **When did MiFID II come into force?**

A December 2016

B July 2017

C January 2018

D July 2018

93   Which one of the following was not one of the key changes introduced by MiFID II?

A   Limiting the size of positions held in commodity derivatives

B   Strengthening transparency before and after financial instruments are traded

C   Widening trading to pure currencies and commodities

D   Creation of Organised Trading Facilities (OTFs)

94   Under the Senior Managers Regime (SMR) which of the following is true of Senior Management Functions (SMFs)?

A   They involve, or might involve, a risk to the authorised person or business

B   Those who fill SMFs have to have at least 10 years' experience

C   They are positions of risk

D   Those who fill SMFs must at least hold a Master's degree

95   Which one of the following does the Certification Regime (CR) not apply to?

A   Functions that used to be 'significant influence functions' but are not covered by the Senior Managers Regime

B   Customer facing roles subject to qualification requirements

C   Functions such as Chairman or Chief Financial Officer

D   Anyone who supervises or manages a certified person but who is not subject to the Senior Managers Regime

96   When was the current Market Abuse Regulation (MAR) introduced?

A   July 2005

B   April 2013

C   July 2016

D   October 2017

97   Which one of the following is not targeted by the UK Criminal Finances Act 2017

A   Corruption

B   Money Laundering

C   Tax avoidance

D   Tax evasion

98   Which one of the following is true of an Organised Trading Facility (OTF)?

A   OTFs are designed to capture trading in bonds and derivatives that would not be traded on organised markets or MTFs

B   It is another term for a multilateral trading facility (MTF)

C   It is a regulated market

D   OTFs are Ordinary Trading Functions

99   **Markets in Financial Instruments Regulation (MiFIR) has strengthened which one of the following?**

A   The number of instruments traded

B   The size of trades

C   Detailed transaction reporting

D   The profitability of trades

100   **Two of the following are excluded under MiFID II. Which two are they?**

     I   Receiving and transmitting of orders

     II   Group Treasury activities

     III   Investment advice

     IV   Insurance companies

A   II and IV

B   II and III

C   I and III

D   I and IV

101   **The Common Reporting Standards (CRS) were developed by the OECD. The idea behind CRS is for authorities to generate an automatic exchange of information. What is the main purpose of these standards?**

A   To fight insider dealing

B   To fight market abuse

C   To fight tax avoidance

D   To fight tax evasion

102   **According to the General Data Protection Regulation (GDPR) there are seven principles with which data controllers must comply. Which one of the following is not one of those principles?**

A   Data must be fairly and lawfully processed

B   Data must be adequate, relevant and limited

C   Data must be accurate and up to date

D   Data may be collected for any purposes

103   **Under UCITS V, which one of the following is not a duty of the depositary?**

A   Safekeeping

B   Investment decisions

C   Cash flow monitoring

D   Delegation

104 **Which of the following is not covered by the Alternative Investment Fund Managers Directive (AIFMD)?**

    A Unit trusts

    B Hedge funds

    C Private equity funds

    D Real estate funds

105 **Under the Senior Managers Regime (SMR) the regulators will pre-approve senior individuals with specific Senior Management Functions (SMFs). When applying for an individual to be approved for an SMF, which of the following will a firm not be required to submit?**

    A Statement of Responsibility

    B Responsibilities Map

    C Handover Arrangements

    D Details of Remuneration

106 **Under the Certification Regime (CR), who is responsible for assessing and certifying that an individual, who could pose significant risk to a firm or its customers, is fit and proper?**

    A The FCA

    B The PRA

    C The firm

    D Her Majesty's Treasury

107 **The EU Market Abuse Regulation (MAR) introduced in 2016, brought in a number of changes. Which one of the following was not one of those changes?**

    A MAR is extended to cover financial instruments traded on MTFs and OTFs

    B MAR is extended to cover abuse outside and within the EU where instruments are traded on an EU venue

    C MAR prohibits attempting to engage in market manipulation

    D MAR introduced for the first time, 'insider dealing' as a form of market abuse

108 **The UK Criminal Finances Act 2017 introduced a new angle on tax evasion. What was that angle?**

    A It made tax evasion a criminal offence whereas before it had only been a civil offence

    B It allowed criminal liability to be ascribed to the firm where tax evasion occurred

    C It exonerated firms from liability where a member of their staff had engaged in tax evasion

    D It introduced fixed penalties for tax evasion offences

109   **Under the Certification Regime (CR), which one of the following activities is not a specific function that an individual would carry out?**

A   Significant management

B   Material risk takers

C   Client dealing

D   Chairman

110   **The FCA requires authorised fund managers to assess the value for money of each of their funds. Which one of the following is not one of the seven criteria, as a minimum, that the firm must consider when assessing value for money?**

A   Fund performance

B   Economies of scale

C   Speed of service

D   Classes of units

111   **What is the maximum criminal sanction for assisting a money launderer?**

A   14 years' imprisonment and a £1 million fine

B   5 years' imprisonment and a £1 million fine

C   14 years' imprisonment and an unlimited fine

D   5 years' imprisonment and an unlimited fine

Answers

1 **A** Where a branch is set up, host state rules will apply for operational matters. In general terms, the home state regulator retains responsibility for the firm's prudential regulation (financial resources, governance etc) and the host state regulator applies its rules in relation to the firm's conduct of business in the host state

2 **A** MiFID II, which came into effect on 3 January 2018, added one additional financial instrument to the list of financial instruments contained within the original MiFID. The following are MiFID II financial instruments:

Transferable securities; money market instruments; and units in collective investment undertakings;

Options, futures, swaps, forward rate agreements and any other derivative contracts relating to securities, currencies, interest rates or yields, emission allowances or other derivative instruments, financial indices or financial measures which may be settled physically or in cash;

Options, futures, swaps, forwards and any other derivative contracts relating to commodities;

Derivative instruments for the transfer of credit risk;

Financial contracts for differences;

Options, futures, swaps, forward rate agreements and any other derivative contracts relating to climatic variables, freight rates or inflation rates or other official economic statistics

3 **B** An organised trading facility (OTF) is a new classification of OTC trading venues categorised under MiFID II

4 **B** Operating a Multilateral Trading Facility (MTF) is one of a number of investment services and activities which are core MiFID activities. The others are excluded from MiFID

5 **A** These requirements are implemented through the single set of rules known as the 'common platform'. These requirements are contained in the Senior Management Arrangements, Systems and Controls (SYSC) Sourcebook of the FCA Handbook. The overriding requirement is that a firm must take reasonable care to establish and maintain such systems and controls as are appropriate to its business. One of the purposes of these requirements is to create a common platform of organisational systems and controls for firms

6 **B** The first statement is describing an EU regulation, where the regulation is immediately binding. An EU decision has the force of law in every state. A directive requires the individual state governments to amend their own national laws within a specified period

7 **A** The European Economic Area (EEA) includes all EU states plus Norway, Iceland and Liechtenstein

8 **C** Contracts of insurance will not be covered under the terms of MiFID. Firms that do not conduct investment services at all are not within the scope of MiFID. They include, insurance undertakings, people administering their own assets, and any firms which do not provide investment services and/or perform investment activities

9 **B** The European Securities and Markets Authority (ESMA) works at the European level alongside the European Banking Authority (EBA) and the European Insurance and Occupational Pensions Authority (EIOPA), and continues the work of the former the Committee of European Securities Regulators (CESR). ESMA aims to ensure the integrity, transparency, efficiency and orderly functioning of securities markets in Europe, as well as enhancing investor protection. ESMA does not have a direct role in the UK regulatory re-structuring

10 **C** The European Market Infrastructure Regulation (EMIR) comprises a set of standards for regulation of OTC derivatives, central counterparties (CCPs) and trade repositories. EMIR introduced new requirements to improve transparency and reduce the risks associated with the derivatives market, and it also established common organisational, conduct of business and prudential standards for CCPs and trade repositories

11 **B** Pension benefits can currently be taken from the age of 55 except where there is a lower protected pension age or in cases of ill-health. Pension flexibility also allowed individuals to enter a flexi-access drawdown plan, where there are no limits on the amount that can be taken from the drawdown fund each year. A lump sum of up to 25% of a pension pot can also be taken when the fund is put into drawdown. Any drawdown payments are taxed as income

12 **D** Undertaking any regulated activity requires authorisation unless exempt from authorisation. Arranging deals in investments, establishing a CIS and sending dematerialised instructions are all defined as regulated activities

13 **A** Investment advice and fund management activities are regarded as regulated activities. Acting as an unremunerated trustee is an excluded activity under FSMA 2000

14 **A** FSMA 2000 states that the innocent party to the agreement will still be able to enforce the agreement against the other party

15 **B** Only the Recognised Investment Exchange (RIE) itself, such as the LSE, is exempt, not the members of the exchange. Appointed representatives are one of the exempt persons, exempt from authorisation

16 **D** The Remunerations Code applies to large banks, building societies, broker-dealers and large alternative investment fund managers and capital adequacy directive (CAD) investment firms. Any guarantees should be exceptional, for new hires only and limited to a year. Non-financial performance metrics should form a significant part of the performance assessment process. At least 50% of variable remuneration (bonus) should consist of shares, ownership interests, share-linked instruments and/or equivalent non-cash instruments that are subject to a retention policy to align incentives with the firm's long-term interests

17 **D** Currencies themselves are not specified investments, only currency futures and options. Generally, specified investments include all investment instruments and rights to those instruments, but exclude physical assets (eg land, antiques and commodities). Regulated mortgages are also deemed specified investments and are thus regulated by the FCA. Following the implementation of MiFID II, structured deposits and emission allowances were added as categories of specified investments

18   **A**   The regulatory changes following the Financial Services (Banking Reform) Act 2013 are not specifically concerned with investor protection. Option A describes one of the aims of the Alternative Investment Fund Managers Directive (AIFMD), as the AIFMD includes organisational and governance requirements, and the regular disclosure of information to investors, hence improving investor protection

19   **B**   The primary purpose of the *Financial Times* is not that of giving investment advice. This is one of the excluded activities, that do not require authorisation.

20   **A**   The FCA is responsible for both conduct and prudential regulation of fund managers

21   **C**   The Panel on Takeovers and Mergers is responsible for enforcing the City Code on Takeovers and Mergers. A mandatory offer is only required when the holding reaches 30% or, in certain situations, the holding is already over 30% and the investor buys one more share. Therefore, any bidder who acquires 30% or more of the voting rights of a company is required to make a cash offer to all other shareholders at the highest price they paid in the previous year

22   **A**   The Pensions Regulator is the regulatory body for work-based pension schemes in the UK. The Pensions Regulator has various objectives that include protecting the benefits of members of occupational schemes and personal pension schemes.

          The Pensions Schemes Act 2021 introduces enhanced enforcement powers for the Pensions Regulator including new climate change risk governance requirements. The Act gives the Pensions Regulator stronger powers and creates a range of new criminal offences and gives the Regulator the ability to issue civil penalties of up to £1 million in certain circumstances. The Regulator will have powers to enforce compliance, including the ability to issue fines of up to £5,000 for an individual trustee and £50,000 for a corporate trustee

23   **A**   Any takeover must remain open for a minimum of 21 calendar days, hence Day 21 is the first closing date, after the initial posting of the offer document. The target company's directors must normally advise shareholders of their views within 14 days after the offer document is sent out. If the bidder's stake in a company reaches 50%, the company is required to keep the offer open for acceptance by the remaining shareholders

24   **D**   If a predator company buys shares in the market during the bid at a price higher than the offer price, they must announce the bid and revise the offer to this new price

25   **B**   There is a £1 charge on all contract notes in shares where the consideration is over £10,000. The PTM levy is payable on trades in securities of companies which are incorporated in the UK, the Channel Islands or the Isle of Man and whose shares are admitted to trading on a UK-regulated market or MTF

26   **A**   Under the default provisions of the Trustee Act 2000, trustees may make any investment of the kind that they could if the funds were their own, with the exception of overseas land. A trustee must normally obtain and consider proper advice, and have regard to the standard investment criteria, which include the suitability to the trust of an investment and also the need to diversify investments as appropriate for the circumstances of the trust

27   **C**   The Competition and Markets Authority (CMA) will consider whether a bid is against the public interest based on the market share of 25% ('share of supply' test). This is the criterion to suggest that there will be a 'substantial lessening of competition'. The turnover test is met if the target company has a UK turnover of £70m or more

28 **B** This is the 'turnover test'. The Competition and Markets Authority (CMA) will investigate all mergers that meet the 'turnover test' or the 'share of supply' test. The turnover test is met if the target company has a UK turnover of £70m or more. The share of supply test is met if the merging parties will together supply at least 25% of goods or services either in the UK as a whole or in a substantial part

29 **B** The City Code on Takeovers and Mergers ('the Code') applies to all publicly quoted companies. The Code applies to private companies in certain cases, eg where they have been public within the last 10 years

30 **C** Failure to comply with a request for information may result in a fine. Regarding Option B, it is the turnover of the acquiree entity being over £70 million that is relevant – not the combined turnover. The CMA will investigate all mergers that meet the 'turnover test' or the 'share of supply' test. The turnover test is met if the target company has a UK turnover of £70m or more. The share of supply test is met if the merging parties will together supply at least 25% of goods or services either in the UK as a whole or in a substantial part

31 **A** Restrictions in the trust deed will override the wider investment powers provided for in the Trustee Act

32 **C** The Perimeter Guidance Manual (PERG) is a Regulatory Guide and is not one of the seven FCA Handbook Blocks. Block 1 – High Level Standards contains the overarching standards expected of authorised persons (firms) and approved persons. Block 3 – Business Standards sets out the requirements that affect firms on a day-to-day basis. Block 5 – Redress deals with the processes for handling complaints and compensation. The Perimeter Guidance Manual (PERG) contains FCA guidance about circumstances in which authorisation is required, or exempt person status is available, including guidance on the activities regulated under the FSMA 2000 and the exclusions that are available

33 **A** Business to be Conducted in a Prudent Manner is a PRA Threshold Condition that is closely equivalent to the FCA's appropriate resources and business model conditions

34 **C** Firms should treat customers 'fairly', but unreasonable charging is not mentioned. The Principles for Businesses state that a firm must conduct its business with due skill, care and diligence; a firm must pay due regard to the interests of its customers and treat them fairly; and finally, a firm must deal with its regulators in an open and cooperative way, and must disclose to the appropriate regulator appropriately anything relating to the firm of which that regulator would reasonably expect notice

35 **A** The Principles for Businesses are for the protection of all customers and apply to all authorised firms

36 **C** Polarisation, an advice-giving regime that was abolished in 2005, is not one of the eleven Principles for Businesses. The Principles include financial prudence, which states that a firm must maintain adequate financial resources. In additional, a firm must arrange adequate protection for clients' assets when it is responsible for them, and a firm must conduct its business with integrity

37 **D** The Principle for Businesses stated is Principle 9. Principle 6 states: 'A firm must pay due regard to the interests of its customers and treat them fairly'. Principle 7 states: 'A firm must pay due regard to the information needs of its clients, and communicate information to them in a way which is clear, fair and not misleading'. Principle 8 states: 'A firm must

manage conflict of interest fairly, both between itself and its customers and between a customer and another client'

38 **C** Senior Management Arrangements, Systems and Controls (SYSC) focuses on the responsibilities of directors and senior management to ensure the firm has appropriate control, supervision and accountability systems in place. SYSC states that a firm must take reasonable care to establish and maintain appropriate systems and controls, in effect this amplifies Principle 3 (PRIN), under which a firm must take reasonable care to organise and control its affairs responsibly and effectively, with adequate risk management systems

39 **C** There are five Individual Conduct Rules that apply to all certified staff (some rules are FCA-only), and there are also four second-tier Senior Manager Conduct Rules.

The Individual Conduct Rules are as follows:

1. You must act with integrity
2. You must act with due care, skill and diligence
3. You must be open and co-operative with the FCA, the PRA and other regulators
4. You must pay due regard to the interests of customers and treat them fairly
5. You must observe proper standards of market conduct

The Senior Manager Conduct Rules are as follows:

SC1. You must take reasonable steps to ensure that the business of the firm for which you are responsible is controlled effectively

SC2. You must take reasonable steps to ensure that the business of the firm for which you are responsible complies with the relevant requirements and standards of the regulatory system

SC3. You must take reasonable steps to ensure that any delegation of your responsibilities is to an appropriate person and that you oversee the discharge of the delegated responsibility effectively

SC4. You must disclose appropriately any information of which the FCA or PRA would reasonably expect notice

40 **D** Retail investment advisers are required to hold a Statement of Professional Standing (SPS) if they want to give independent or restricted advice. This rule has applied since the end of 2012, when the RDR changes came into effect. Advisers must hold a Statement of Professional Standing (SPS) from an accredited body. Accredited bodies will inform the FCA of any advisers who are not meeting the standards required to obtain the SPS

41 **D** The Senior Manager Conduct rules consist of four rules, including SC4 - you must disclose appropriately any information of which the FCA or PRA would reasonably expect notice. The five Individual Conduct Rules are as follows: 1. You must act with integrity; 2. You must act with due care, skill and diligence; 3. You must be open and co-operative with the FCA, the PRA and other regulators; 4. You must pay due regard to the interests of customers and treat them fairly; 5. You must observe proper standards of market conduct

42 **A** You must observe proper standards of market conduct is an Individual Conduct rule. The other three rules stated are second-tier Senior Manager Conduct Rules. The four Senior Manager Conduct Rules are as follows: SC1. You must take reasonable steps to ensure that the business of the firm for which you are responsible is controlled effectively; SC2. You must take reasonable steps to ensure that the business of the firm for which you are responsible complies with the relevant requirements and standards of the regulatory system; SC3. You must take reasonable steps to ensure that any delegation of your

responsibilities is to an appropriate person and that you oversee the discharge of the delegated responsibility effectively; SC4. You must disclose appropriately any information of which the FCA or PRA would reasonably expect notice

43   **B**   Retail investment advisers must carry out at least 35 hours of CPD annually, of which 21 hours must be structured. If Amanda completes 5 hours of structured CPD, she will have met the requirement. Structured learning activities include seminars, lectures, conferences, workshops or courses, and completing appropriate e-learning activities

44   **B**   Running an investment exchange is a regulated activity (arranging deals in investments), but Recognised Investment Exchange (RIE) status exempts an exchange from the requirement to be authorised

45   **B**   The power to make temporary rules, without the normal consultations, can be used if the FCA considers that the delay involved in complying with the requirement would be prejudicial to the interests of consumers

46   **C**   Churning and switching relate to the deliberate overtrading of client accounts for the purpose of generating commission. Churning involves dealing too frequently (in investments) than is in the client's best interests. Switching involves trading within or between packaged products

47   **C**   Appropriateness rules apply where investment services are provided, other than making a personal recommendation and managing investments and where the investments are deemed to be 'complex', such as warrants

48   **C**   A large undertaking for MiFID business must have two of the following:
- €20 million balance sheet total
- €40 million net turnover
- €2 million own funds

49   **D**   Operating a research payment account (RPA) will require new policies, systems and controls, as well as additional disclosures, including all of these areas listed, as follows: Regular assessment of the quality of the research purchased, based on robust quality criteria and its ability to contribute to better investment decisions; Detailed policies (provided to clients) for assessing quality and the benefit to client portfolios, and for the fair allocation of costs to clients; Appropriate controls and senior management oversight of assessment of the need for third party research, and the allocation of the budget to ensure that it is managed and used in the best interests of clients, with a clear audit trail of payments made to research providers and how these were determined with reference to the quality criteria; Reporting to clients both in advance and on at least an annual basis

50   **C**   The FCA'S Principle for Businesses 10 (PRIN 10 - Clients' assets) requires a firm to arrange adequate protection for clients' assets when the firm is responsible for them. An essential part of that protection is the proper accounting and treatment of client money

51   **B**   The adviser charging rules do not apply to 'basic' pre-scripted advice on stakeholder products. Since 1 January 2013, a firm making a personal recommendation to a retail client in the UK to invest in a retail investment product can no longer earn commission set by the product provider. Instead, the firm is paid an adviser charge agreed with the client in advance. These rules apply equally to independent and restricted advice, but not to basic advice (advice on stakeholder products using pre-scripted questions) where advisers are

still able to earn commission on sales. Non-advised services, or execution-only sales, where no advice or recommendation is given, also fall outside the adviser-charging regime

52   **D**   The category of 'retail investment products' (RIPs) extends beyond the existing definition of packaged products to cover products in a packaged form that modifies the exposure to underlying assets compared with a direct holding of the financial asset. A building society deposit is not encompassed by the definition. Personal pension plans including SIPPs, stakeholder pension plans and OEIC shares are all within the definition of RIPs

53   **C**   When research is provided to clients, the firm generally cannot act upon it until their clients have had a reasonable opportunity to react to the research. A financial analyst or anyone else having knowledge of the timing or content of investment research is not permitted to deal ahead – also known as 'front running'. The exceptions to this are a market-maker acting in good faith, and with regard to the execution of an unsolicited client order

54   **A**   The fund manager must prepare both a prospectus and a Key Investor Information (KII) document and, as a short document, the KII document is likely to better meet Gemma's requirements than the prospectus

55   **D**   Age 55 is the normal age at which the uncrystallised funds pension lump sum (UFPLS) becomes available. 75% of a UFPLS payment is taxable; 25% of the payment is tax-free. The UFPLS option applies to defined contribution pension plans. Ad hoc UFPLS payments can be taken in the future while there are still funds in the plan

56   **A**   Although the client probably satisfies the qualitative test, we are unable to show that they satisfy two of the following criteria for the quantitative test:

- The client has carried out at least ten 'significant' transactions per quarter on the relevant market, over the last four quarters

- The client's portfolio, including cash deposits, exceeds €500,000

- The client has knowledge of the transactions envisaged from at least one year's professional work in the financial sector

We must therefore treat Nazmi as a retail client

57   **A**   Advertisements do not each need to be approved by the FCA, which would of course be quite an onerous task for the regulator. Financial promotions require to be issued by an authorised firm, or approved for issuance by an authorised firm, in line with section 21 of FSMA 2000

58   **D**   The requirement to declare the FCA as the regulator only applies for direct offer financial promotions

59   **B**   A firm is required to apply the financial promotions rules to its appointed representatives, for example a non-written financial promotion such as a personal visit or telephone call. Exempt promotions include generic promotions, where the financial promotion itself must not relate to a controlled investment provided by a person who is identified in it, nor must it identify any person as someone who carries on any controlled activity. Another example of an exempt promotion is to investment professionals, where this exemption applies to financial promotions made only to, or directed only at, certain types of person who are informed enough to understand the risks involved

60   **B**   Cold/unsolicited calls are not allowed unless an existing customer envisages such a call, or the call relates to generally marketable packaged products, or it relates to a controlled

activity/service regarding readily realisable securities. The adviser should identify himself and his firm, and should call 'at an appropriate time of day'. There is no rule specifically about calling after having made unsuccessful calls on the same day

61   **C**   A suitability letter is not supplied if the client is making the transaction on an 'execution-only basis', as advice is then 'neither being sought nor given'. Firms providing investment advisory or discretionary portfolio management services are required to assess suitability for all retail clients and for professional clients

62   **A**   An appropriateness check is not required for certain non-complex financial instruments. Non-complex products include shares listed on a regulated market, money market instruments and units in a UCITS collective investment scheme. Complex products include warrants, derivatives and unlisted shares

63   **A**   The maximum period of reflection is 30 calendar days in this case. A retail client has a right to cancel a packaged product within 14 days, except for life policies and pension (including personal and stakeholder pension) schemes where the cancellation period is 30 days

64   **D**   Pre-publication drafts can be previewed by the issuer only for the purpose of verifying compliance. In addition, the firm, the financial analysts or any other relevant person involved in the production of investment research must not accept inducements from those with a material interest in the subject matter of the research

65   **C**   The requirement to state the research firm's holding in the subject or *vice versa* starts at 5%. A firm must, in a research recommendation produced by it, disclose clearly and prominently the identity of the person responsible for its production, and in particular the name and job title of the individual who prepared the research recommendation. A financial analyst's remuneration should not be linked to any recommendations contained in the research. Finally, when referred to as investment research, it is presented as an objective or independent manner

66   **C**   The rule on inducements applies to retail and professional clients. Inducements cover fees, commissions and non-monetary benefits paid to or by the client or someone on their behalf. Minor non-monetary benefits are only allowed if they are capable of enhancing the quality of the service provided, they do not impair compliance with the firm's duty to act in the best interests of the client and are clearly disclosed in the conflicts of interest policy

67   **C**   Prudent segregation is associated with client money, not with safe custody assets. The term refers to a firm's segregation of an amount of money as client money

68   **B**   The firm may operate a client bank account as a general client bank account, a designated client bank account, or a designated client fund account

69   **A**   A short report and a long report must be prepared half-yearly and annually. The short report is to be sent to all unitholders, and the long report is to be made available to unitholders on request

70   **D**   Dual regulation refers to the regulation of prudentially significant firms by both the PRA (for prudential regulation) and the FCA (for conduct regulation). The FCA's supervision model is based on the three pillars:

   1.   Firm systematic framework (FSF): preventative work through structured conduct assessment of firms;

2.   Event-driven work: dealing with problems that are emerging or have happened, and securing customer redress or other remedial work where necessary. This will cover issues that occur outside the firm assessment cycle;

3.   Issues and products: intensive campaigns on sectors of the market or products within a sector that are putting or may put consumers at risk

71   C   Given that the firm is investing on its own account without apparent problem, it is unlikely that the regulator will cancel the firm's Part 4A permission. However, because the firm has not offered advice for over 12 months, the regulator is likely to vary the firm's permission to stop them offering advice

72   D   Only certain kinds of claim are eligible for compensation. A professional client who is a large company is not an eligible claimant

73   B   A summary of complaints should be reported to the regulator every six months. Most firms must also provide the FCA with a biannual report (every 6 months) on the number of complaints, completions of complaints within four weeks, eight weeks and over eight weeks from receipt, and the number of complaints accepted as valid by the firm

74   D   The Financial Ombudsman Service (FOS) is an alternative to the courts for an eligible complainant when a firm has failed to deal with a complaint to their satisfaction. The maximum money award the FOS can make is £375,000 for complaints referred after 1 April 2022. If the complainant accepts the award, it is binding on the firm

75   C   The firm is bound by the Financial Ombudsman Service's (FOS) ruling. If the complainant accepts the FOS determination, it is binding on the firm, but if the complainant rejects the determination, the firm is not bound by it. For awards over £375,000, the firm is invited to pay the excess, but is not compelled to do so

76   A   A firm receiving a complaint must, by the end of eight weeks after its receipt of the complaint, send the complainant a final response, or a written response. The written response will explain why the firm is not in a position to make a final response and indicates when it expects to be able to provide one. The response will also inform the complainant that they may now refer the complaint to the FOS, and also include a copy of the standard explanatory leaflet

77   C   The complainant must first take their complaint to the firm. If it is not resolved to their satisfaction, they may go to the Financial Ombudsman Service (FOS)

78   C   The Temporary Product Intervention Rules (TPIRs) may only last for up to 12 months. They may be used where complex or niche products are sold to the mass market. There is no specific requirement for the FCA to consult the PRA regarding TPIRs

79   A   The Proceeds of Crime Act (POCA) 2002 supersedes the Criminal Justice Act (CJA) 1993. The various money laundering offences includes assistance - any person assisting money laundering is punishable on conviction by a maximum of 14 years' jail, or an unlimited fine, or both; tipping-off - where a person informs anyone connected with an investigation into money laundering that such an investigation is occurring. If the offence is committed by someone in the regulated sector, the punishment on conviction is a maximum of five years' jail, or an unlimited fine, or both; and a failure to report - where a person fails to report knowledge or suspicion of money laundering, the punishment on conviction is a maximum of five years' jail, or an unlimited fine, or both

80 **B**   A market maker is not 'an insider', as long as the dealing is in the course of normal market-making activities and the market maker acted in good faith, ie did not change their prices as a result of the information they were aware of. This is a special defence against the charge of insider dealing

81 **C**   The Criminal Justice Act (CJA) 1993 legislation is the responsibility of HM Treasury. Investigation and prosecution are the responsibility of the LSE and the FCA respectively

82 **B**   The investments covered by the CJA 1993 include shares, debentures, options, warrants and public sector debt instruments. Unit trusts (and OEICs), in which there is no secondary market, are excluded from the legislation, as is currency and commodities

83 **A**   A special defence for insider dealing is a market-maker that had inside information in the course of their business, but acted genuinely for that business. This is only as long as they are 'acting in good faith', otherwise, they may be prosecuted

84 **D**   Enhanced due diligence (EDD) is for higher-risk situations, including politically exposed persons (PEPs), a category that includes high-ranking non-UK public officials. EDD applies in four circumstances:

  1.   Where business is conducted on a non-face-to-face basis;

  2.   In respect of correspondent banking relationships;

  3.   Where a situation by its nature can present a higher risk of money laundering or terrorist financing;

  4.   Where the customer is a politically exposed person (PEP).

There are also additional high-risk factors to be considered when assessing the need for enhanced due diligence. These may occur where:

  • There are relevant transactions between parties based in high-risk third countries;

  • The customer is the beneficiary of a life insurance policy;

  • The customer is a third-country national seeking residence rights or citizenship in exchange for transfers of capital, purchase of a property, governments bonds or investment in corporate entities;

  • Non face-to-face business relationships or transactions without certain safeguards, such as concerning the electronic identification processes; and

  • Transactions related to oil, arms, precious metals, tobacco products, cultural artefacts, ivory or other items related to protected species, or archaeological, historical, cultural and religious significance, or of rare scientific value

85 **D**   You may be a benchmark administrator if you provide indices used in investment funds, mortgage and consumer credit contracts and financial instruments traded on EU trading venues or systematic internalisers

86 **B**   A deposit account does not fall within the PRIIPs definition (other than structured deposits as defined in MiFID II). The others are all considered retail products that would fall within the PRIIPs definition

87 **B**   The four distinct phases of the product governance cycle for both manufacturers and distributors are design and approval, development and implementation, launch and promotion and monitoring and review

88 **C** The FCA has created a process for recognising industry codes for unregulated financial markets and activities, known as 'FCA recognition'. The codes that have been recognised by the FCA are:

FX Global Code – this Code sets global principles of good practice standards in the foreign exchange (FX) market, promoting the integrity and effective functioning of the wholesale foreign exchange market

UK Money Markets Code (MM) – this sets standards and best practice expected from participants in the deposit, repo and securities lending markets in the UK

Standards of Lending Practice for business customers – these standards set the benchmark for good lending practice in the UK, outlining the way registered firms are expected to deal with their business customers throughout the entire product life cycle

89 **D** MiFIR has a wider scope than MiFID II, hence it covers a greater number of assets. It sets out a number of reporting requirements in relation to the disclosure of trade data to the public and competent authorities. MiFID's scope is extending under MiFIR to cover more asset classes, so more firms will be caught by the reporting obligations

90 **A** UCITS V, which enhanced the rules on the responsibilities of depositaries and introduced remuneration policy requirements for UCITS fund managers, was implemented into UK law in March 2016. The statements regarding the widened the list of products that could be included in a fund, and also that UCITS introduced the need for higher qualifications for fund managers, have no relevance to UCITS V

91 **C** GDPR has seven principles. The GDPR requires anyone who handles personal information to comply with the seven principles.

The GDPR requires anyone who handles personal information to comply with seven principles. The principles are to ensure that personal data is:

1. Processed lawfully, fairly and in a transparent manner in relation to individuals;

2. Collected for specified, explicit and legitimate purposes and not further processed in a manner that is incompatible with those purposes; further processing for archiving purposes in the public interest, scientific or historical research purposes or statistical purposes shall not be considered to be incompatible with the initial purposes;

3. Adequate, relevant and limited to what is necessary in relation to the purposes for which they are processed;

4. Accurate and, where necessary, kept up to date; every reasonable step must be taken to ensure that personal data that are inaccurate, having regard to the purposes for which they are processed, are erased or rectified without delay;

5. Kept in a form which permits identification of data subjects for no longer than is necessary for the purposes for which the personal data are processed; personal data may be stored for longer periods insofar as the personal data will be processed solely for archiving purposes in the public interest, scientific or historical research purposes or statistical purposes, subject to implementation of the appropriate technical and organisational measures required by the GDPR in order to safeguard the rights and freedoms of individuals;

6. Processed in a manner that ensures appropriate security of the personal data, including protection against unauthorised or unlawful processing and against accidental loss, destruction or damage, using appropriate technical or organisational measures; and

7. Handled by those that are accountable. That is, to take responsibility for what they do with personal data and how they comply with the other principles. They must also have appropriate measures and records in place to be able to demonstrate their compliance

92   **C**   MiFID II was introduced in January 2018

93   **C**   MiFID II did not extend trading to currencies and commodities. The key changes that MiFID II has introduced are as follows:

- A regulated organised trading facility (OTF) to capture unregulated trades that are executed on non-regulated platforms. OTFs will exist alongside existing trading platforms such as traditional stock exchanges

- Strengthening the transparency requirements that apply before and after financial instruments are traded

- Limiting the size of positions held in commodity derivatives to reduce speculation in basic products such as agriculture

94   **A**   Senior Management Functions (SMFs) are functions that 'involve, or might involve, a risk of serious consequences for the authorised person, or for business or other interests in the UK'. This may include the functions carried out by non-executive directors or directors in other group entities that participate in making decisions for the firm

95   **C**   Senior Management Functions (SMFs), such as Chairman or Chief Financial Officers are subject to the Senior Managers Regime (SMR)

96   **C**   The current Market Abuse Regulation (MAR) was introduced in July 2016. Market Abuse Regulation was first introduced in July 2005 implementing the Market Abuse Directive

97   **C**   The UK Criminal Finances Act 2017 targets corruption, money laundering and tax evasion. It aims to make it easier to seize funds obtained through criminal means. Tax avoidance is a legal activity and is not a target of the UK Criminal Finances Act 2017. It is tax evasion that is illegal

98   **A**   Organised Trading Facilities (OTFs) are indeed designed to capture trading on bonds and derivatives that would not be traded on organised markets or Multilateral Trading Facilities (MTFs)

99   **C**   MiFIR strengthened compulsory transparency requirements which apply before and after financial instruments are traded. Such strengthening includes more detailed transaction reporting

100   **A**   The receiving and transmitting of orders, and investment advice ARE examples of services and activities included under MiFID II

101   **D**   The Common Reporting Standard (CRS) is an information standard that aims to fight tax evasion. The CRS is for the exchange of tax and financial information on a global level. Tax avoidance is not illegal and is not the focus of the CRS

102 **D**   The second (of the seven) GDPR principles is to ensure that personal data are 'collected for specified, explicit and legitimate purposes and not further processed in a manner that is incompatible with those purposes; further processing for archiving purposes in the public interest, scientific or historical research purposes or statistical purposes shall not be considered to be incompatible with the initial purposes'

103 **B**   Investment decisions would the responsibility of the Authorised Corporate Director (ACD) but not the Depositary

104 **A**   An alternative investment fund (AIF) is a collective investment undertaking that is not subject to the UCITS Directives and includes hedge funds, private equity funds, retail investment funds, investment companies and real estate funds. Unit trusts are covered by UCITS

105 **D**   The firm will be required to submit a statement of responsibility, which sets out the responsibilities that the senior manager is to perform as part of their controlled function, and how they fit in with the firm's overall governance and management arrangements. The firm must also provide a responsibilities map, which sets out how the various responsibilities have been allocated (and to make sure there are no gaps in accountability). Although other information needs to be submitted such as CVs, job descriptions, organisational charts and development plans, there is no requirement to submit remuneration details

106 **C**   Under the Certification Regime, it is the firms themselves who are responsible for assessing and certifying that individuals are fit and proper

107 **D**   The changes introduced by MAR include:

- Extending the scope of the EU market abuse regime to financial instruments traded on MTFs or other OTFs and certain OTC activities (including derivatives and credit default swaps)

- MAR also extends the market abuse regime to cover behaviour both within and outside the EU in relation to instruments admitted to trading on an EU-trading venue

- A prohibition on attempting to engage in market manipulation. Such an attempt may include situations where the activity is started but is not completed, for example as a result of a technical failure

'Insider dealing' has always been considered a form of market abuse – even prior to the introduction of MAR in 2016.

108 **B**   Tax evasion has always been a criminal offence. Rather than exonerating firms, the UK Criminal Finances Act 2017 makes them potentially criminally liable. Prosecution could lead to unlimited fines. A corporation may be prosecuted for failure to prevent the facilitation of UK tax evasion

109 **D**   The Certification Regime applies to those individuals carrying out specific functions (Certification Functions) for a firm that can have a significant impact on the firm or its customers but are not senior management functions. These include significant management, material risk takers, client dealing, as well as CASS oversight, proprietary trading, and algorithmic trading. The Chairman and chief financial officer are examples of senior management functions

110 **C** The FCA require authorised fund managers to assess the value for money of each of their funds. The FCA require authorised fund managers (AFMs) to assess the value for money of each fund, take corrective action if it does not offer good value for money; and explain the assessment annually in a public report. The FCA sets out seven criteria as the minimum that firms must consider when assessing the value for money of each fund, as follows: Quality of service (not speed of service): the range and quality of services provided to investors, Fund performance, AFM costs, Economies of scale, Comparable market rates, Comparable services and Classes of units

111 **C** The maximum penalty for the offence of assistance of a money launderer is 14 years' imprisonment and an unlimited fine, when found guilty in a Crown Court

4 Legal Concepts

Questions

1   **Which of the following terms is not an essential element in the formation of a valid contract?**

   A   Process

   B   Intention

   C   Agreement

   D   Consideration

2   **Where a company has its affairs wound up leading to its dissolution, how is this best described?**

   A   Receivership

   B   Liquidation

   C   Administration

   D   Bankruptcy

3   **Ben Schwartz has been discussing taking out a life assurance policy. With such a policy, which part of the contract constitutes the 'offer'?**

   A   An insurer's acknowledgement of receipt of a proposal form

   B   An advertisement in an insurer's shop window

   C   A postal offer of life assurance with a free gift

   D   A completed proposal form

4   **To be a fully binding agreement, which of the following attributes does a contract not necessarily need to have?**

   A   Offer and acceptance

   B   Intention to create legal relations

   C   Consideration

   D   Expressed in writing

5   **Which of the following is not necessarily a feature of the relationship between an agent and a principal?**

   A   The agent receives payment from the principal

   B   The agent has a duty to avoid conflicts of interest with the principal

   C   The agent must hand over any benefit to the principal unless the principal agrees otherwise

   D   The agent must keep what he knows of the principal's affairs confidential even after the agency relationship ceases

6   **A retail investment adviser who offers advice and recommendations to a client from a full range of products is acting:**

    A   As agent of the client

    B   As agents of the product provider

    C   As an attorney

    D   As an appointed representative

7   **An attorney (in a lasting power of attorney (LPA)) may be defined as:**

    A   A person who has been given authority to act on another person's behalf

    B   The person who takes possession of the assets of a bankrupt and distributes them to creditors

    C   A person who is not mentally capable of handling their own affairs

    D   A person who signs documents on behalf of someone else but, in so doing, does not have the authority to enter into a contract

8   **An Enduring Power of Attorney (EPA) that has not yet been registered:**

    A   Cannot be changed but can be registered

    B   Is established under the Mental Capacity Act 2005

    C   Covers personal health and welfare decisions relating to the donor

    D   Is void and must be replaced by a Lasting Power of Attorney (LPA)

9   **Which UK Act of Parliament specifies a 'decision-specific' test which assesses whether a person will be able to take a particular decision at a particular time?**

    A   Trustee Act 2000

    B   Financial Services and Markets Act 2000

    C   Mental Capacity Act 2005

    D   Financial Services Act 2012

10   **Minka wishes to register a lasting power of attorney (LPA) which would allow his brother to make decisions on his behalf in the event that he becomes physically incapacitated by a progressive disease that he is suffering from. With which body would he need to register the LPA?**

    A   The Financial Conduct Authority

    B   The Ministry of Justice

    C   The Office of the Public Guardian

    D   The Attorney General's Office

11 **Mr and Mrs Entwhistle are each liable as individuals for the whole of their joint mortgage. This is most likely to be so because they are:**

A   Joint tenants

B   Equal tenants

C   Tenants in common

D   Common tenants

12 **If one of two joint tenants dies, the property will automatically:**

A   Belong to the estate of the deceased

B   Be inherited by any children

C   Be held in trust until the death of the survivor

D   Belong to the survivor

13 **A Bankruptcy Order could not be brought against:**

A   A retail investment adviser who is a sole practitioner

B   A limited company providing security services to a Government agency

C   A partner in a firm of solicitors

D   A Member of Parliament

14 **Mr M. Patel has substantial debts and finds himself unable to pay a number of bills which are now due. A supplier who is owed £4,000 of unsecured debt is considering petitioning for bankruptcy to recover the funds. Lawyers looking into Mr Patel's potential bankruptcy are also examining the case of a company that is in financial difficulty and have been late in paying a number of outstanding bills. The court will not entertain the petition of the supplier. Which of the following is the most likely reason?**

A   Mr Patel would need to have been in debt for at least three years

B   £4,000 of unsecured debt is not a sufficient sum

C   Mr Patel is a private individual and not a company

D   Individual creditors cannot petition for a bankruptcy order

15 **Which of the following most accurately describes the basic aim or aims of insolvency law?**

A   Balancing the interests of competing groups and encouraging 'rescue' operations

B   Absolving the directors from responsibility for the company's collapse

C   Protecting the shareholders and directors of the company

D   Encouraging 'rescue' operations and protecting the shareholders of the company

16   A trust is established with a sole beneficiary. The beneficiary of the trust has the absolute and immediate right to both the income and capital from the trust. This form of trust can be described as a:

A   Bare trust

B   Lifetime trust

C   Charitable trust

D   Discretionary trust

17   A trust is established which gives the income beneficiary of the trust the legal right to live in a property during her lifetime. On her death the property will be held for the benefit of the second class beneficiary. This form of trust can be described as a:

A   Bare trust

B   Simple trust

C   Interest in possession trust

D   Charitable trust

18   A will is not invalidated by the testator:

A   Being a minor

B   Having a criminal record

C   Lacking mental capacity

D   Having been pressured into including some parts of the will

19   With regard to an individual voluntary arrangement (IVA), what percentage of creditors is required to vote in favour of the IVA proposal?

A   50%

B   75%

C   90%

D   100%

20   Which one of the following types of trust is most suited to giving the trustees greater freedom in decision making about distributions of income and capital for a group of beneficiaries?

A   A bare trust

B   An absolute trust

C   An interest in possession trust

D   A discretionary trust

Answers

1   **A**   A valid contract required an acceptance, following an offer, as there must be a willingness from the accepting party to enter into the contract. In order to make the contract complete, there must also be specific terms and conditions set out and accepted. Consideration and an intention to make the agreement legally binding are also required

2   **B**   Liquidation means that the company must be brought to an end, with the liquidator acting mainly in the interests of unsecured creditors. A liquidator is appointed to take control of the company, collect in all its assets, pay all its debts and distribute any surplus between members. The company is then dissolved and removed from the Register of Companies. The terms liquidation and winding-up both describe the process by which a company ceases to exist

3   **D**   A completed proposal form constitutes an offer in the legal contractual sense. For any contract to be considered legally binding, the elements of offer and acceptance must exist. The origin of a contract or agreement will begin with an off er and aft er the offer is accepted unconditionally, the contract is then formed

4   **D**   A contract does not have to be in writing for it to be binding, although a contract to sell land (ie property, including a house) or tenancy agreements, must be in writing

5   **A**   Reward is not a necessary feature of the agency relationship, although it is often present. An important consideration is the agency relationship, where a financial services entity acts on behalf of their clients, essentially acting as an agent. Laws of contract and ownership must also be fully understood to appreciate the significance of the agency relationship

6   **A**   The adviser owes a duty of care to the client, and acts as his or her agent

7   **A**   The attorney, who is given 'power of attorney' to handle someone's affairs, has the authority to enter into contracts. A power of attorney is a legal document that allows a person to give another person the power to make decisions about their financial affairs and/or their health and personal welfare. It can take two forms: either an enduring power of attorney (EPA) or a lasting power of attorney (LPA). The LPA was created in 2007 under the Mental Capacity Act 2005 and replaces the previous EPA, although any EPAs created before 2007 still remain valid. There are two types of LPA, being a property and affairs LPA that gives a person the ability to make decisions about somebody else's financial affairs, and secondly a personal welfare LPA that gives a person the ability to make decisions relating to somebody else's personal healthcare and welfare, including decisions to give or refuse consent to treatment on their behalf

8   **A**   The Mental Capacity Act 2005 replaced the procedure for setting up Enduring Powers of Attorney (EPA) with a Lasting Power of Attorney (LPA). Pre-existing EPAs can still be registered, although they cannot be changed

9   **C**   The Mental Capacity Act 2005 specifies such a test, as the Lasting Power of Attorney (LPA) which was created under the Mental Capacity Act 2005, allows a person to give another person the power to make decisions about their financial affairs and/or their health and personal welfare

10   **C**   A Lasting Power of Attorney (LPA) must be registered with the Office of the Public Guardian (OPG) to be effective, before it can be used

11   **A**   With the form of joint ownership known as joint tenancy, the survivor will automatically inherit the whole of the property. Each joint tenant will normally be liable for the whole mortgage. On the death of a joint tenant, their share passes to the other joint tenant

12   **D**   Joint tenancy means that the survivor inherits the deceased's share of the property, rather like a joint bank account. Joint tenants have equal ownership of the property and a joint tenant can only dispose of their interest during their lifetime by giving notice to the other joint tenant

13   **B**   A Bankruptcy Order may apply to individuals, sole traders or members of a partnership. Corporate insolvency law will apply to a limited company. Companies can be insolvent but not legally bankrupt

14   **B**   Anyone can apply to the court to become bankrupt, including individuals, sole traders and members of a partnership. There are different bankruptcy procedures for companies and partnerships. A person's creditors can usually petition the court to use a bankruptcy order if the person owes more than £5,000. The court will not hear a petition for less than £5,000

15   **A**   The basic aims of insolvency law would include controlling or punishing directors rather than removing their responsibilities, and protecting creditors rather than shareholders of the company

16   **A**   A bare trust is also known as a simple trust or an absolute trust. The trustee has no discretion over payment of income or capital to the beneficiary. The income and any capital gains are treated as the beneficiary's for tax purposes. This type of trust is typically used when a proposed beneficiary is a child or incapable of dealing with money

17   **C**   This is an interest in possession trust. These trusts are also known as 'life interest' trusts because the beneficiary has an interest in the benefits of the assets held in trust until their death. Where the assets in the trust are invested, one party, has the right to the income, or occupation of property

18   **B**   For a will to be valid, certain conditions have to be met. It must be in writing. It must be signed and witnessed by two persons. The person must be over 18 when it is made (ie not a minor). The person must have the mental capacity to make the will and understand the effect it will have. The person must not have made it as a result of pressure from someone else

19   **B**   An alternative to bankruptcy is for a debtor to seek an individual voluntary arrangement (IVA). To decide whether an IVA is acceptable, a creditors' meeting is called, and a vote is taken. Creditors representing at least 75% of those who vote need to vote in favour of the IVA proposal for it to go ahead. Once the IVA is approved, creditors are unable to take any legal action to recover the debt

20   **D**   With a discretionary trust, the trust property can be held for the benefit of group of beneficiaries and the trustees have discretion about how much to give to which beneficiaries and when. This is most suited when the beneficiaries are the settlor's children and/or grandchildren, with the trustees having discretion over payment of income until each child becomes entitled to their share in the estate at a given age. With a discretionary trust, the trustees use their discretion to decide which of the intended beneficiaries should receive income or capital from the trust

5 Client Advice

Questions

1   **The liabilities of pension funds are predominantly:**

A   Long-term real liabilities

B   Long-term fixed liabilities

C   Short-term real liabilities

D   Short-term fixed liabilities

2   **Brian is 38 years old and owns a two-bedroom flat in Cambridge. He has a mortgage that is provided by a bank. The flat was new when Brian bought it ten years ago.**

Gwenn is 49 years old and lives in a terraced house in Oxford. She has taken out two loans on the property. One was taken out to finance the purchase. The second mortgage was taken out to finance improvements which enhanced the value of the property.

Over a recent period, both Brian and Gwenn have both seen their loan-to-value ratio fall.

Which of the following statements is the most likely explanation of why Brian's loan-to-value ratio has, over the period in question, fallen less than Gwenn's loan to value ratio has fallen?

A   House prices have risen more in Cambridge than Oxford

B   House prices have risen in Cambridge but have fallen in Oxford

C   House prices have risen more in Oxford than Cambridge

D   House prices have risen in Oxford but have fallen in Cambridge

3   **Which of the following is not a reason for the decline in defined benefit (DB) pension schemes and the rise of defined contribution (DC) schemes?**

A   Higher liabilities in DB schemes

B   Decreased longevity

C   Falling returns on pension scheme assets

D   Increasing pension deficits

4   **Which of the following best describes strategic asset allocation?**

A   Strategic asset allocation is the practice of adjusting portfolio weights, when the portfolio manager believes that the relationship between asset classes will change during the near future

B   Strategic asset allocation is the process of attempting to identify the intrinsic value of a share

C   Strategic asset allocation is the process of allocating a portfolio among available assets in order to achieve the objectives of the portfolio

D   Strategic asset allocation is the process of attempting to exploit recurring and predictable share price movements

5 **Which of the following statements about life assurance funds is/are incorrect?**

      I   Any contributions paid into the life assurance fund are paid net of tax

      II   Capital gains within the fund are not taxable

      III   Any interest accumulated within the fund is not taxable

A I, II and III

B II only

C II and III

D III only

6 **If a pension fund is said to be a mature pension fund, this means that:**

A The pension fund has invested in assets that are said to be mature assets due to the age of the asset being invested in

B The pension fund has individuals who contribute into the pension fund who are mature in age

C The pension fund has been in existence for longer than other similar funds in the same peer group

D The pension fund has invested in government-backed bonds which are near to maturity, when the redemption proceeds will be received in order to meet a particular liability

7 **Which of the following types of fund is most likely to purchase index-linked gilts?**

A Investment trust companies

B Authorised unit trusts

C Pension funds

D Life assurance companies

8 **Which of the following are likely to be liability-driven investors?**

      I   General insurance funds

      II   Someone saving for school fees

      III   Unit trusts

A I and II

B I and III

C II and III

D I, II and III

9 **Which of the following is likely to be most suitable for a return-maximising investor who is prepared to take on a relatively high level of risk?**

A Pension fund

B Exchange-traded fund

C Investment trust

D General insurance fund

10   Denby Shotover is an investment firm with a range of institutional clients, an asset management arm and a newly acquired private client business. Which of the following of the firm's clients is likely to have the most complex objectives?

    A   A venture capital trust

    B   A wealthy private client

    C   An exchange-traded fund

    D   A pension fund

11   Which of the following are nominal liabilities?

        I   Bank loan

        II   Future college fees

        III   Credit card liabilities

    A   I and II

    B   I and III

    C   II and III

    D   I, II and III

12   Which of the following are real liabilities?

        I   School fees

        II   A defined benefit pension scheme

        III   Income provision for children

    A   I and II

    B   I and III

    C   II and III

    D   I, II and III

13   Which of the following matters in a fact-find is most likely to be described in terms of soft facts?

    A   Bank overdraft

    B   Current investment holdings

    C   Client aspirations

    D   Current income

14   What is the best description of shortfall risk?

    A   Potential variability of inflation rates

    B   Potential variability of interest rates

    C   Potential variability of current fund values

    D   Potential variability of future fund values

15   Edward and Edwina Smith are in their mid-30s and are hoping to retire before they reach 60 and still be able to maintain their lifestyles. Neither of them has any pension arrangement. Which of the following will be the best starting point for giving advice?

A   An analysis of household income

B   An analysis of their existing life assurance policies

C   Details of their children

D   Details of their expense claims

16   Your client, Bob, is in his mid-30s and has listed his financial objectives as follows.

–   **Retire at age 60**
–   **Protect his family in the event of his death or ill health**
–   **Repay his mortgage within 10 years**

Having costed these options, you find that Bob has insufficient income to afford all of these objectives. What advice would you offer him?

A   That he can achieve all objectives he sets himself

B   Regulations require that a fully funded pension must take priority

C   That his mortgage lender can determine his priorities

D   That he must choose which objectives to prioritise

17   If a portfolio is managed so that it grows through a combination of income and capital gain, its investment objective can be best described as:

A   Capital preservation

B   Long/short

C   Total return

D   Liability-driven

18   Hanna is a retail client who works as a junior hospital doctor. She has little time to spend on organising her financial affairs. She now has saved money which she wishes to invest over the medium and long term.

What is the least important consideration if you are to recommend an investment in a collective investment scheme for Hanna?

A   Historical performance of the fund relative to peers

B   Management and other charges

C   Whether the fund is structured as a Unit Trust or an OEIC

D   Riskiness of the sector in which the fund is invested

19   Which of the following is not a stage in the financial planning process?

A   Analyse

B   Review

C   Purchase

D   Collect

20 **Which one of the following is less likely to be an example of a vulnerable client, as determined by the FCA?**

A   A client with a lack of English language skills

B   A client with mental health problems

C   A client who cares for an elderly relative, and has a Last Power of Attorney (LPA)

D   A 70-year old client, with poor eyesight

Answers

1   **A**   There is typically a long-term time horizon, with liabilities being affected by inflation

2   **C**   The equity that a homeowner has in the home increases as the loan-to-value (LTV) ratio decreases. House price rises will tend to reduce the loan-to-value ratio of the borrower. House price falls will increase the homeowner's LTV, which is not the case for either Brian or Gwenn

3   **B**   Along with the other factors, such as higher liabilities in a DB scheme, falling returns on pension scheme assets and increased pension deficits, increased (not decreased) longevity is one of the reasons for the decline in defined benefit schemes

4   **C**   The strategic asset allocation is not fixed permanently, nor is it changed regularly. In the UK, it is common to review the strategic asset allocation once every three years. Asset allocation refers to the mix of underlying asset classes held within a portfolio. The main asset classes are cash, fixed-interest securities, property and equities. Each asset class behaves differently and has very different risk characteristics. A number of academic studies have shown that asset allocation is the single most important factor in determining the returns of an investment portfolio. The implication is therefore that other factors, such as individual security, fund selection or market timing, are less important

5   **C**   Life assurance funds have a different tax position from that of pension funds. The investment returns within a life assurance fund are subject to both income tax and capital gains tax. Also, any contributions paid into the fund by an investor will be paid out of their post-tax income

6   **B**   The maturity of a pension fund is with reference to the average age of the individuals who contribute into the pension fund. The two extremes would be a 'young' pension fund, where the pension fund has a longer time horizon, and a 'mature' pension fund, where the pension fund has a shorter time horizon to consider

7   **C**   Index-linked gilts are most likely to be purchased by pension funds, as they are trying to meet a 'real' liability in the future rather than a 'nominal' liability, and so an index-linked gilt that offers an inflation-protected, real return would be an ideal investment to buy

8   **A**   A unit trust will seek to maximise returns. An insurance fund will have short-term liabilities in general, due to the nature of insurance, such as motor insurance or home insurance. If saving for school fees, the timing of the liability is known with some certainty, as an investor would be able to identify the time period of a child attending school

9   **C**   An investment trust companies will generally seek to maximise returns and some may focus on sectors that are higher risk, while other funds will aim to achieve matching, such as an ETFs matching an index, and not seeking outperformance

10 **B**   A wealthy private client is likely to have several objectives to meet, perhaps with similar priorities. The funds will each have one primary objective. Every individual investor has different investment objectives related to their particular circumstances, attitudes and constraints. There are three main factors that are important in determining an investor's needs and objectives, which as time horizons, return requirements and risk tolerance. This is likely to make for complex objectives

BPP LEARNING MEDIA

11   **B**   Future college fees represent a real liability, as these are likely to rise with inflation in the economy, indicating a real liability. A nominal liability is one that remains the same, irrespective of inflation, such as a bank loan, specifically a mortgage

12   **D**   All are real liabilities, as these are likely to rise with inflation

13   **C**   Client aspirations are subjective, being incapable of objective quantification, hence are described as soft facts in a fact-finding exercise. Current levels of income, existing liabilities and current investments are all deemed to be hard facts. Other examples include personal information, such as name, address, date of birth, National Insurance number, state of health, marital status, residence and domicile status, employment details and family details

14   **D**   The risks described are, respectively, inflation risk, interest rate risk, capital risk, shortfall risk. Shortfall risk is the risk that the investment return will literally fall short of the amount required for the investor to meet their objectives. The response in anticipation of a shortfall could be to reduce the target amount, increase the amount currently invested or extend the time horizon, in an attempt to reduce the shortfall

15   **A**   Affordability will be the primary concern, and hence household income is the most important. Affordability is a real constraint that means that clients often have to prioritise their financial goals. Affordability can be established by preparing a cash flow statement showing all of the client's income and expenditure. A surplus indicates capital available for pension plans, or maybe repaying mortgage debt

16   **D**   An individual's financial priorities are for that individual to determine themselves. Affordability can be a concern, and a client will often have to prioritise their financial goals themselves. Many clients may need assistance in understanding the financial implications of prioritising objectives and agreeing either revised financial targets or amended timescales to achieve these

17   **C**   Total returns are a combination of income and capital gains

18   **C**   The technical differences between OEICs and unit trusts are less important than the other reasons quoted, such as past performance, management charges and the risk profile of the sector that the fund is investing in. These are more important factors to be considered before investing in a particular fund

19   **C**   The stages of the financial planning process are Establish, Collect, Analyse, Develop, Implement and Review. The financial planning process should follow a six-step process: 1. Establish and define the client–personal financial planner relationship. 2. Gather client data and determine goals and expectations. 3. Analyse and evaluate the client's financial status. 4. Develop and present the plan. 5. Implement the financial planning recommendations. 6. Monitor the financial plan and the financial planning relationship

20   **D**   A vulnerable client, as determined by the FCA, includes a client with a lack of English language skills, a client with mental health problems, and also a client who cares for an elderly relative, and has a Last Power of Attorney (LPA). However, the FCA suggest that an 80-year old client (rather than a 70-year old), which is correlated with a physical or mental impairment is also a vulnerable client

6 Taxation in the UK

Questions

1 **Which individual is exempt from paying national insurance contributions?**

A Alex, who is self-employed

B Jared, who is above the state pension age

C Afrah, who is aged 17 and works for a bank

D Samir, who works 25 hours per week

2 **In the financial year 2022, the 19% rate of corporation tax applies to companies which earn profits of:**

A Less than £1,500,000 only

B Between £150,000 and £300,000 only

C Less than £300,000 only

D Any amount

3 **Which of the following is not tax-free income for an individual?**

A Interest on gilts

B Proceeds of a qualifying life assurance policy

C Income from an Individual Savings Account

D Interest on National Savings & Investments (NS&I) Savings Certificates

4 **Emma, who is 62 years old, earns a salary of £49,000. Which of the following is true in relation to Emma's tax situation in the current fiscal year?**

A Emma's personal allowance is £12,300 and her marginal rate of tax is 10%

B Emma's personal allowance is £12,300 and her marginal rate of tax is 40%

C Emma's personal allowance is £12,570 and her marginal rate of tax is 20%

D Emma's personal allowance is £12,570 and her marginal rate of tax is 40%

5 **Ivan Seeger has made two chargeable disposals in the current fiscal year. The chargeable gains have been calculated as £13,400 and £5,300. Neither is eligible for entrepreneurs' relief. There are brought forward losses of £2,000. Ivan has taxable income of £34,500. What is the capital gains tax payable for the current fiscal year (in pounds, to the nearest £1)? The capital gains tax annual exempt amount is £12,300. The taxable income basic rate tax band is from £0 to £37,700.**

Important! You should enter the answer only in numbers strictly using this format: 000

Do not include spaces, letters or symbols (but decimal points and commas should be used if indicated).

6   The tax rate on dividends for an additional-rate taxpayer is 39.35%. This taxpayer receives a dividend of 16p per share on their holding of 50,000 shares; what tax is due to be paid on the dividend, in pounds to the nearest £1? The taxpayer receives no other dividends.

Important! You should enter the answer only in numbers strictly using this format: 0,000

Do not include spaces, letters or symbols (but decimal points and commas should be used if indicated).

7   An individual disposes of shares in company A for £61,700 and shares in company B for £30,300, having purchased them for £48,000 and £31,000 respectively. If income tax is paid at the higher rate, the capital gains tax exempt amount is £12,300, and entrepreneurs' relief is not available, what CGT is payable?

A   £140

B   £126

C   £70

D   £0

8   In October of the current tax year, Sally buys a four-bedroom house for £650,000. How much stamp duty land tax (SDLT) must she pay?

A   £13,000

B   £22,500

C   £20,000

D   £32,500

9   On which of the following does CGT have an impact?

I   Savings accounts
II   UK Government bonds
III Equities

A   III only

B   I and II

C   II and III

D   I, II and III

10   From which of the following sources is any income free of income tax?

I   NS&I Savings Certificates
II   NS&I Direct Saver Account
III Individual Savings Account

A   I, II and III

B   II and III

C   I and III

D   None of I, II and III

11   **Which of the following disposals is/are not chargeable to capital gains tax?**

      I   Sale of gilts

      II   Sale of Eurobonds

      III   Sale of convertible debt denominated in sterling

  A I, II and III

  B I and II

  C I and III

  D I only

12   **A capital gains tax liability may not be reduced by the cost of:**

  A Acquiring the asset

  B Maintaining the asset

  C Improving the asset

  D Disposing of the asset

13   **Kevin makes a gift of £175,000 to a trust in July of the current tax year. He had previously made a chargeable transfer of £145,000 within the last ten years and another transfer of £173,000 six years ago. The trustees agree to pay the lifetime tax. How much do the trustees have to pay on the gift made in July, in pounds to the nearest £1?**

Important! You should enter the answer only in numbers strictly using this format: 0,000

Do not include spaces, letters or symbols (but decimal points and commas should be used if indicated).

14   **What is the highest rate of tax that discretionary trusts may be required to pay on their dividend income?**

  A 20%

  B 33.75%

  C 39.35%

  D 50%

15   **What are the rates of capital gains tax on UK share sales for (1) basic rate taxpayers, (2) higher rate taxpayers, (3) additional rate taxpayers, and (4) trustees, in the current fiscal year?**

  A (1) 8.75%; (2) 33.75%; (3) 39.35%; (4) 39.35%

  B (1) 10%; (2) 20%; (3) 20%; (4) 20%

  C (1) 18%; (2) 28%; (3) 28%; (4) 18%

  D (1) 10%; (2) 20%; (3) 28%; (4) 18%

16   What is the standard rate of VAT?

A   0%

B   5%

C   17.5%

D   20%

17   At what rate is Stamp Duty Reserve Tax (SDRT) charged?

A   0.5%

B   1%

C   3%

D   4%

18   On which dates are first and second self-assessment payments on account for 2022/23 due?

A   31 July 2022 and 31 January 2023

B   31 January 2023 and 31 July 2023

C   31 January 2023 and 31 January 2024

D   31 July 2023 and 31 January 2024

19   Darren, aged 50, has a personal pension plan into which he has made maximum tax-relievable contributions in each of the last five years, up to and including the current year. How much can he contribute into the plan and obtain tax relief in the current fiscal year?

A   The higher of £3,600 and his earnings in the tax year, subject to a cap of £40,000

B   The lower of £3,600 and his earnings in the tax year

C   The higher of £3,600 and his earnings in the tax year, subject to a cap of £150,000

D   £3,600 if he is a non-taxpayer and £50,000 if he is a taxpayer

20   Ronan has made contributions of £8,000 into a stocks and shares ISA in the current tax year. What is the maximum amount, in pounds, that he can contribute to a cash ISA in the same tax year?

Important! You should enter the answer only in numbers strictly using this format: 00,000

Do not include spaces, letters or symbols (but decimal points and commas should be used if indicated).

21   Which of the following is not true of Real Estate Investment Trusts (REITs)?

A   REITs are listed companies

B   REITs may elect for their property income to be exempt from corporation tax

C   It is not possible to hold a REIT in an ISA

D   Disposals of REIT shares may be subject to CGT

22 **The Junior ISA is best described as:**

A A way to take advantage of a government payment for a child born after 2 January 2011

B A way for a child born before 3 January 2011 and holding a Child Trust Fund to continue to receive an annual government payment

C A scheme of tax-free investment on behalf of a child in which £9,000 can be invested in the current fiscal year

D A scheme of tax-free investment on behalf of a child in which £3,600 can be invested in the current fiscal year

23 **An investor sells shares that he purchased ten years ago. Which of the following statements regarding tax allowances on the sale is correct?**

A The investor will receive a CGT exemption allowance only

B The investor will receive no CGT exemption allowance nor any other allowance

C The investor will receive a CGT exemption allowance and an allowance for inflation only

D The investor will receive a CGT exemption allowance and an allowance related to the period the shares were held only

24 **Which of the following would incur a CGT liability on sale?**

A Private car

B Gilts

C Currency in a foreign exchange trading account

D Shares in an ISA wrapper

Use the following information to answer Questions 25 to 28.

Bill Swinson is a higher rate taxpayer with a salary of £85,000 per year. During the current fiscal year, he also received £9,000 in coupon interest from an investment in bonds, and dividends of £7,200 from his investments in shares.

25 **How much (in pounds, to the nearest £1) is Bill's personal allowance for income tax purposes?**

Important! You should enter the answer only in numbers strictly using this format: 00,000

Do not include spaces, letters or symbols (but decimal points and commas should be used if indicated).

26 **How much tax (in pounds, to the nearest £1) is Bill liable to pay in respect of the bond coupon interest?**

Important! You should enter the answer only in numbers strictly using this format: 0,000

Do not include spaces, letters or symbols (but decimal points and commas should be used if indicated).

27 **How much tax is Bill liable to pay in respect of his dividend income, in pounds to the nearest £1?**

Important! You should enter the answer only in numbers strictly using this format: 0,000

Do not include spaces, letters or symbols (but decimal points and commas should be used if indicated).

---

28 **What was Bill's total tax liability for the current fiscal year, in pounds to the nearest £1?**

Important! You should enter the answer only in numbers strictly using this format: 00,000

Do not include spaces, letters or symbols (but decimal points and commas should be used if indicated).

---

29 **Which of the following proposals would be least appropriate as a method of potentially minimising an individual's CGT liability?**

A   Transfer the ownership of assets to a spouse or civil partner who is in a lower tax bracket or may have unused CGT annual exempt allowance

B   Phase asset disposals over more than one tax year

C   Transfer the CGT annual exempt allowance to a spouse or civil partner

D   Realise gains within the CGT annual exempt amount, and repurchase a similar asset

---

30 **Which of the following is least likely to be recommended as a tax-efficient investment?**

A   Personal Pension Plan

B   Individual Savings Account

C   High Interest Savings Account

D   Enterprise Investment Scheme

---

31 **An investor owns a rental property which provides income (after allowable expenses) of £28,000 per year. On 5 April, she transfers 50% ownership of the property to her husband, who has no other income. How much income tax liability will the husband have, in pounds to the nearest £1, after the transfer, in the current fiscal year?**

Important! You should enter the answer only in numbers strictly using this format: 000

Do not include spaces, letters or symbols (but decimal points and commas should be used if indicated).

---

32 **Which of the following would be treated as a gift with reservation (GWR) for IHT purposes?**

A Giving away a holiday cottage but continuing to spend long holidays there while paying a market rent

B Giving away a house but continuing to live in it while paying rent of £1 per annum

C Giving away a painting

D Creating a trust from which you do not benefit

---

33 **Florence Devere died on 1 November 2019 leaving £162,500 to her surviving spouse Kevin and the remaining £195,000 of her estate to her only child. The IHT nil rate band in the year of death and also in the current fiscal year is £325,000. Which of the following is correct?**

A On his death, Kevin's estate cannot take advantage of any transfer of Florence's nil rate band

B On his death, Kevin's estate can take advantage of 40% additional nil rate band as a result of Florence's nil rate band being transferred

C On his death, Kevin's estate can take advantage of 50% additional nil rate band as a result of Florence's nil rate band being transferred

D On his death, Kevin's estate can take advantage of 60% additional nil rate band as a result of Florence's nil rate band being transferred

Use the following information to answer Questions 34 to 37.

Ashley and Cheryl, a married couple, have asked you to provide them with investment advice. During the fact-find process you have determined their existing investments, set out in the table below. All the investments are presently in Ashley's name.

Ashley has taxable income of £58,000 and Cheryl has taxable income of £13,500. The annual capital gains tax (CGT) exemption is £12,300 in the current tax year.

Type of asset	Current value £	Purchase price £
Gilts	18,500	12,000
Shares in Big Boots plc	16,000	20,000
Vintage wine	30,000	9,000
Bank savings account	25,000	22,000
Buy to let flat	400,000	250,000

Give your answers to the nearest £1.

---

34 **What would be the CGT liability if the vintage wine were sold by Ashley, assuming that he made no other disposals in the current fiscal year, in pounds to the nearest £1?**

Important! You should enter the answer only in numbers strictly using this format: 0,000

Do not include spaces, letters or symbols (but decimal points and commas should be used if indicated).

35 What would be the total CGT liability if the shares in Big Boots Plc were sold in the current fiscal year, as well as the vintage wine, in pounds to the nearest £1?

Important! You should enter the answer only in numbers strictly using this format: 000

Do not include spaces, letters or symbols (but decimal points and commas should be used if indicated).

```

```

36 What would be the CGT liability if the wine were sold by Cheryl after being fully transferred into Cheryl's name, in pounds to the nearest £1?

Important! You should enter the answer only in numbers strictly using this format: 000

Do not include spaces, letters or symbols (but decimal points and commas should be used if indicated).

```

```

37 How much CGT is saved by transferring the wine into Cheryl's name before selling, in pounds to the nearest £1?

Important! You should enter the answer only in numbers strictly using this format: 000

Do not include spaces, letters or symbols (but decimal points and commas should be used if indicated).

```

```

38 What is the pension lifetime allowance for the current fiscal year?

A   £1,000,000

B   £400,000

C   £325,000

D   £1,073,100

39 What is the rate of tax deducted from a dividend distributed by a REIT?

A   0%

B   10%

C   20%

D   The rate of tax deducted will depend upon the tax status of the investor

40 If a five-bedroom residential house is purchased in December of the current tax year for £950,000, how much stamp duty land tax (SDLT) is payable?

A   £37,500

B   £16,000

C   £40,000

D   £38,750

Answers

1   **B**   NICs are not payable by those who are older than the State pension age. Depending on the individual's income level, NICs may be payable by full-time or part-time workers, and by those who are self-employed

2   **D**   For the financial year 2022 (1 April 2022 to 31 March 2023), companies must pay a single rate of corporation tax at 19% of their profits. A UK-resident company is liable to corporation tax on its worldwide profits and chargeable gains arising in an accounting period

3   **A**   Gilt interest is normally paid gross but is still liable to income tax. ISAs produce non-taxable income. Other tax-free investments include NS&I savings certificates and NS&I children's bonds. There is also a tax-free pension commencement lump sum (PCLS) of up to 25% can be taken from a pension fund upon retirement. Any proceeds from a qualifying life assurance policy are usually free of income tax and CGT for the original beneficiary

4   **C**   Emma is entitled to a personal allowance (PA) of £12,570. The basic rate (20%) band applies to the first £37,700 of taxable income (2022/23). Taxable income is calculated after the personal allowance has been deducted, therefore, an individual could earn a salary of up to £50,270, and be treated as a basic rate tax payer

5   **560**

	£
Chargeable gains	18,700
Less: loss brought forward	(2,000)
Less: CGT annual exemption	(12,300)
	4,400

Since the investor has taxable income (which is after the income tax personal allowance has been deducted) of £34,500 (£3,200 below the higher rate threshold of £37,700), the capital gains tax payable is calculated as:

(10% × £3,200 falling into the basic rate band) + (20% × £1,200 falling into the higher rate band) = £320 + £240 = £560 CGT

6   **2,361**   The total dividend is 50,000 shares × 16p = £8,000. The dividend allowance is £2,000, and is available to all taxpayers

£8,000 − £2,000 = £6,000. Therefore, £6,000 × 39.35% = £2,361

7   **A**   (£61,700 − £48,000) + (£30,300 − £31,000) − £12,300 annual exemption = £700

Applying the capital gains tax rate of 20% (as a higher rate taxpayer) gives CGT of £700 × 20% = £140

8 **B** The nil rate band threshold of £125,000 is relevant for the current tax year, followed by the next £125,000 band at 2%, and the next £675,000 band at 5%. Therefore, the SDLT payable, on a house worth £650,000, is as follows:

(£125,000 × 0%) + (£125,000 × 2%) + (£400,000 × 5%) = £0 + £2,500 + £20,000 = £22,500

Residential SDLT rates

£0 to £125,000 at 0%; £125,001 to £250,000 at 2%; £250,001 to £925,000 at 5%;

£925,001 to £1,500,000 at 10%; Over £1,500,000 at 12%

9 **A** Capital gains tax will not impact on savings or deposit accounts because the capital remains unchanged – these are subject to income tax on the interest earned. Capital gains tax (CGT) is paid by UK residents on the sale of an asset. Most assets are chargeable, including shares and property. However, some assets are exempt from CGT, including UK Government bonds and most corporate bonds

10 **C** National Savings & Investments (NS&I) Savings Certificates, NS&I children's bonds, and Individual Savings Accounts (ISAs) pay income free of UK income tax. Interest paid on a NS&I Direct Saver account is paid gross and is taxable

11 **D** Capital gains on Eurobonds and convertible bonds are subject to capital gains tax. UK Government bonds, known as gilts, and most corporate bonds (non-convertible) are exempt from CGT

12 **B** Running and maintenance costs are not allowable as a reduction in the CGT calculation, however the cost of acquiring the asset, as well as any improvements to the asset, and costs incurred in selling the asset can be deducted

13 **3,400** Most transfers into trusts are immediately liable to IHT if the transfer exceeds the donor's available nil rate band. These are known as Chargeable Lifetime Transfers (CLTs). CLTs are subject to an immediate 20% IHT charge if the reduction in the value of the donor's estate (after any allowable deductions, such as the £3,000 annual exemption (AE), exceeds the available nil rate band (this will also be reduced by any CLTs made within the past seven years, such as the gift of £173,000). The gift of £145,000 was made more than 7 years ago, and this is not included in the calculation

Transfer of value July of the current tax year

	£	£
Cash gift		175,000
Less AE current year		(3,000)
AE previous year (brought forward)		(3,000)
Gross transfer of value		169,000
Nil rate band available at date of gift	325,000	
Less: chargeable transfers in the 7 years before gift	(173,000)	
Nil rate band remaining (after CLT)		(152,000)
Taxable		17,000
Tax @ 20% (as this is a chargeable lifetime transfer, as it is a gift into a trust)		3,400

14   C   The dividend income within a discretionary trust is taxed at what is known as the 'dividend trust rate' of 39.35%. This is the equivalent rate of tax for an additional rate taxpayer (2022/23). All other income such as property or savings is taxed at 45%, known as the 'trust rate'

15   B   There are two rates of CGT for individuals – 10% (for basic rate taxpayers) and 20% (for higher and additional rate tax payers) – and trusts pay the same CGT rate as higher and additional rate taxpayers

16   D   The 20% VAT rate (called the 'standard rate' of VAT) applies to most goods and services. A zero-rated supply (such as children's clothes and printed books) is different from VAT exempt items. This is because businesses supplying zero-rated items can reclaim VAT on any of their purchases, whereas a business supplying exempt items cannot reclaim VAT. The 5% VAT rate applies to energy products and services.

17   A   0.5%. The amount of SDRT paid by an investor is worked out at a flat rate of 0.5% (rounded up or down to the nearest penny) based on what the investor paid for the shares, not what the shares are currently worth. For a cash transaction, SDRT is based on the amount of cash paid, eg if an investor buys shares for £1,000, they will pay £5 in SDRT no matter the value of the shares

18   B   The tax payer will make two equal payments which are due on 31 January in the tax year, and on 31 July after the tax year ends

19   A   An individual, who is under the age of 75, is entitled to tax relief on contributions made into a pension scheme during the tax year. The maximum contributions that can be made are the higher of the individual's relevant earnings subject to an annual cap of £40,000 (2022/23 fiscal year); or a basic amount of £3,600. Unused annual allowances from the three previous tax years can be carried forward, but this individual has no unused allowances from these years. Non-taxpayers can contribute £3,600 gross, the basic amount

20   12,000   ISAs generally have an annual investment limit of £20,000 (2022/23). This limit is flexible and can be split between the various types of ISA as desired – such as £14,000 in a cash ISA and £6,000 in a stocks and shares ISA. Therefore, if £8,000 has already been invested, the remaining available contribution is £12,000 for this current fiscal year

21   C   REITs can be held in an ISA. They are listed companies (on the LSE) and any rental income and capital gains are exempt from tax at the REIT level, however are taxed at the investor level when they are paid as dividends. If the investor sells these shares, there will also be a potential CGT liability

22   C   There are no government payments for Junior ISA holders. Junior ISAs are available to children under the age of 18 who were either born after 2 January 2011 or who were not eligible for a child trust fund (CTF). The maximum investment in a Junior ISA is £9,000 per tax year (2022/23), which may be split between a cash Junior ISA and a stocks and shares Junior ISA as desired. A child can have a maximum of two Junior ISAs (one of each type) over their childhood

23   A   Investors receive an annual allowance on capital gains, only. No other allowances are permitted when disposing of shares

24   **C**   Gilts do not incur CGT liability and any assets in an Individual Savings Account (ISA) are free of any tax. A car is generally considered a wasting asset which incurs no CGT. However, currency gains made via a trading account would be subject to CGT. Foreign currency for personal use, such as a holiday overseas is exempt

25   **11,970**   Bill's earned income is £85,000. We are told that he received coupon interest of £9,000. Bill received £7,200 in dividend income. Total income = £85,000 + £9,000 + £7,200 = £101,200. This exceeds £100,000 by £1,200, thus reducing the standard personal allowance of £12,570 by £1,200/2 = £600. Thus, Bill's revised personal allowance is £11,970, being £12,570 less the restriction of £600

26   **3,400**   Bill received gross interest of £9,000. As a higher rate taxpayer, Bill has a personal savings allowance (PSA) of £500, as he is a higher rate taxpayer. Therefore, he will need to pay 40% on £8,500 (£9,000 - £500 PSA), which equals £3,400

27   **1,755**   The dividend is £7,200, less the dividend allowance of £2,000 equals £5,200. As a higher rate taxpayer, Bill must pay 33.75% on £5,200 (£7,200 - £2,000 dividend allowance), which equals £1,755

28   **26,827**   The answer is calculated in the following table. Note that the question asks for the total tax liability, and not the total tax due

	Earnings £	Interest £	Dividends £
Total earnings	85,000		
Interest		9,000	
Dividends			7,200
Less personal allowance (£600 reduction)	(11,970)		
Taxable income	73,030	9,000	7,200
	£		
Tax on first £37,700 @ 20%	7,540		
Tax on next £35,330 @ 40%	14,132		
Tax on £500 @ 0%		0	
Tax on £8,500 @ 40%		3,400	
Tax on £2,000 @ 0%			0
Tax on £5,200 @ 33.75%			1,755
Total tax liability			**26,827**

29   **C**   The annual CGT exempt allowance cannot be transferred. However, there are some common strategies to reduce CGT such as sharing ownership of assets between family members to make use of the maximum number of annual exempt amounts (transfers between spouses are free from CGT); phasing of disposals over different tax years to benefit from more than one annual exempt amount (two separate disposals made in late March 2023 (2022/23) and early April 2023 (2023/24)) would make use of two annual exempt amounts; and realising capital losses to reduce gains that would otherwise exceed the annual exempt amount and then become taxable

30   **C**   While the other investments all offer tax reductions, there is no such reduction for an ordinary high interest savings account that is not within a tax wrapper, and the interest will be charged to income tax

31 **286** Each will be taxed on the rental income (£28,000 × 50% = £14,000) as though they own 50% of the property as joint owners. The husband's liability will therefore be (£14,000 – £12,570 personal allowance) = £1,430 × 20% = £286

32 **B** Gifts with reservation (GWR) occur when an individual gifts property and continues to enjoy the benefit of the asset, either rent free or at reduced cost, or the person getting the gift does so with conditions attached. Therefore, it is still considered to be part of their estate no matter how long they live after making the gift. If someone gives their house to their children, but carries on living there without paying a full market rent, then the value of the house will be included in their estate and liable to IHT

33 **B** The transfer to Kevin is exempt from IHT. The remaining transfer to the child amounts to 60% of Florence's nil rate band (as £195,000 / £325,000 = 60%), leaving the remaining percentage of the nil rate band, 40%, to transfer to Kevin, the surviving spouse. It is always the remaining percentage that is transferred, and not the monetary amount

34 **1,740** The vintage wine gain on disposal is £21,000 (£30,000 value - £9,000 cost). The first £12,300 is covered by the annual CGT exemption. The taxable gain is therefore £8,700 (£21,000 - £12,300) at 20% CGT = £1,740, as Ashley is a higher rate tax payer

35 **940** The total gain is now £17,000. This is made up of (£16,000 value of shares - £20,000 cost) = £4,000 loss on disposal of the shares plus £21,000 gain from the vintage wine. The loss on the shares partially offsets the gain on the wine. The first £12,300 is exempt from CGT, leaving a taxable gain of £4,700 (£17,000 - £12,300), taxable at the higher rate of 20% = £940

36 **870** Taxable gain = (£30,000 value of wine – £9,000 cost) – £12,300 annual exemption = £8,700. The taxable gain is therefore £8,700 (£21,000 - £12,300) at 10% CGT = £870, as Cheryl is a basic rate tax payer

37 **870** £1,740 CGT incurred at higher rate (20% CGT) less £870 at lower rate (10% CGT)

38 **D** The pension lifetime allowance for the current fiscal year is £1,073,100. This is normally indexed annually in line with the consumer price index (CPI) to reflect the inflationary uplift, however it is to remain unchanged at this current level of £1,073,100 up to and including the 2025/26 fiscal year

39 **C** Basic-rate tax at 20% is generally withheld from the dividend, with the dividend then taxed as property income at the investor's marginal tax rate, with the benefit of a credit for the tax withheld

40 **D** If a house is purchased for £950,000, then the SDLT payable is as follows:

(£125,000 at 0%) + (£125,000 at 2%) + (£675,000 at 5%) + (£25,000 at 10%) = £38,750

Residential SDLT rates

£0 to £125,000 at 0%; £125,001 to £250,000 at 2%; £250,001 to £925,000 at 5%;

£925,001 to £1,500,000 at 10%; Over £1,500,000 at 12%

Practice Examinations

Contents

	Page Number	
	Questions	Answers
Practice Examination 1	93	111
Practice Examination 2	121	139
Practice Examination 3	147	164
Practice Examination 4	173	191
Practice Examination 5	201	219

The Unit 1 examination *The Investment Environment* consists of 85 questions, to be answered in 1 hour and 40 minutes. There will be a small number of additional questions which will not be marked as these are new questions included for evaluation purposes. Your examination is therefore based on 85 marked questions, although you will not be informed which are marked and which are not.

Most of the questions will be four-part multiple-choice questions but the exam will also contain a number of gap-fill questions for numerical areas. With a gap-fill question, no selection of possible answers is offered: you must enter your answer in the space provided.

Each of the five Practice Examinations presented here has 85 questions (the number that is marked in the examination) and you should allow yourself a time limit of 1 hour and 40 minutes for each exam.

Practice Examination 1

(85 questions in 1 hour and 40 minutes)

1   Which of the following is not one of the objectives of the Financial Conduct Authority, as provided in FSMA 2000?

A   Securing an appropriate degree of protection for consumers

B   Ensuring that the relevant markets function well

C   Ensuring stable prices and confidence in the currency

D   Promoting effective competition in the market for regulated financial services

2   What is the standard settlement term on shares traded through the London Stock Exchange?

A   T + 1

B   T + 2

C   T + 3

D   T + 5

3   Which of the following is not true with regard to asset allocation?

A   It is designed to achieve better risk/return outcomes than from just investing in one asset class

B   It is the final stage of the investment management process

C   It would include consideration of investing in cash

D   It is influenced by a client's objectives and constraints

4   How would you describe the typical risks of investing in cash?

A   Capital risk

B   Interest rate risk

C   Capital and interest rate risk

D   Neither capital nor interest rate risk

5   What is the main reason why a pension fund would hold equities?

A   To immunise the portfolio

B   To hedge the inflation risk in the liabilities

C   Because the fund manager believes that the return will match the fund's future liabilities

D   To match the risk profile of the fund's liabilities

6   **Jared is a higher rate taxpayer He receives £1,750 in dividends from ordinary shares in listed companies in the current tax year. The shares are not held in an Individual Savings Account. How much tax must he pay on the dividends, in pounds sterling?**

        Important! You should enter the answer only in numbers strictly using this format: 0.00

        Do not include spaces, letters or symbols (but decimal points and commas should be used if indicated).


```
┌─────────────────────────────────────┐
│                                     │
└─────────────────────────────────────┘
```

---

7   **What is the last stage of the process of investing a retail client's funds?**

     A   Asset allocation

     B   Fact find

     C   Fund selection

     D   Market timing

---

8   **Against which of the following company's annual profits can this year's losses be offset for corporation tax purposes?**

        I   Profits of this year

        II   Future year's gains from the same trade

        III   Last year's profits

     A   I and II

     B   I and III

     C   II and III

     D   I, II and III

---

9   **Which of the following conduct rules apply only to senior managers?**

     A   You must act with due care, skill and diligence

     B   You must take reasonable steps to ensure that the business of the firm for which you are responsible is controlled effectively

     C   You must observe proper standards of market conduct

     D   You must be open and co-operative with the FCA, the PRA and other regulators

---

10   **How are Eurobonds normally traded in the secondary market?**

     A   Over the counter

     B   Via Clearstream

     C   Via Euroclear

     D   Through the ECB

11   **In the context of company meetings, which of the following is/are correct with regards to proxies?**

       I   The proxy must be able to vote in two ways on each issue

       II   The proxy form must state that the member gives consent for the proxy to vote on their behalf

       III   The proxy form must state in which direction the proxy must vote

A II only

B I and II

C I and III

D I, II and III

---

12   **Under the CFA Institute Code and Principles, which of the following is most accurate with regard to an employee leaving their current firm and joining a rival?**

A The employee may take information with regards to the current clients of their existing firm

B The employee may take a valuation model which was developed at the firm where they currently work for which the employee was involved in the development of

C The employee may take partly complete research reports which the employee was working on before leaving their current firm

D The employee may take knowledge gained from attending a training course whilst employed at their current firm

---

13   **Under the CFA Code and Principles, which of the following would be most likely to be considered market manipulation?**

A Buying shares in a company after having recommended to clients to buy the same company's shares

B Selling share in a company after having recommended to clients to sell the shares in the same company

C Buying shares in a company on behalf of clients to push the share price up before selling personal holdings of shares

D Buying shares in a company before buying shares on behalf of your clients

---

14   **Which pair of words most closely describe a 'financial promotion'?**

A Advertisement/encouragement

B Incentive/publicity

C Invitation/inducement

D Prospectus/upgrade

15   **Under the CFA Code and Principles, if an adviser is about to recommend buying shares which the adviser holds herself, what is the most appropriate action to be taken?**

A   The adviser should sell her own shares before making the recommendation

B   The adviser should not make the recommendation since she owns shares herself

C   The adviser should disclose to her clients that she owns shares themselves

D   The adviser is not required to do anything with regard to making this recommendation

16   **With whom is a lasting power of attorney (LPA) required to be registered?**

A   The Crown Court

B   The Attorney Agency

C   The Ministry of Justice

D   The Office of the Public Guardian

17   **Which of the following are covered by the FCA's Principles for Businesses?**

I   Protection of client assets

II   Communication of relevant information to clients

III   Skill, care and diligence

A   II and III

B   I and II

C   I and III

D   I, II and III

18   **The FCA suspects that a new computer system implemented by Sweetwater & Cranley, an authorised firm, will be insufficient to deal with the trading volume of the business and will most likely lead to inefficient execution of client trades. In this case:**

A   The firm can be punished because a principle has been broken

B   The firm can be punished because a principle will be broken

C   The firm cannot be punished because a principle has not been broken yet

D   The firm cannot be punished because a principle will not be broken

19   **Which of the following promotions would not be covered by the financial promotions order rules?**

A   A direct offer financial promotion to a retail client

B   An offer to a group of business angels to buy 50% of the shares of a company

C   An email to all of a firm's existing clients with regards to a new product they are offering

D   An advert on a billboard relating to a firm's existing product range

20 **Which of the following would be considered by the FCA in relation to a firm's application for authorisation?**

      I   The firm's business model

      II   The applicant's fitness and propriety

      III   Close links that the applicant has to other firms

A II only

B I and II

C I and III

D I, II and III

21 **How can Dubois Carhaix, a French investment firm, who wishes to open up a branch in the UK, obtain the necessary regulatory approval?**

A Apply for a waiver from the FCA

B Apply for Part 4A permission from the FCA

C Apply to the French regulator for authorisation

D Passport into the UK via MiFID

22 **Under the CFA Code and Standards, which of the following statements is correct with regard to a new investment fund? The fund has created a simulated portfolio of how they would have traded over the last three years.**

A The performance of the simulated portfolio cannot be included in any promotional material because it is only simulated

B The performance of the simulated portfolio cannot be included in any promotional material since it only covers three years

C The performance of the simulated portfolio can be included so long as it is clearly disclosed that the performance was not actually achieved

D There are no additional disclosure requirements

23 **The FCA believes that an adviser has been purchasing and selling shares too frequently within a client's portfolio. This practice is an example of:**

A Churning

B Switching

C Money laundering

D Front running

24 **Which one of the following is the maximum jail sentence for insider dealing offences?**

A 2 years

B 5 years

C 7 years

D 14 years

25 **Which of the following could normally generate a capital gains tax liability on disposal?**

A Government bonds

B An individual's main home

C Antique jewellery

D A car that is four years old

26 **Which of the following is correct with regards to a fact find?**

A The fact find must be completed prior to any meeting between investment adviser and client

B The fact find has to be documented and kept up to date on an annual basis

C All factual data must be verified before the provision of any investment advice

D There are no specific regulatory requirements with regard to a fact find

27 **Mr Dunwoody has a number of financial objectives, among which, in descending order of priority, are to be mortgage-free, to be able to send his only child to private school, and to be able to take three foreign holidays a year.**
Mr Dunwoody currently owes £12,000 in credit card debt, on which he pays an APR of 15.5%. Which of the following is most likely to be what you would advise Mr Dunwoody to do with some surplus cash savings which he has?

A Reduce his credit card debt

B Take out a larger life assurance policy

C Repay some of the principal on the loan he used to buy his current home

D Invest in zero coupon bonds which mature when his child is ready to start private school

28 **International financial reporting standards require derivatives to be valued on the company's balance sheet at:**

A Cost

B Amortised cost

C Fair value

D Market value

29 **Variation margin is best described as:**

A The maximum probable one-day loss on the current open positions

B A good faith deposit to demonstrate to the clearing house that you can pay your losses

C The amount of money required to be paid into a margin account to cover the previous day's losses

D The amount of money that can be taken out of a margin account represented by the previous day's trading gains

30 **The person who gains from the performance of the assets held in a discretionary trust is:**

A The settler

B The trustee

C The beneficiary

D The remainderman

31 **Which of the following is a financial intermediary?**

I An investment trust company

II A building society

III A defined benefit pension scheme

A I only

B II only

C I and II

D I, II and III

32 **How should an authorised firm initially categorise a client that is a corporate body with assets of £1,000,000 and income of £10,000, that wishes to conduct non-MiFID business?**

A Eligible counterparty

B Professional client

C Retail client

D Authorised client

33 **The Bank of England has responsibility for the supervision of all of the following, except which one?**

A Aquis Stock Exchange (AQSI)

B LME Clear Limited

C ICE Clear Europe

D LCH Ltd

34 **Which of the following are required with regard to a prospectus for a rights issue by a listed company?**

I The prospectus must be made public

II The prospectus must be approved by the UKLA

III The prospectus must be approved by the LSE

A I and II

B I and III

C II and III

D I, II and III

35   **A firm wishing to engage in stock lending of a client's assets:**

A   Is not obliged to inform clients that it is engaging in stock lending using clients' assets

B   May do so after it has made a general disclosure to clients that it may engage in stock lending using clients' assets

C   Must obtain specific prior consent from the client to lend their stock

D   Is not allowed to do so unless the client is an eligible counterparty

36   **Victoria has passed an appropriate examination which permits her to give advice on retail investment products, and another appropriate examination which permits her to give advice on regulated mortgage contracts. She does not hold any further appropriate examinations passes. In which of the following client transactions is Victoria not qualified to give advice?**

A   A personal pension plan

B   A home reversion plan

C   A re-mortgage

D   A unit-linked whole of life policy

37   **What is the rate of income tax payable by a higher rate tax payer on dividend income that is not covered by any allowances?**

A   8.75%

B   25%

C   33.75%

D   39.35%

38   **Jane Dickson has an estate of £520,000 on her death. Calculate her inheritance tax liability, in pounds to the nearest £1, assuming that 50% of her husband's inheritance tax nil rate band was unused when he died 5 years ago. The current level of the nil rate band is £325,000.**

Important! You should enter the answer only in numbers strictly using this format: 00,000

Do not include spaces, letters or symbols (but decimal points and commas should be used if indicated).

39   **The following are all Conduct Rules included in the Code of Conduct sourcebook (COCON). Which one of these rules is a second-tier Senior Management Conduct Rule?**

A   You must be open and co-operative with the FCA, PRA and other regulators

B   You must act with due skill, care and diligence

C   You must disclose appropriately any information of which the FCA or PRA would reasonably expect notice

D   You must act with integrity

40   **Mr and Mrs Renwick plan to transfer ownership of their home to their three children. What rules may have the result that this transfer has no inheritance tax advantage?**

    A   Benefit in interest rules

    B   Gifts with reservation rules

    C   Chargeable lifetime transfer rules

    D   Potentially exempt transfer rules

41   **Nigel Thwaite and Lucy Reese have lived together for six years. They may get married in the future, but have no plans to do so soon.**

    In addition to inheritance tax, what tax should Nigel consider when he transfers ownership of assets to Lucy?

    A   Value Added Tax

    B   National Insurance Contributions

    C   Income Tax

    D   Capital Gains Tax

42   **An investment adviser is likely to consider a liability-driven investment approach for:**

    I   Providing for school fees

    II   Repaying a mortgage

    III   Investing uncommitted income

    A   I and II

    B   I and III

    C   II and III

    D   I, II and III

43   **Julio prefers to invest in equities and Maria prefers to invest in gilts. What can be deduced about their attitudes towards risk?**

    A   Julio is more risk-tolerant than Maria

    B   Maria is more risk-tolerant than Julio

    C   Julio and Maria are both equally risk-tolerant

    D   Maria is more a risk-taker than Julio

44   **An investment adviser holds an initial meeting with a new client in which the adviser obtains information from the client about their salary, investment objectives and attitudes towards risk. What is the usual name of the document in which this information would be recorded?**

    A   Fact-find

    B   Client summary

    C   Power of attorney

    D   Investment mandate

45   **Which of the following would be classified as a hard fact?**

        I   Details of salary

        II   Attitude towards risk

        III   Desire to repay mortgage within the next ten years

        IV   Current value of outstanding mortgage balance

  A   I, II and III

  B   I, II and IV

  C   II and III

  D   I and IV

46   **Key provisions of the Foreign Account Tax Compliance Act (FATCA) include the requirement for:**

        I   Foreign financial institutions to provide information about accounts held by US citizens to the US tax authorities

        II   Payment of 30% tax on all monies held in offshore accounts by US citizens

        III   US payers making payments to non-compliant foreign financial institutions to withhold 30% of gross payments

        IV   All funds held in offshore accounts belonging to US citizens to be repatriated to the US

  A   I, II and III

  B   I, II and IV

  C   I and III

  D   II and IV

47   **Which of the following is not a feature of retirement savings accounts held with the National Employment Savings Trust (NEST)?**

  A   Freedom to transfer into and out of NEST

  B   Auto-enrolment for eligible jobholders if an employer selects NEST as the qualifying scheme for employees

  C   Required employer contributions

  D   Minimum annual contribution levels

48   **Ainsley Peacock is a MiFID firm that is subject to CASS. For how long must the firm keep its client money records?**

  A   One year

  B   Three years

  C   Five years

  D   Seven years

49   **The least important consideration when recommending a collective investment scheme for a retail client is:**

A   Historical performance relative to peers

B   Management and other charges

C   Whether the fund is structured as a Unit Trust or an OEIC

D   Riskiness of the sector in which the fund invests

50   **Your role is that of a Financial Adviser at Renfrew, a company that has set an objective of growing its advisory business by 25% each year for the next three years.**

You have completed a client fact find and you have prepared a statement of recommendations for the client. The client has indicated that she does not have much time to consider personal financial matters because of her demanding role as a Senior Graphic Designer with a nationally known advertising agency. When you explain your recommendations to the client, she has her pen ready in order to sign the necessary forms and does not ask any questions. You have the impression that she wants to keep the meeting as short as possible.

What is the most appropriate action you should take in this situation?

A   Ask the client questions to check that she has understood your recommendations before asking her to sign

B   Advise the client that you do not think it appropriate to proceed and suggest that she seek advice elsewhere

C   Given the firm's objective of growing the business, consult with your compliance officer before proceeding

D   Give the client the opportunity to sign as soon as you have explained your recommendations

51   **Hoolihan Investments Ltd are registered in the UK and intend to offer investment advice for high net worth individuals. The firm currently employs twelve analysts who all have a number of years working for larger firms in the same sector.**

Which of the following bodies is it most appropriate for the firm to approach in order to get authorisation to offer investment advice?

A   HMRC

B   The FCA

C   The Bank of England

D   The PRA

52   **In which of the following circumstances must a director report their own transactions in shares of the company of which they are the director?**

A   Any purchase or sale of shares

B   Any purchase only of shares

C   Any purchase or sale that takes his holding above 3% of the company's issued share capital

D   Any purchase or sale only in a takeover situation

53   **A team supervisor at Peawhite Investments is conducting a discussion of the Bribery Act 2010 (BA 2010) with his team. During the discussion, team members mention various statements that they have heard about the new Act. Which of the following statements by team members is least correct?**

    A   Arnie mentions that firms will be subject to BA 2010 only if they have a 'demonstrable business presence' in the UK

    B   Colin states that guidance for firms on adequate procedures to prevent bribery has been issued by the Ministry of Justice

    C   Thea states that the Financial Conduct Authority is responsible for enforcing the criminal offences in BA 2010 for authorised firms

    D   Gemma says that firms can be prosecuted for failing to prevent bribery, if a person associated with it bribes another person on its behalf

54   **At a barbecue party, Mitra overhears Miranda complaining that her husband is always home late because he is CEO of a company that has just been approached with a hostile takeover bid. The next day Mitra buys share for herself and for her clients. According to the CFA Institute's Standards of Practice, which of the following is correct?**

    A   Mitra has not breached the standards because she heard the information in a non-work context

    B   Mitra has breached the standards because she bought shares for herself as well as her clients. She should only have traded for her clients

    C   Mitra has breached the standards because she traded on the basis of non-public information

    D   Mitra has breached the standards because she failed to make the information public

55   **An analyst is compiling a research report. Which of the following is correct according to the CFA Institute Standards of Practice?**

    A   She can use quotations from well-known economists without attributing them

    B   She can use spreadsheet models without referencing the source as long as she does her own analysis

    C   She can use excerpts from journals if the source is quoted

    D   She can reproduce the work of other analysts without reference to them as long as she is consistent with their conclusions

56   **Kim is a basic rate taxpayer and her husband Rupert is a higher rate taxpayer. Both Kim and Rupert receive bank interest that exceeds their personal savings allowance. They also both own gilts, within and outside their ISAs. Which of the following is the least tax-efficient action in respect of the gilts?**

    A   Rupert transfers his gilts outside of his ISA to Kim

    B   Rupert transfers his gilts from inside his ISA to outside his ISA

    C   Kim transfers her gilts outside her ISA to Rupert

    D   Kim transfers her gilts from inside her ISA to outside her ISA

57   **A pension fund's Statement of Investment Principles (SIPs) is the responsibility of:**

A   The actuary

B   The trustees

C   The investment advisers

D   The auditors

58   **Bruce is concerned that his current investments will not enable him to pay off his interest-only mortgage which matures in 15 years.**

Which asset would be most appropriate for him to invest in if he wants the best chance of producing the highest sum to pay off the mortgage?

A   Bank deposit account

B   Gilt-edged securities

C   Equities unit trust

D   Corporate bond fund

59   **What is the name of the risk that an investor is exposed to if they are concerned that the value of their investment will not grow to a suitable amount to meet the liability?**

A   Shortfall risk

B   Capital risk

C   Inflation risk

D   Sovereign risk

60   **Life insurance companies often have a significant amount of their assets invested in long-term bonds. This is because long-term bonds:**

A   Are expected to generate a higher return than other asset classes

B   Have more exposure to interest rate risk

C   Provide matching cashflows for annuity liabilities

D   Provide real returns

61   **Caitlin is an adviser who sometimes receives requests for advice beyond her area of expertise. She passes these requests from her clients on to a larger firm and receives a referral fee in return. According to the CFA Institute Standards of Practice:**

A   This arrangement is not acceptable due to the inherent conflict of interest

B   Caitlin can receive referral fees without disclosure as she could not have performed the work herself

C   Caitlin cannot receive referral fees unless the arrangement is once-only

D   Caitlin can receive the referral fees as long as disclosure is made to her clients

62 Arnold Schwartz and Christian Merriweather live together as civil partners. They currently live in a rented flat in Dorset, England. The landlord has agreed to sell the freehold to Arnold and Christian for £325,000. Arnold and Christian will be paying £45,000 towards the purchase cost and are seeking a repayment mortgage to fund the remainder of the purchase. What is the best way of establishing affordability of the mortgage for Arnold and Christian?

A Reviewing the last three months' payslips of Arnold and Christian

B Performing an analysis of monthly household income and outgoings

C Reviewing the current assets and liabilities of Arnold and Christian

D Undertaking an analysis of the risk profiles of Arnold and Christian

63 At what percentage of voting rights held by one shareholder would a listed company be required to make a public announcement?

Important! You should enter the answer only in numbers strictly using this format: 0.0

Do not include spaces, letters or symbols (but decimal points and commas should be used if indicated).

64 A man died leaving half of his £499,200 estate to his children and the rest to his wife, at a time when the inheritance nil-rate band was £312,000. Three years later, his wife dies leaving a total estate of £695,000 to their children when the nil-rate band is £325,000. How much inheritance tax will be payable, in pounds to the nearest £1?

Important! You should enter the answer only in numbers strictly using this format: 000,000

Do not include spaces, letters or symbols (but decimal points and commas should be used if indicated).

The following information relates to Questions 65 to 67.

Barlow & Barlow (B&B) is a firm of financial advisers offering services to a wide variety of clients including large firms, investment banks and small individual private investors. They primarily offer research and advice into specialist areas including the pharmaceutical sector, but also offer more general financial advice. B&B's largest client is Jump plc, with whom they carry out non-MiFID business. Jump plc has a balance sheet total of €15,000,000 and 150 full-time employees. Last year Jump plc had a turnover of €20,000,000.

65 Based on the information available, what would be the most appropriate initial client categorisation for Jump plc?

A Private client

B Retail client

C Per se professional client

D Per se eligible counterparty

66   **Patrick is a retail client of B&B with a portfolio worth £450,000 who requests in writing that he be treated as an elective professional client with respect to share purchases. Patrick has worked for a major bank for nine months carrying out daily transactions in equity dealing. B&B should treat Patrick:**

   A   As a retail client for the reason that he does not satisfy the quantitative test for MiFID business

   B   As a retail client for the reason that he does not satisfy the qualitative test

   C   As a per se professional client

   D   As an elective professional client

67   **When doing business with one of its clients, B&B provided the client with a basic agreement. The business involved arranging for the client to opt out of their work pension scheme and into a private scheme, four years ago. For how long does B&B need to keep a record of this agreement?**

   A   Two years

   B   Five years

   C   Seven years

   D   Indefinitely

68   **COBS rules require communications with clients about designated investment business to meet a number of key criteria. Which of the following is not explicitly stated as one of these criteria?**

   A   Not misleading

   B   Clear

   C   Comprehensive

   D   Fair

69   **Which one of the following sections within the UK Corporate Governance Code can be used to highlight the importance of promoting a combination of gender diversity as well as varying social and ethnic backgrounds?**

   A   Section 1: Board Leadership

   B   Section 2: Division of Responsibilities

   C   Section 3: Composition, Succession and Evaluation

   D   Section 4: Audit, Risk and Internal Control

70   **Which of the following is the maximum penalty for the directors of an institution which fails to implement internal reporting procedures in respect of money laundering?**

   A   Two years' imprisonment or an unlimited fine

   B   Five years' imprisonment and an unlimited fine

   C   Two years' imprisonment and an unlimited fine

   D   Six months' imprisonment and the statutory fine

71 **What is the standard settlement term for gilts traded through the London Stock Exchange?**

A T + 1

B T + 2

C T + 3

D T + 5

72 **Which is the most significant asset class for meeting the objectives of pension funds?**

A Bonds

B Equity

C Cash

D Antiques

73 **A client has a complaint against an authorised firm. Normally, to whom should the complaint be addressed initially?**

A The Financial Conduct Authority (FCA)

B The Financial Ombudsman Service (FOS)

C The Competition and Markets Authority (CMA)

D The authorised firm

74 **With respect to a defined benefit pension fund, who is responsible for preparing the Statement of Funding Principles?**

A The depositary

B The investment manager

C The plan sponsor

D The trustee

75 **Which of the following is not a MiFID core service or activity?**

A Advising on investment

B Discretionary management

C Dealing as principal

D Providing safeguarding services

76 **An additional rate taxpayer has savings income of £780 from a bank deposit. What is the total amount of income tax payable on this income?**

Important! You should enter the answer only in numbers strictly using this format: 000.00

Do not include spaces, letters or symbols (but decimal points and commas should be used if indicated).

77   The three stages of money laundering are Placement, Layering and Integration. In which stages could an investment manager typically be used?

          I   Placement
          II   Layering
          III   Integration

A   I and II
B   I and III
C   II and III
D   I, II and III

78   In the context of authorisation by the FCA, which of the following is an exempt person?

A   An appointed representative
B   A private client adviser
C   A broker/dealer
D   A market maker

79   Within what time period must a firm send a written acknowledgement of a complaint?

A   Promptly
B   Five calendar days
C   Seven business days
D   Seven calendar days

80   How long will the Competition and Markets Authority (CMA) have to reach an initial 'Phase I' decision about a takeover?

A   40 working days
B   3 months
C   24 weeks
D   There is no stipulated time frame

81   Which of the following can be a defence against a charge of insider dealing under the Criminal Justice Act (CJA) 1993?

A   I only sold to prevent a loss
B   Other investors who did not have the information acted in a similar way
C   I believed the information to be widely known
D   I only bought shares for my clients

82 **Under POCA 2002, a court is required to take into account Joint Money Laundering Steering Group (JMLSG) guidance because the guidance has received approval from:**

A The Bar Council

B The Financial Conduct Authority

C HM Treasury

D The British Bankers Association

83 **Which of the following are true with respect to the suitability rule?**

    I   The rule applies to retail clients only

    II   The rule applies when advising clients

    III   The rule applies when conducting discretionary management

A I and II

B I and III

C II and III

D I, II and III

84 **How often should a firm report to the FCA with reference to complaints received?**

A Every month

B Quarterly

C Twice a year

D Annually

85 **ABC Investments have prepared a research report which they are planning to make available to their clients. Under which of the following circumstances can the firm deal ahead of releasing the research report?**

    I   In anticipation of client orders

    II   When acting as a market maker

    III   When executing an unsolicited client trade

A I and II

B I and III

C II and III

D I, II and III

Answers

1   **C**   Ensuring stable prices and confidence in the currency is part of the task of the Bank of England, in its core purpose of monetary stability. Ensuring the markets function well is the FCA's single strategic objective. Protection for consumers and promoting effective competition are operational objectives of the FCA

2   **B**   The standard settlement period for equities traded through the London Stock Exchange is two business days after the trade date, or T + 2

3   **B**   Asset allocation refers to the mix of underlying asset classes held within a portfolio. The main asset classes are cash, fixed-interest securities, property and equities. Each asset class behaves differently and has very different risk characteristics. A number of academic studies have shown that asset allocation is the single most important factor in determining the returns of an investment portfolio. The implication is therefore that other factors, such as individual security or fund selection, are less important. The last stage of the investment management process is stock or fund selection, and occurs after the asset allocation stage

4   **B**   When investing in cash there is no capital risk, as the value of the cash investment is not at risk. However, a cash investment will typically be subject to interest rate risk, so as interest rates fall, less interest will be earned on the cash deposit

5   **C**   The investments made by a pension fund manager are all made with the aim of matching the liabilities of the pension fund and, as such, if the fund manager has invested in equity, then it will be because they believe this will help them to achieve the aim of matching the fund's liabilities

6   **0.00**   All taxpayers have a tax-free dividend allowance of £2,000. Once the dividend income exceeds this allowance, dividend income is taxed at 8.75% within the basic-rate band, at 33.75% within the higher-rate band and then at a 39.35% additional tax rate. Dividend income is taken as a taxpayer's top slice of income, so it is taxable at a taxpayer's highest marginal rate

7   **C**   Fund selection is the last stage of the investment process. Fund selection comes after asset allocation. The range of funds available to an adviser depends on whether they are tied to a specific provider or are independent and therefore free to choose from the whole of the market. However wide or narrow the choice is, there are various factors that should be taken into account as part of the fund selection process, such as past performance, charges and even the stability of the provider

8   **D**   The year's losses can be offset against this year's profits, last year's profits and future profits of the same trade

9   **B**   There are two tiers of the Conduct Rules. The first tier, consisting of five rules, applies to everyone. The second tier, consisting of four rules, applies only to senior managers.

            Individual Conduct Rules

            1. You must act with integrity. 2. You must act with due care, skill and diligence. 3. You must be open and co-operative with the FCA, the PRA and other regulators. 4. You must pay due regard to the interests of customers and treat them fairly. 5. You must observe proper standards of market conduct

Senior Manager Conduct Rules

SC1. You must take reasonable steps to ensure that the business of the firm for which you are responsible is controlled effectively. SC2. You must take reasonable steps to ensure that the business of the firm for which you are responsible complies with the relevant requirements and standards of the regulatory system. SC3. You must take reasonable steps to ensure that any delegation of your responsibilities is to an appropriate person and that you oversee the discharge of the delegated responsibility effectively. SC4. You must disclose appropriately any information of which the FCA or PRA would reasonably expect notice. Firms must provide training to all staff. This training should ensure that staff are notified of the rules that apply to them, and that those staff understand how the rules apply to them. Training records, such as a certificate or training log, must be maintained

10   **A**   In the secondary market, Eurobonds are traded OTC. Major markets for Eurobonds exist in London, Frankfurt, Zurich and Amsterdam

11   **A**   A proxy can be either in the form whereby the proxy decides on the best way to vote in a resolution, or to be able to only vote in one particular way. A general proxy involves appointing a person to vote as they think fit, bearing in mind what is said at the meeting. A special proxy involves appointing a person to vote for or against a particular resolution (this is also known as a 'two-way proxy')

12   **D**   An employee is not permitted to take anything with them when they leave a firm which is considered the property of the firm. The knowledge that the employee has is not the property of the firm

13   **C**   In this set of transactions, the clients' holding has been purchased with the sole purpose of pushing the share price up. This is considered market manipulation

14   **C**   The FCA's own description uses the words 'invitation' and 'inducement'. A financial promotion is an invitation or inducement that aims to persuade the recipient to engage in investment activity

15   **C**   The adviser can make this recommendation so long as their shareholding is disclosed to allow the clients to place the advice of the adviser its correct context

16   **D**   A lasting power of attorney (LPA) must be registered with the Office of the Public Guardian (OPG) for the LPA to be effective

17   **D**   All of these matters are covered by the FCA's Principles for Businesses

18   **A**   Principles have already been breached: those of skill, care and diligence and management and control. This is because the firm has not put an appropriate dealing system in place

19   **B**   A financial promotion made to sophisticated investors (which includes business angels) is not covered by the financial promotions order rules. A certified sophisticated investor as a person who has a certificate in the required form confirming that they have been assessed by a firm as being sufficiently knowledgeable to understand the risk of a particular investment. In addition, a retail investor can be a self-certified sophisticated investor if they can state that they are a member of a network or syndicate of business angels, and have been so for at least six months prior to the signature date

20   **D**   Within the threshold conditions are suitability, business model and effective supervision (including close links), so all of these factors would be considered in an application of authorisation

21 **B** The French firm will now have to apply to the FCA for Part 4A permission, after Brexit, where the UK left the EEA. The Temporary Permissions Regime (TPR) allows European Economic Area (EEA)-based financial services firms who were formally using a 'passport' to continue to operate in the UK for a limited period of time following the end of the transition period, while they seek authorisation from UK regulators – known as Part 4A permission. Previously, before Brexit, a French firm conducting investment business would have been able to open up a branch in the UK (host) under the passporting arrangement contained within MiFID

22 **C** A simulated (or hypothetical) portfolio's performance can be included if clients are made aware that this is simulated performance and was not actually achieved

23 **A** When a firm is overtrading investments, such as securities, too frequently within a client's account, to no benefit for the clients, this is referred to as churning. Switching refers to overtrading within and between packaged products

24 **C** The maximum jail sentence for insider dealing is 7 years, under the Criminal Justice Act (CJA) 1993. It is worth noting that an individual found guilty of insider dealing shall be liable, on summary conviction, in a Magistrates' court, to a fine not exceeding the statutory maximum or imprisonment for a period not exceeding six months, or both. However, on conviction or indictment, in a Crown court, an individual found guilty of insider dealing shall be liable to a fine or imprisonment for a period not exceeding seven years, or both

25 **C** A capital gains tax liability will not be created on the disposal of the principal primary residence (main home), or on the disposal of gilts, nor on a wasting asset such as a car, as these are exempt from CGT

26 **D** A fact-find usually take the form of a questionnaire or structured discussion, which will ascertain a client's current financial circumstances, financial requirements and attitude to risk, however there are no specific legal or regulatory requirements with regards to the completion of a fact find

27 **A** The client's primary investment objective is to be mortgage-free, but – given the high APR on his credit card borrowing – it makes more sense to reduce the credit card balance than to repay some of the outstanding mortgage balance or make other investments

28 **C** The International Financial Reporting Standard (IFRS) that impacts upon derivatives is IFRS 9, which requires derivatives to be measured at fair value, with changes in fair value recognised either in profit or loss or in reserves, depending on whether the company uses hedging. Where the derivative is used to offset risk and certain hedging conditions are met, changes in fair value can be recognised separately in reserves

29 **C** Variation margin is additional margin that must be paid to cover the previous day's trading losses. This is in addition to the initial margin payment

30 **C** The beneficiary gains for the assets held in a discretionary trust. With a discretionary trust, the trust property is held for the benefit of the beneficiaries and the trustees have discretion about how much to give to which beneficiaries and when

31 **D** All of these are considered to be financial intermediaries

32 **C** A per se professional clients, in relation to business that is not MiFID business, includes a large undertaking such a corporate body that has called up share capital of at least £5m

33   **A**   The FCA recognises a number of exchanges (RIEs), including the London Stock Exchange, the Aquis Stock Exchange, the London Metal Exchange and ICE Futures Europe. The Bank of England recognises a number of clearing houses (RCHs) including ICE Clear Europe, LME Clear, LCH Ltd and CME Clearing Europe

34   **A**   The prospectus must be approved by both the UKLA and the LSE, as well as being made available to the public. The prospectus must be approved by the UKLA/FCA. In conjunction with this, an application is made to the LSE to have the securities admitted for trading and meet their admission and disclosure standards rather than the LSE actually approving the prospectus. Where the securities are not to be offered to the public, a prospectus is not required but listing particulars still need to be approved and published by the listing authority.

35   **C**   A firm cannot engage in stock lending using a client's assets unless that client has given express prior consent for their assets to be used in this way

36   **B**   A home reversion plan will require an equity release qualification. The other options will be covered by retail investment products (pensions and life policies) and mortgage advice qualifications

37   **C**   The rate of income tax payable by a higher rate taxpayer on dividend income is 33.75%. An additional rate tax payer would pay 39.35%

38   **13,000**   Jane can make use of her own nil rate band and also the unused proportion (50%) of her husband's nil rate band, making a total of £487,500 (£325,000 + (£325,000 × 0.50)). Once this is deducted from the total value of Jane's estate of £520,000, it leaves £32,500 that is subject to inheritance tax. The inheritance tax rate is 40%, and so the IHT liability will be £13,000 (£32,500 x 40%)

39   **C**   The first-tier Individual Conduct Rules are as follows:

        1. You must act with integrity. 2. You must act with due care, skill and diligence. 3. You must be open and co-operative with the FCA, the PRA and other regulators. 4. You must pay due regard to the interests of customers and treat them fairly. 5. You must observe proper standards of market conduct

40   **B**   The gifts with reservation rules mean that, if a transfer of the legal ownership of an asset takes place, but the original owner still retains some rights with regards to that asset (for example, living in a house rent-free) then, for the purposes of inheritance tax, the transfer will be deemed to have not taken place

41   **D**   From the point of view of capital gains tax, this transfer will be treated as a chargeable disposal (as they are not yet married) and so may generate a capital gains tax liability

42   **A**   A liability-driven investment (LDI) strategy involves taking future liabilities as given and building a portfolio of assets that are required to meet those future liabilities. Uncommitted income is, by definition, not targeted towards any commitment, hence will be managed to maximise returns. Mortgage and school fees suggest a future liability

43   **A**   Equities are riskier than gilts. Since Julio prefers investing in the more risky equities asset class, he is more tolerant of risk than Maria

44   **A**   Information gathered from a client should be documented in a fact find. A fact-find usually take the form of a questionnaire or structured discussion, which will ascertain a client's current financial circumstances, financial requirements and attitude to risk. A lot of background information is needed in order to understand a client's current position, and so a fact find is often carried out as part of this process, to gather both hard-facts and soft-facts

45   **D**   Salary details and the outstanding balance on a mortgage are two examples of 'hard' factual topics. A fact-find covers personal information, such as name, address, date of birth, National Insurance number, state of health, marital status, residence and domicile status, employment details and family details. These are all examples of 'hard-facts'. A fact-find also collects financial information, such as income, including earned income, savings income and pensions; investments and other assets; liabilities, such as mortgages and credit card balances; and financial dependants

46   **C**   The Foreign Account Tax Compliance Act (FATCA) legislation came into US law in 2010. Its main aim is in combating tax evasion by US taxpayers holding foreign accounts or offshore banking facilities. FATCA created a tax information and reporting and withholding regime to gain information about US persons rather than to raise revenue

47   **A**   The Government set up the National Employment Savings Trust (NEST), so that all employers can have access to a suitable pension scheme if they do not have a quality scheme in place. All eligible jobholders (those between age 22 and State pension age with annual earnings over £10,000) to be enrolled into a qualifying scheme. Transfers in and out of NEST are not allowed except in specific limited circumstances

48   **C**   The records should be retained for five years – the usual MiFID record-keeping requirement

49   **C**   Past performance, charges and risk profile of a fund are more important considerations in the selection of a fund. The technical differences between an OEIC and a unit trust structure are less important than the other reasons quoted

50   **A**   It is important to ensure that the client has understood what you have said, even though she seems to want the meeting to be as short as possible. The firm's objective to grow its business is not relevant to the action you should take, as you should act in the client's best interests

51   **B**   FSMA 2000 creates the authorisation regime for regulated activities such as offering investment advice. A firm of this type would seek authorisation from the FCA

52   **A**   Disclosure rules require that all transactions are reported. Listed companies are subject to the FCA's disclosure rules and transparency rules (DTR). The DTRs deal with reporting transactions in a company's securities, including derivatives, by 'persons discharging managerial responsibilities' (PDMRs), which includes directors. PDMRs and their connected persons must notify the listed company concerned of a transaction (both sale and purchase of any value) within four business days of the transaction

53   **C**   The regulator is not responsible for enforcement under Bribery Act 2010 (BA 2010). Where the FCA finds evidence of criminal matters, it will refer them to the Serious Fraud Office, who are the UK lead agency for criminal prosecutions for corruption. However, authorised firms who fail to address corruption and bribery risks adequately remain liable to regulatory action by the FCA

54	**C**	Mitra should not have traded on the basis of this material, non-public information. This is related to Standard II: Integrity of capital markets. Members and candidates who possess material non-public information, that could affect the value of an investment, must not act or cause others to act on the information. 'Material' means that disclosure is likely to have an impact on the price of a security, or that reasonable investors would want to know the information before making an investment decision. 'Non-public' information means that the information has not been disseminated in the market and investors have not had a chance to react to it
55	**C**	This relates to Standard I: Professionalism - Misrepresentation. These are all examples of plagiarism, apart from using excerpts from journals and quoting the source. Examples of plagiarism include basing a report on another analyst's report; using excerpts from an article; and using charts, graphs or proprietary spreadsheets without referring to the original source or without the required permission. This Standard not only covers plagiarism in written materials, but also in oral communications, such as in client meetings or presentations
56	**B**	The least tax-efficient scenario is for Rupert to go from paying no tax (within the ISA) to paying higher rate tax on the income from the gilts
57	**B**	The Statement of Investment Principles (SIPs) is required to be prepared by the trustees. The SIP sets out the principles governing how decisions about investments are made, and must include the scheme's policy on choosing investments, the kinds of investments to be held, and the balance between different investments held, as well as how risk is to be measured and managed, and the expected return on investments
58	**C**	The asset classes of cash, gilts and bonds are less likely than equities to be able to provide the necessary capital growth that Bruce requires. Equities carry risk and so losses are possible, and volatility can be expected. We are asked which asset class produces the 'best chance'
59	**A**	This is the definition of shortfall risk. Shortfall risk is the risk that the investment return will literally fall short of the amount required for the investor to meet their objectives. The response in anticipation of a shortfall could be to reduce the target, increase the amount invested or extend the time horizon
60	**C**	If life companies have sold annuities, they are subject to long-term regular cash outflows. Long-term bonds provide long-term regular inflows to match this
61	**D**	Referral fees could lead to a conflict of interest but the requirement for disclosure should reduce this, as clients can then make up their own minds on the situation. Although not asked about in the question, the RDR charging rules would need to be considered
62	**B**	The best way of establishing affordability is to prepare a cashflow analysis, which can be in the form of an analysis of monthly household income and outgoings. This will establish whether the client's goals are realistic
63	**3.0**	3% is a material interest and would require a listed company to make an announcement to the market. An investor must notify a company within two business days when it acquires 3% or more of that company's shares. Further disclosures are required at increments of more than 1% above the initial 3%. The listed company must then notify the market as soon as possible thereafter, and no later than the end of the following business day. This notification must be through a primary information provider (PIP)

64 **122,000** The unused portion of the husband's tax-free band (here (£312,000 – (£499,200 x 50%) = £62,400), which equates to 20% of the nil rate band (in the year of the husband's death)) is transferred to the wife. On her death, the estate benefits from her tax-free band and the unused portion (20%) of his tax-free band at rates prevailing on the second death. Inheritance tax payable is (£695,000 – (£325,000 × 120%)) × 40% = £122,000

65 **B** The test for professional clients when carrying out non-MiFID business requires two of the following:

€12,500,000 balance sheet total

€25,000,000 net turnover

250 average number of employees in the year

So, the company would not be treated as a *per se* professional client and, as such, would be treated as a retail client

66 **A** While it is likely that the client satisfies the qualitative test, we are unable to show that they satisfy two of the three criteria for the quantitative test, which are:

–   The client has carried out at least ten 'significant' transactions per quarter on the relevant market, over the last four quarters

–   The client's portfolio, including cash deposits, exceeds €500,000

–   The client has knowledge of the transactions envisaged from at least one year's professional work in the financial sector

B&B must therefore treat Patrick as a retail client

67 **D** A record of the client agreement should be kept for five years, or for the duration of the relationship with the client, if longer. But, for pensions transfers, opt-outs or FSAVCs, the record should be kept indefinitely

68 **C** FCA Principles for Businesses 7 (PRIN) requires firms to ensure that all communication is fair, clear and not misleading. Additionally, COBS for communications (including financial promotions) require clear, fair and not misleading communication, and set out a number of requirements for financial promotions

69 **C** Section 3: Composition, Succession and Evaluation of the UK Corporate Governance Code highlights the importance of promoting diversity of gender, social and ethnic backgrounds, as well as cognitive and personal strengths when considering the composition of the board. This section of the Code suggests that the board and its committees should have a combination of skills, experience and knowledge. Annual evaluation of the board should consider its composition, diversity and how effectively members work together to achieve objectives

70 **C** The maximum penalty would be a prison sentence together with a fine. Therefore, two years in jail and an unlimited fine. Remember, liability does not require money laundering to have happened; simply not having the appropriate procedures in place is deemed to be serious enough

71 **A** Gilts settle the same day or the next day, and so the best answer is T + 1

72 **B** This depends on the type of pension fund since those with a young client base will tend to invest more heavily in equities while those with a more mature client base will typically make more use of bonds. However, UK pension funds invest heavily in equities when considered overall. Since equities offer a suitable match for longer time horizon pension fund liabilities, equity investments, including direct UK and foreign equity holdings, are most likely. Fixed income securities play a smaller role in the overall picture

73 **D** Initially, a client should address the complaint with the firm. It might be that the client later takes the complaint to the Financial Ombudsman Service (FOS) but this is only if they do not achieve resolution with the firm first

74 **D** The trustee is responsible for preparing the Statement of Funding Principles. The trustees prepare the statement of funding principles specific to each scheme, setting out how the statutory funding objective will be met. The statement of funding principles must be reviewed every three years

75 **D** Under MiFID II, ancillary services include safekeeping and administration of financial instruments for the accounts of clients, including custodianship and related services, such as cash/collateral management

76 **351.00** An additional taxpayer has no personal savings allowance (PSA), and pays 45% income tax in the additional rate tax bracket

£780 × 45% = £351

The personal savings allowance (PSA) available depends on a person's income tax rate, with a basic-rate taxpayers receiving a PSA of £1,000, and a higher-rate taxpayer receiving a PSA of £500, however an additional-rate taxpayer does not receive any allowance

77 **C** Placement usually involves a deposit-taking institution, such as a bank and a building society. Investment businesses are more likely to find that they are used in the second and third stages of money laundering, being layering and integration respectively

78 **A** The mnemonic APRIL can help you to recall the list of exempt persons

A – Appointed representatives

P – Professions – where a person is a member of a designated professional body (eg an accountant or solicitor) and is carrying on certain regulated activities in a manner that is incidental to the normal business of the profession

R – Recognised institutions (RIEs and RCHs)

I – Institutions (given special exemption)

L – Lloyd's members

79 **A** A firm must send to the complainant a prompt written acknowledgement providing 'early reassurance'. A firm receiving a complaint must, within eight weeks after its receipt of the complaint, send the complainant either a final response, or a written response that explains the delay

80 **A** The CMA has up to 40 days to undertake an initial (phase one) study of a merger. If the CMA believes the merger will lead to a 'substantial lessening of competition', then it will normally move to a phase two investigation

81   **C**   Insider dealing is the dealing in a public company's shares by individuals with access to material non-public information about the company. If the information is widely available, a general defence is that the information was not non-public information

82   **C**   JMLSG guidance has received HM Treasury approval. When considering whether to take disciplinary action against an FCA-regulated firm in respect of a breach of the relevant provisions of SYSC, the FCA will have regard to whether a firm has followed relevant provisions in this guidance. When considering whether to bring a criminal prosecution in relation to a breach of the ML Regulations, the FCA may also have regard to whether the person concerned has followed this guidance

83   **C**   Firms providing investment advisory or discretionary portfolio management services are required to assess suitability for all retail clients and professional clients. To make an assessment of suitability, a firm needs to obtain the necessary information in relation to the client to assess their investment objectives, including risk tolerance; their financial situation, including ability to bear losses; and their knowledge and experience

84   **C**   Firms must provide the FCA with a biannual report (every 6 months) on the number of complaints, the completions of complaints within four weeks, eight weeks and over eight weeks from receipt, and the number of complaints accepted as valid by the firm

85   **C**   If a market maker is not prepared to deal, that in itself might lead to suspicions of something being announced. The market maker is required to act 'in good faith'. Since (in III) the client approaches the firm, the firm is allowed to conduct the trade, because again a refusal will arouse suspicions

Practice Examination 2

(85 questions in 1 hour and 40 minutes)

1   **Mrs Mandava is working in an investment bank and receives an unusual order for a deal of over £500,000 from a relatively new client to transfer the monies recently placed in the account. Mrs Mandava is suspicious that the funds could be the proceeds of criminal activity. What action should Mrs Mandava take?**

A   Inform the National Crime Agency

B   Contact the Competition and Markets Authority

C   Inform her firm's Money Laundering Reporting Officer

D   Contact the Financial Conduct Authority

2   **Four prospective clients are considering whether to engage with your firm in business that is non-MiFID business.**

Which would be deemed to be a 'large undertaking' based on the following information, for the purposes of categorising these clients?

A   Articall, a company with a €10 million balance sheet total and €30 million turnover

B   Greenby Engineering, which has called-up share capital of £10 million and an average number of employees of 160 in the year

C   Mega-Mall Enterprises, with €15 million balance sheet total and €20 million turnover

D   Landscape Print, which has €30 million turnover and an average number of employees of 200 in the year

3   **For which one of the following would a suitability report not be required?**

A   A pension transfer

B   A decision to transfer to making income withdrawals from a short-term annuity

C   Buy units in a regulated collective investment scheme

D   If the firm acts as investment manager and recommends a regulated collective investment scheme

4   **In the current fiscal year, an individual has capital gains of £34,300 and income of £87,000. How much capital gains tax will be payable, in pounds to the nearest £1? The annual exempt allowance is £12,300.**

Important! You should enter the answer only in numbers strictly using this format: 0,000

Do not include spaces, letters or symbols (but decimal points and commas should be used if indicated).

5   **A large company has decided to undertake a review of its responsibilities to its stakeholders. Which of the following might it reasonably conclude are among its stakeholders?**

I   Employees
II   Suppliers
III   Customers

A   I and III

B   I and II

C   II and III

D   I, II and III

6   **In the absence of knowledge of the recipient's suitability, cold (unsolicited) calls are allowed for:**

I   Authorised unit trusts
II   Unauthorised unit trusts
III   Derivatives

A   I only

B   II and III

C   I and III

D   I, II and III

7   **Which of the following is not a threshold condition for becoming authorised by the FCA?**

A   Custody of investments

B   Location of company's offices

C   Appropriate resources

D   Business model

8   **Mr Chang has decided to invest £50,000 into ordinary shares of a company for which he subsequently provides consultancy services, and he becomes privy to inside information. Which of the following courses of action is advisable for Mr Chang to take, in order to avoid committing market abuse?**

A   Mr Chang retains the shares

B   Immediately, Mr Chang disposes of the shares

C   Mr Chang declares to the market the information that he holds

D   Mr Chang buys further shares in the company to close out his position

9   **UCITS status allows for a fund:**

A   A passport across the EEA for collective investment schemes

B   A passport across the EU for collective investment schemes

C   To guarantee outperformance

D   To guarantee lower charges and outperformance

10   An individual dies during the current fiscal year, leaving an estate of £319,000 to his two children. In the previous year he had made gifts to them of £8,000 each. These were not wedding gifts. He made no other gifts in the previous seven years. How much inheritance tax is payable?

A   £1,800

B   £1,600

C   £720

D   £0

11   Under the Certification Regime for bank employees, employees are certified by:

A   The employee

B   The regulator

C   The employing bank

D   An accredited professional body

12   Which of the following is not an offence under insider dealing legislation?

A   Dealing in shares when in possession of inside information

B   Encouraging another person to deal when in possession of inside information

C   Dealing as a market maker when in possession of inside information

D   Disclosing inside information to another person

13   Graham is an analyst who becomes aware of price-sensitive inside information that is not available to the general public. Which of the following courses of action by Graham would not amount to market abuse in this case?

A   Recommend to clients that they trade in the security concerned

B   Take no further action

C   Switch discretionary funds under the firm's management into this security

D   Recommend to clients that they do not trade in the security concerned

14   Which of the following is correct regarding the appointment of a proxy at a company general meeting?

A   The proxy is valid for the meeting but not for any adjournment

B   A general proxy may vote as he thinks fit, considering anything that is discussed at the meeting

C   A proxy is unable to vote on a show of hands

D   A proxy does not have the right to speak

15   A UK-listed mortgage lender operates through agents in a number of foreign countries. The lender has identified bribery risks associated with its reliance on agents and is considering what action it should take to ensure compliance with anti-bribery legislation. Which of the following is not an appropriate measure for the firm to adopt in pursuit of this objective?

A   Explain its intentions to strengthen anti-bribery procedures through written communications to all of its agents

B   Provide for its staff a confidential channel of communication through which to raise any concerns they may have about bribery

C   Include in its procedures manual a disclaimer of responsibility for any actions of its agents in which bribery is involved where they are based outside the UK

D   Communicate its anti-bribery message periodically through external channels such as trade publications and industry fairs

16   You are working for a new employer. Your firm operates a suspicious transaction reporting system which identifies suspicious transactions for further investigation by a number of criteria, including the amount of the transaction. You have been assigned to work in the department that investigates these transactions.

Selina, your supervisor, has explained that external auditors often test samples of transactions in order to assess whether errors may be 'material' to the business of the firm. Selina routinely disregards most items on the report. She proposes that, given time pressures, you should adopt a similar approach to investigating the suspicious transactions: she tells you to pick one out of ten transactions randomly, for further investigation.

What should you do, taking into account ethical requirements?

A   Investigate all of the cases of suspicious transactions reported, while telling the Compliance Department of Selina's proposed procedure

B   Report Selina's actions to the regulatory authority

C   Follow Selina's approach, since most of the transactions are small relative to the size of the firm

D   Follow Selina's approach, since commercial realities must be balanced with regulatory compliance

17   According to the UKLA Listing Rules, what is the minimum market capitalisation for a listed company on issue of equity?

A   At least £300,000

B   At least £500,000

C   At least £30,000,000

D   At least £100,000,000

18   In the context of authorisation by the regulator, which of the following is an exempt person?

A   Recognised Investment Exchange

B   Employee share scheme

C   Dealing as principal

D   Overseas person

19 **Clive Woodley is a professional client who requests to opt down to be afforded greater protection in its dealings with your firm.**

Which one of the following applies?

A   Clive can be treated as a retail customer without notification

B   Clive can be categorised as a retail customer but must be notified by the firm

C   Clive cannot opt down

D   The firm must pay attention to the experience, expertise and knowledge of Clive before deciding if the client can opt down

20 **Carl, a Financial Adviser, has approached Andy to discuss pensions following a referral from Carl's customer, Peter. Andy asks who suggested that he might be interested in pensions.**

What should Carl do?

A   Decline to answer Andy's question

B   Give Peter's name, having obtained his permission at the outset to do so

C   Give Peter's name and explain briefly the nature of Peter's business with the company

D   State that he must first obtain his client's permission to reveal his name

21 **Your firm is reviewing the financial promotions that it issues. Which of the following financial promotions would not fall under the territorial scope of the FCA's Financial Promotions regulations?**

A   A financial promotion made to an investor based in the UK

B   An unwritten cold call made to an investor based outside of the UK

C   Approving a financial promotion of an overseas person communicated at investors in the UK

D   A solicited unwritten financial promotion made to an overseas person

22 **The application of Jarrow Smith Advisers for a change in permission is refused by the FCA. To whom can the firm appeal?**

A   The Upper Tribunal

B   The Regulatory Decisions Committee

C   The Financial Conduct Authority

D   The Treasury

23 **Which one of the following is not classified as a regulated activity?**

A   Accepting deposits

B   Lloyd's market-related activities

C   Sending dematerialised instructions

D   Dealing as a principal (where not holding oneself out to the market)

24 **What is the most important consequence for regulated firms of the FCA's adoption of a 'principles-based' approach to regulation?**

A Firms should have fewer detailed FCA rules to follow but must follow higher-level principles

B Firms must formulate a set of principles and must disclose these principles to private customers before they do business

C Firms can expect more regular compliance checks from the FCA, whether or not their activities are regarded as risky

D Firms will decide which detailed rules to follow based on whether the rules are in accord with the firm's principles

25 **Which of the following is not a per se eligible counterparty?**

A Insurance company

B Pension fund of a large company

C Central bank of a major nation

D Treasury department of a large oil company

26 **The Competition and Markets Authority (CMA) may investigate a merger if it creates a market share of:**

A 10% or more

B 20% or more

C 25% or more

D 30% or more

27 **Which of the following would be a general defence against the charge of insider dealing under the Criminal Justice Act 1993?**

   I   Not expecting to make a profit
   II   Dealing only in treasury bonds
   III   Believed the information was published

A I and III

B II only

C II and III

D I, II and III

28 **What best describes the purpose of the client categorisation rules?**

A To ensure that those who take most risk receive the most protection

B To ensure that clients receive the correct protection given their level of knowledge and understanding

C To enable firms to decide which rules are applicable

D To assist with decisions relating to client money

29 **How long must a firm keep its records on client orders and transactions, in relation to its MiFID business?**

A   One year

B   Three years

C   Five years

D   Six years

30 **When implementing the 'best execution criteria', the firm must take into account all of the following characteristics, except:**

A   The client order

B   How long the client has been a client of the firm

C   The execution venues

D   The financial instruments

31 **The trading process for equity shares in companies that are in the FTSE All Share Index is:**

A   Open outcry

B   Order-driven

C   Quote-driven

D   Price-driven

32 **All of the following are recognised as stages in the money laundering process, except:**

A   Placement of cash in the financial system by depositing money a bank account

B   Conducting a complex series of financial transactions to separate legitimate from illegitimate funds

C   Selling banned drugs for profit

D   Purchasing income-generating financial assets with previously invested illegal funds

33 **Which of the following can the shareholders normally do at an AGM?**

    I   Approve the accounts

    II   Remove the directors

    III   Increase the dividend recommended by the directors

A   I only

B   I and II

C   I and III

D   I, II and III

34   **What percentage of the accumulated value of a personal pension plan can normally be taken as a tax-free lump sum when benefits are commenced?**

A   0%

B   10%

C   20%

D   25%

35   **An investor, who is an additional rate taxpayer, buys two investments, generating a chargeable gain of £12,800. The CGT annual exempt amount is £12,300. Calculate the capital gains tax payable, in pounds to the nearest £1.**

Important! You should enter the answer only in numbers strictly using this format: 000

Do not include spaces, letters or symbols (but decimal points and commas should be used if indicated).

36   **Victoria and Kevin are advisers who have each spent time during the last week making some unsolicited calls ('cold calls') to prospective clients. Both advisers have been in their roles for one year, and are working for the same firm, with the same supervisor. The supervisor has reviewed their cold calling practices and found that Victoria's calls contravened the regulators' rules on call calling, while Kevin's appeared to be compliant.**

Which of the following alternative scenarios could explains the supervisor's review findings?

A   Victoria's calls related to self-invested personal pensions. Kevin's calls related to stakeholder pension plans

B   Victoria and Kevin were both calling prospective clients about the same product type. Kevin made his calls between 10am and 4pm on weekdays. Victoria's calls were at various times, including Saturday and Sunday evenings between 21:00 and 22:00

C   Victoria's calls related to life policies. Kevin's calls related to investment trust savings schemes

D   Victoria's and Kevin's were all to prospective clients about a new range of unit trusts that their firm has added to the list of products on which it gives advice. Victoria's calls related to making an investment within child trust funds. Kevin's calls related to making an investment outside tax wrappers

37   **Which of the following activities are excluded from regulation the Financial Services and Markets Act 2000?**

A   Acting as a broker

B   Accepting deposits

C   Giving investment advice

D   Acting as an unremunerated trustee

38   **Which of the following is/are true of the Financial Ombudsman Service (FOS)?**

    I   Firms are required to cooperate with the Financial Ombudsman Service (FOS)

    II   There is no limit on the amount which the FOS can require a firm pays to a complainant

    III If the FOS makes a decision which the complainant wishes to enforce then it is binding on the firm

A I, II and III

B I only

C III only

D I and III

39   Andrea opened an Individual Savings Account (ISA) in the current fiscal year and she plans to **make the maximum ISA contribution during the current tax year. What is the maximum percentage of the total ISA allowance for the year that Andrea can invest in a cash ISA?**

A 100%

B 75%

C 50%

D 20%

40   **A direct offer financial promotion might be best described as an offer to:**

A Enter into an agreement with a high net worth individual without receiving further information

B Discuss an agreement with a new potential customer without receiving further information

C Investors to purchase investments directly 'off-the-page' without receiving further information

D Extend an agreement with an existing customer without receiving further information

41   **Which of the following provide(s) a route to authorisation under the Financial Services and Markets Act 2000?**

    I   Permission from the FCA

    II   Membership of a designated professional body

    III Authorisation to carry out investment business in a member state of the EU (other than the UK)

A I and II

B I and III

C II and III

D I, II and III

42 **Giuliana is a financial adviser with the authorised firm Compass 360 Advisers. One of Giuliana's clients wishes to discuss building a portfolio of direct stock market investments. Giuliana's experience is almost entirely within the area of insurance-based products and she does not feel confident about the areas of investment that the client wishes to discuss, although she is authorised to do so. What should Giuliana do?**

A Offer advice at a 'basic' level and ask the client to sign that they have received an appropriate disclaimer

B Propose a meeting jointly with the client and another adviser within the firm who has more relevant experience

C State clearly that she is unable to act and apologise to the client for any inconvenience

D Persuade the client to consider the product types of which she has more experience

43 **For a listed UK company, the ex-dividend date falls on a:**

A Tuesday

B Wednesday

C Thursday

D Friday

44 **You are asked to brief a group of colleagues on your firm's activities. Regarding a client fact find, it is correct to state that:**

A The nature and content of a fact find is not governed by requirements of the FCA

B If a personal recommendation is made, the FCA requires that a fact find be completed and fully disclosed to the client

C It is a regulatory requirement that the client fact find is prepared in writing

D The FCA requires that a fact find be completed by the client before their first meeting with an adviser

45 **Which of the following statements about periodic statements is/are correct?**

I   They must include the name/designation of a retail client's account

II   For a retail client, they are required semi-annually for a securities portfolio

III For a retail client involved in a leveraged portfolio, they should be provided once every three months

A I and II

B II and III

C III only

D II only

46 **Which of the following is an exempt person under the Financial Services and Markets Act (FSMA) 2000?**

   A A person authorised in another EU state

   B The London Stock Exchange

   C The Law Society

   D The New York Stock Exchange

47 **As a member of a professional body in the financial services industry, you have agreed to its Code of Ethics. As an approved person, you are subject to the regulatory requirements.**

   What is the best description of how you will act in an ethical manner?

   A You will make sure that you have passed all appropriate examinations and that your approved person status is maintained

   B You will act in accordance with the wishes of your client at all times, above all else

   C You will act in accordance with your commitment to the highest standards of personal integrity in carrying out professional work

   D You will act in accordance with all of the regulator's rules on business conduct

48 **An individual dies leaving an estate of £340,000 that is left to their civil partner. The nil rate band is £325,000 in the current fiscal year. How much inheritance tax is payable?**

   A £15,000

   B £7,500

   C £6,000

   D £0

49 **Harry Yeung died leaving half of his £436,800 estate to his children and the rest to his wife, when the inheritance tax nil rate band was £312,000. Harry's wife dies in May of the current tax year, leaving a total estate of £478,000 to their children. The nil rate band is £325,000. How much inheritance tax will be payable on the wife's death?**

   A £11,100

   B £22,200

   C £23,760

   D £55,500

50 **Which of the following is most appropriately described as a returns-maximising fund?**

   A Defined benefit pension fund

   B Life assurance fund

   C Open-ended investment company

   D General insurance fund

51 **Which of the following are nominal liabilities?**

        I   Mortgage principal

        II   Index-linked pension

        III   Credit card balance

  A I and II

  B I and III

  C II and III

  D I, II and III

52 **Under the Market Abuse Regulation (MAR), inside information is information that:**

  A Is of an imprecise nature and has been made public

  B Is of a precise nature and has been made public

  C Is of an imprecise nature and has not been made public

  D Is of a precise nature and has not been made public

53 **In October of the current fiscal year, a house is bought for owner-occupation at a price of £587,000. What will be the stamp duty land tax (SDLT) payable by the buyer?**

  A £0

  B £19,350

  C £23,100

  D £29,350

54 **Who is responsible for supervising recognised clearing houses (RCHs)?**

  A The Bank of England

  B The Treasury

  C The Financial Conduct Authority

  D The Prudential Regulation Authority

55 **If the outcome of a Financial Ombudsman Service (FOS) investigation is accepted by the complainant, then it is:**

  A At the discretion of the firm to comply

  B Implemented by HMT

  C Binding on the firm

  D Binding on the customer

56 **Which of the following dealings is not covered by the insider dealing legislation?**

  A Trading in a Eurobond that is for the purpose of price stabilisation

  B Trading in shares on a foreign stock exchange where those shares are listed on the LSE

  C Trading in advertised securities off a recognised exchange

  D Trading in shares in a recognised exchange other than the LSE

57   **Which of the following would be an offence under the provisions of the insider dealing legislation?**

    A   A predator company buying shares in the target company prior to announcement of the bid

    B   An individual using inside information to their advantage that is not from a known source

    C   A person using inside information but not to gain a profit or avoid a loss

    D   An institutional investor buying shares without having announced their intention to do so

---

The following information relates to Questions 58 to 63.

Samson Industries is a manufacturer of certain specialist lines of sporting equipment. Samson currently controls 14% of its market sector. Samson hopes to take over Delilah Sporting Goods which has a market value of £60 million. Delilah's shares are currently trading at £2.60. Samson Industries intends to offer £3.00 per share to Delilah shareholders. Samson aims to purchase all shares in the Delilah.

58   **Which is the largest market share Delilah could have control of, before any takeover, that will normally avoid the Competition and Markets Authority (CMA) instigating an investigation?**

    A   1%

    B   10%

    C   25%

    D   30%

---

59   **If an investigation is started into the merger, a failure by Samson Industries to provide requested information relating to the acquisition could lead to a fine being imposed by:**

    A   The Information Commissioner

    B   The Competition and Markets Authority

    C   The Secretary of State for Business, Energy & Industrial Strategy

    D   The Takeover Panel

---

60   **What is the Takeover Panel levy payable by the seller of shares of shares in Delilah Sporting Goods for consideration of £31,000 through the LSE? Give your answer in pounds and pence.**

Important! You should enter the answer only in numbers strictly using this format: 0.00

Do not include spaces, letters or symbols (but decimal points and commas should be used if indicated).

---

61   **Under the terms of the Takeover Code, what is the least time that Samson must leave the offer on the table for Delilah shareholders before they can remove their bid?**

    A   14 days

    B   21 days

    C   28 days

    D   60 days

62   **The shareholders of Delilah are unenthusiastic about the offer and the number of shareholders accepting the bid falls short of that required by Samson. After 60 days, Samson withdraws its bid. How long will it be before Samson is able to make a further bid?**

    A   90 days

    B   6 months

    C   12 months

    D   10 years

63   **What is the least percentage (%) of shares that Samson will need to purchase to guarantee that it can buy all of the Delilah shares?**

    Important! You should enter the answer only in numbers strictly using this format: 00

    Do not include spaces, letters or symbols (but decimal points and commas should be used if indicated).

64   **What is the maximum custodial sentence for an individual failing to report suspicions of money laundering?**

    A   14 years

    B   7 years

    C   5 years

    D   2 years

65   **The purpose of probate is:**

    A   To determine the distribution of the estate of an individual who dies intestate

    B   To establish ownership of the estate before the assets of a deceased person are distributed

    C   To establish the assets and liabilities of a person in the course of bankruptcy proceedings

    D   To enable a person to allow another person to take control of their financial affairs

66   **For a new retail client in respect of designated investment business, when must a firm normally provide the retail client with the terms of the agreement they are obliged to provide?**

    A   Within five business days of starting business

    B   Before the client is bound by any agreement

    C   Immediately after the client is bound by the agreement

    D   It is not necessary to provide the terms of agreement

67   **When must an authorised firm assess appropriateness?**

    A   When executing a warrants transaction for a retail client as a result of a direct offer financial promotion

    B   For a life insurance investment when the client has declined advice

    C   For an authorised collective investment scheme

    D   For all transactions with retail clients

68   **If a higher rate taxpaying investor earning a salary of £80,000 also receives total UK dividends of £600, what additional tax is payable?**

    A   £120

    B   £150

    C   £195

    D   £0

69   **You have taken over a list of 30 clients from an adviser who has recently left your firm. In one case, it is clear to you that investments have been switched in order to generate additional commissions. In another case, investments have been included in a client's portfolio that are unsuitable in the light of the client's risk profile, in order to generate higher commissions. Which of the following actions or sets of actions is most appropriate in these circumstances?**

    A   Review approximately ten further clients' files and, if they all appear satisfactory, treat the two dubious cases as isolated incidents and take no further action

    B   Raise the issue with a supervisor or senior manager so that a full review of this adviser's client list can be implemented, and compensate the clients for losses arising from the unsuitable investments

    C   Raise the issue with a supervisor or senior manager so that a full review of this adviser's client list can be implemented; contact the providers of the mis-sold products and demand that they compensate the clients

    D   Contact the providers of the mis-sold products and demand that they compensate the clients; review approximately ten further clients' files and, if they all appear satisfactory, treat the two dubious cases as isolated incidents

70   **Which body will deal with a company's application to join the UK Official List?**

    A   Bank of England

    B   Department of Business, Energy & Industrial Strategy

    C   United Kingdom Listing Authority

    D   London Stock Exchange

71   **Which of the following would not normally be deemed to be a criminal activity?**

    A   Tax avoidance

    B   Tax evasion

    C   Failing to report suspicions of money laundering

    D   Insider dealing

72   **What will normally follow the issue of an EU directive, to make it effective in the UK?**

    A   The UK Parliament will alter its national laws to conform with the Directive

    B   The EU will issue Regulations that alter UK laws

    C   The Directive will become effective in the UK if it is not vetoed by the UK Parliament

    D   The EU will issue a Decision on the applicability of the Directive to member States

73 **Under the CFA Code and Principles, which of the following is the most correct course of action if an order for multiple clients is not filled?**

A   Fill the order of the biggest client first

B   Fill the order of the smallest client first

C   Fill the order of the clients who have recently suffered losses first

D   Fill the orders on a pro rata basis

74 **Which of the following are 'packaged products'?**

    I   Life policies

    II   Units in a regulated CIS

    III   Structured 'capital-at-risk' products (SCARPs)

A   I and II

B   II and III

C   II only

D   I, II and III

75 **The Compliance Officer at QWR Investors is drafting a procedures manual for the firm's investment advisers. Among other topics, the manual will set out to enable advisers to understand the main FCA principles, rules and requirements relating to the provision of investment advice and product disclosure, including in relation to the assessment of client suitability requirements.**

When preparing suitability reports to comply with the regulator's rules, which of the following is not correct?

A   A suitability report will need to be prepared if basic scripted advice is given on a stakeholder product

B   If a personal pension plan is recommended, an explanation should be included of why it is at least as suitable as a stakeholder pension

C   Suitability should result from keeping to the 'know your customer' rule

D   A suitability report is required when the firm makes a recommendation and the client enters into a pension transfer

76 **A basic written agreement concerning designated investment business is always required for:**

A   An eligible counterparty

B   An eligible client

C   A professional client

D   A retail client

77   Which of the following is/are 'specified investments'?

      I   Bonds

      II   Shares

      III   Options on shares

A   I and II

B   I only

C   III only

D   I, II and III

78   Which of the following are part of the criteria that the firm would consider when looking to test the fitness and propriety of an individual being considered under the Certification Regime?

      I   Honesty, integrity and reputation

      II   Competence and capability

      III   Past performance in certification functions

A   III only

B   I and II

C   I and III

D   I, II and III

79   Gail Faulkner is preparing a research report on a small biotech company for public distribution. Her supervisor sees a rough draft with favourable earnings projections. Faulkner later obtains revised data and lowers the favourable projections. Just before the report is published, Faulkner sees that her supervisor has substituted her earlier, more favourable projections in place of the less favourable projections. According to CFA Institute Code and Standards Faulkner should:

A   Immediately report the incident to the regulatory authorities

B   Require either inclusion of the unfavourable earnings projections or removal of her name from the report

C   Request that the report include a disclaimer with respect to the earnings projections

D   Allow the report to be distributed without revision, but prepare and release a second report that includes the lower earnings projection

80   Which of the following is not one of the exemptions set out in the Financial Promotions Order?

A   Promotions that are subject to the Takeover Code

B   Financial promotions communicated only to members of the Designated Professional Bodies

C   Financial promotions communicated only to investment professionals

D   Promotions to associations of high net worth individuals

81   **Which of the following is not a 'core' activity under MiFID?**

A   Receipt and transmission of orders

B   Operating a multilateral trading facility

C   Safeguarding and administration of financial instruments

D   Discretionary management of investment portfolios

82   **When treating a retail client as an elective professional client for a transaction, the regulator requires an investment manager to assess all of the following, except which one?**

A   Whether the client has adequate expertise, experience and knowledge

B   Whether the client is capable of making their own investment decisions

C   Whether the client understands the risks involved

D   Whether the client owes money to the firm

83   **Which of the following is not one of the basic aims of insolvency law?**

A   Balancing the interests of competing groups

B   Making shareholders responsible for all liabilities of the company

C   Protecting the creditors of the company

D   Encouraging 'rescue' operations

84   **Which of the following is not one of the types of behaviour that can constitute market abuse under the Market Abuse Regulation?**

A   Market soundings

B   Unlawful disclosure of inside information

C   Market manipulation

D   Insider dealing

85   **With regard to investigations by the FCA, the regulator may do all of the following, except which one?**

A   Require an authorised firm and its employees to provide all relevant documents to the investigators

B   Issue a warrant where access to a firm's premises is refused

C   Require employees of the authorised firm to attend a questioning by an investigator

D   Extend its investigation beyond the regulated activities of the firm

Answers

1 **C** If a person suspects a person of money laundering, then they should inform the police or, more usually, an appropriate officer in their workplace. This person is usually the Money Laundering Reporting Officer (MLRO)

2 **B** In this question the business is not MiFID business, so we are looking for two out of the three limits: €12,500,000 balance sheet total, €25,000,000 net turnover, and 250 average number of employees in the year. Alternatively, called up share capital of at least £5,000,000 – as is the case with Greenby Engineering – qualifies an undertaking as 'large'

3 **D** A suitability report would not be required where a firm is acting as investment manager and recommends a regulated collective investment scheme. A firm must provide a suitability report to a retail client if the firm makes a personal recommendation and the client: Buys or sells shares or units in a regulated collective investment scheme; Buys or sells shares through an investment trust savings scheme; Buys, sells, surrenders or cancels rights in, or suspends contributions to, a personal or stakeholder pension scheme; Elects to make income withdrawals from a short-term annuity; Enters into a pension transfer or pension opt-out; Enters into any transaction in relation to a life policy

4 **4,400** (£34,300 – £12,300 annual exemption) = £22,000. Then £22,000 × 20% (higher rate of CGT) = £4,400 CGT

5 **D** Large companies are increasingly being held to account for their interactions with all stakeholder groups that their activities touch. Corporate governance essentially involves balancing the interests of a company's many stakeholders, which include the shareholders, management, customers, suppliers, financiers, Government departments and the wider community

6 **A** Firms are restricted in what they can sell through cold calls. They are permitted for generally marketed packaged products. A firm must not make a cold call regarding a higher volatility fund, or a life policy that is linked to a higher volatility fund

7 **A** Custody is covered by the regulated activity of safeguarding and administration of investments but is not one of the threshold conditions

8 **A** Mr Chang was not an insider when the investment was made, and so there has been no market abuse. On becoming an insider, there is no need to dispose of the shares, nor is there a need to declare information to the market. The option to close out the position is a distractor that does not make sense

9 **A** The Undertakings for Collective Investment in Transferable Securities (UCITS) Directive allows open-ended funds, such as unit trusts and OEICs, to be passported across the EEA

| 10 | **B** | Inheritance tax is payable on the death estate plus the lifetime transfers within seven years of death. |

Taxable transfer	£
Life-time transfer in last seven years	
– Last year (£8,000 x 2)	16,000
Annual gift exemption	
– Last year	(3,000)
– Year before, carried forward	(3,000)
(can carry forward one year)	
	10,000
Estate upon death	319,000
Taxable transfer	329,000
Inheritance tax payable	£
£325,000 at 0%	0
£4,000 at 40%	1,600
Total IHT payable	1,600

11   **C**   The relevant bank (or firm) will have responsibility for certifying these individuals, who will no longer be approved by the regulator. The Certification Regime applies to those individuals carrying out specific functions (Certification Functions) for a firm that can have a significant impact on the firm or its customers but are not Senior Management Functions (SMFs). The Certification Regime requires a firm to take reasonable care to ensure that none of its employees perform a Certification Function unless that employee has a valid certificate issued by the firm

12   **C**   Market makers carrying out their normal business have a special defence. The defence against insider dealing is that the market-maker had inside information in the course of their business, but acted genuinely for that business – ie the market maker 'acted in good faith'

13   **B**   Taking no further action is an appropriate way for an analyst to deal with such a situation and is not an offence of market abuse

14   **B**   A proxy is valid for the meeting and any adjournment. The ability to vote either way is known as a general proxy. Following CA 2006 changes, proxies may exercise all the powers the member would have if they were present in person, including the right to speak, and to vote on a show of hands or on a poll

15   **C**   A firm that explains its intentions to strengthen anti-bribery procedures, provide for its staff a confidential channel of communication through which to raise any concerns, and communicating an anti-bribery message may all serve to promote proportionate anti-bribery procedures, in line with the Bribery Act 2010. A disclaimer of responsibility is likely to be ineffective and does not form part of 'adequate procedures' as required by the anti-bribery legislation

16   **A**   The suspicious transactions report identifies transactions for further investigation, and so you should investigate each one. Financial crime compliance requirements impose requirements that firms will investigate suspicious transactions, and materiality to the business is not relevant

17   **C**   For either a premium or standard listing, the minimum market capitalisation is £30,000,000 for equities. The market value securities to be listed must be at least £200,000 for debt securities

18   **A**   Recognised Investment Exchanges (RIEs) such as the LSE, LME and ICE Futures, known as 'exempt persons' are exempt from the need to be authorised. All the others are types of excluded activities

19   **B**   If a professional client requests to opt down (to a retail client status), then the firm must allow this

20   **B**   The name of the person making the referral should be given to the client

21   **D**   As the overseas person has solicited the unwritten communication, the FCA rules do not apply. The rules only apply outside the UK in relation to financial promotions that are cold calls

22   **A**   The firm has a right to appeal to the Tax and Chancery Chamber of the Upper Tribunal. The Upper Tribunal is a body independent of the FCA

23   **D**   The requirement to seek authorisation does not apply to personal dealings of unauthorised persons for their own account – this is an excluded activity. Accepting deposits, Lloyd's market related activities and sending dematerialised instructions are all examples of regulated activities that would require authorisation

24   **A**   The 'principles-based' approach goes hand-in-hand with the 'risk-based' approach. There should be fewer detailed rules and more emphasis on higher-level principles

25   **D**   The Treasury department of a large oil company would be treated as a professional client. It could, if it so requests, be treated as an elective eligible counterparty but only with respect of eligible counterparty business. The others are included in the list of per se eligible counterparties

26   **C**   This is the 'share of supply' test. The CMA will investigate all mergers that meet the turnover test or the 'share of supply test'. The turnover test is met if the target company has a UK turnover of £70m or more. The 'share of supply' test is met if the merging parties will together supply at least 25% of goods or services either in the UK as a whole or in a substantial part

27   **A**   The CJA 1993 provides general defences for insider dealing. The main defences to insider dealing include where an individual passed on information in the proper performance of their duties but did not expect the recipient to deal; the deal was not done to make a profit or avoid a loss; a new issue was stabilised under the FCA's stabilisation rules; a market-maker had inside information in the course of their business, but acted in good faith. Dealing in treasury bonds is not one of them

28   **B**   The main purpose of the client categorisation rules is to ensure that clients receive the correct protection, based upon their categorisation. Firms being able to decide which rules apply is a consequence of categorising clients but it is not the main purpose of the rule

29   **C**   The record keeping requirement in relation to MiFID business is five years. Non-MiFID business record requirements are three years

30   **B**   The length of time a client has been a client of the firm is not a relevant factor. Firms must take all reasonable steps to obtain the 'best possible result' for their clients when executing orders. Firms must establish and implement a best execution policy that will obtain the best possible result. When determining what the best possible result is, firms must take into

account price, costs, speed, likelihood of execution and settlement, size, nature or any other consideration that is relevant to the execution of the order

31   **B**   Trading on SETS, including for FTSE All Share constituents, is order driven. SETS is an electronic limit order book used to trade stocks including FTSE 100, FTSE 250 and FTSE Small Cap constituents, as well as many of the most-traded AIM and Irish securities

32   **C**   The three stages in the money laundering process are placement, layering and integration. The criminal activity to get the funds in the first place is not a part of laundering the money

33   **B**   At the Annual General Meeting, the shareholders can approve or reject the proposed dividend, approve the accounts, reappoint directors and reappoint auditors. However, under the Model Articles, they cannot increase the dividend that has been declared by the directors

34   **D**   Up to 25% of the pension fund can be taken as a tax-free pension commencement lump sum

35   **100**

	£
Chargeable gain	12,800
Less annual exemption	(12,300)
Gain subject to CGT	500

The higher rate for CGT is 20%, making a CGT liability of £500 x 20% CGT = **£100**

36   **B**   Cold calls are permitted for both SIPPs (a type of personal pension plan) and stakeholder pension plans: these are packaged products. Although the regulator does not lay down specific permitted times of day for cold calls, it is stipulated that calls should be made at 'an appropriate time of day'. Calls between 9pm and 10pm at weekends could be considered inappropriate. Cold calls are permitted for both life policies and investment trust savings plans: these are packaged products

37   **D**   Trustees, where they are not deemed to be experts holding themselves out to the general public and are not separately remunerated, are excluded from the requirement to seek authorisation. Acting as a broker, giving investment advice and accepting deposits are all examples of regulated activities

38   **D**   FCA-authorised firms are required to participate in the Financial Ombudsman Service (FOS) and to cooperate with the Ombudsman. If the complainant accepts the FOS determination, it is binding on the firm, but if the complainant rejects the determination, the firm is not bound by it. The maximum money award the FOS can make is £375,000 for complaints referred after 1 April 2022. For awards over this, the firm is invited to pay the excess, but is not compelled to do so

39   **A**   There is no separate limit for Cash ISAs: the investor can allocate money between cash ISAs and stocks and shares ISAs however they want. ISAs have an annual investment limit of £20,000 in the current tax year. This limit is flexible and can be split between the various types of ISA as desired – such as £12,000 in a cash ISA and £8,000 in a stocks and shares ISA

40   **C**   A direct offer financial promotion must contain appropriate disclosures and for non-MiFID business additional information so that the client is reasonably able to understand the risks and make investment decisions on an informed basis

41 **B** Membership of a designated professional body exempts an entity from the requirement to seek authorisation if the regulated activities it conducts are incidental to its main business

42 **B** The adviser should aim to ensure that the client is still assisted by the firm. Therefore, proposing a joint meeting with the client and another adviser within the firm who has more relevant experience is the best suggestion

43 **C** The ex-dividend date will always be a Thursday. The record date, also known as the 'books closed date' will be a Friday. As equities settle T+2, a trade on the Wednesday is referred to as 'cum-div', as the buyer will receive the dividend, as they will own the share on the record date, being the Friday, as settlement is two business days after the trade

44 **A** The client fact-find, although a common tool for advisers, is not governed by regulatory provisions. The fact-find usually take the form of a questionnaire or structured discussion, which will ascertain a client's current financial circumstances, financial requirements and attitude to risk. The FCA have identified some examples of good and poor practice in fact find process, however it should be noted that there are no specific regulatory requirements regarding the form a fact find takes

45 **A** In the case of a leveraged portfolio, the statement should be sent out once a month, not every 3 months. A security-based portfolio statement is sent out every six months

46 **B** The LSE is an example of a Recognised Investment Exchange (RIE), and therefore exempt from the requirement to seek authorisation. The RIE is an example of an 'exempt person'

47 **C** Exam passes and approved person status do not ensure that you act ethically (Option A). Sometimes other legal requirements, such as to report suspicions of money laundering or other financial crime, must override your duty to a client, including the duty to act with confidentiality (Option B). Acting ethically involves more than compliance with rules (Option D)

48 **D** Inheritance tax is not payable when the estate passes to a spouse or civil partner. If a person's estate passes to their civil partner (or spouse) and they are both domiciled in the UK, there is no IHT to pay even if the estate is above the nil rate band of £325,000. This exemption applies to lifetime gifts and to estates passing on death

49 **B** The unused portion of the husband's tax-free band (here, £312,000 – (£436,800 x 50%) = £93,600, which equates to 30% of the £312,000 nil rate band) is transferred to the wife. On the wife's death (being the second death), the estate benefits from her tax-free band and the unused 30% portion of his tax-free band at rates prevailing on the second death. Inheritance tax payable is (£478,000 – (£325,000 × 130%)) × 40% = £55,500 × 40% = £22,200

50 **C** The others funds match liabilities. Pension funds, life assurance funds tend to have longer dated liabilities, and insurance funds, such as motor insurance, have shorter dated liabilities

51 **B** An index-linked pension is a real liability as it will rise as inflation rises and is not fixed in cash (nominal) terms. Nominal liabilities do not change, and are fixed, irrespective of inflation

52 **D** Inside information is information that is of a precise nature and is not available to the public. Two further elements are that the information relates to particular financial instruments and, if it were to be made public, would be likely to have a significant effect on the prices of those financial instruments

53   **B**   Stamp duty land tax (SDLT) is payable on that part of the £587,000 purchase price falling within each band. (0% × £125,000) + (2% x next £125,000) + (5% × £337,000) = (£0 + £2,500 + £16,850) = £19,350.

           Residential SDLT rates

           £0 to £125,000 at 0%; £125,001 to £250,000 at 2%; £250,001 to £925,000 at 5%;

           £925,001 to £1,500,000 at 10%; Over £1,500,000 at 12%

54   **A**   Following the changes introduced in the Financial Services Act 2012 (FSA 2012), the Bank of England has responsibility for regulating settlement systems and recognised clearing houses (RCHs)

55   **C**   The firm must comply. If the complainant accepts the FOS determination, it is binding on the firm, but if the complainant rejects the determination, the firm is not bound by it. An FOS determination can be a monetary award or a direction. The maximum money award the FOS can make is £375,000 for complaints referred after 1 April 2022

56   **A**   Stabilisation is a specific exemption and will not constitute insider dealing, where the stabilisation process is carried out in accordance with the strict terms of the FCA's stabilisation rules

57   **B**   This is the best answer as the individual does not need to know the exact source – just that it was an inside source. There are three main insider dealing offences, with are dealing whilst in possession of inside information, encouraging another to deal, and disclosing information to another other than in the proper performance of one's duties

58   **B**   The CMA would investigate if the combined enterprise controlled at least 25%. If Samson controls 14%, this suggests that an investigation should be avoided if Delilah currently controls around 10% or less of the sector (since 10% + 14% = 24%, which is below the 25% threshold). This is known as the 'share of supply test' where the merging parties will together supply at least 25% of goods or services

59   **B**   The Competition and Markets Authority (CMA) has the power to impose fines for failure to provide requested information. The CMA was established under the Enterprise and Regulatory Reform Act 2013. The framework of control of mergers in the UK involves the CMA acting as an independent competition authority

60   **1.00**   The PTM levy is £1 for both buyers and sellers on transactions over £10,000

61   **B**   The first day that a bid may close is Day 21. If it then goes 'unconditional', then the offer must remain on the table for further 14 days. Any offer must remain open for a minimum period of 21 days after the initial posting (Day 21). The target company's directors must normally advise shareholders of their views within 14 days after the offer document is sent

62   **C**   Once a bid has lapsed, the bidding company may not launch a further bid for at least one year

63   **90**   At 90%, a company may invoke a compulsory purchase order, which forces any minority shareholders to sell their share

64   **C**   Failure to report, which is where a person fails to report knowledge or suspicion of money laundering (under POCA 2002), is punishable with a maximum of five years' imprisonment and an unlimited fine

65 **B** Executors need to obtain a Grant of Probate from the Probate Registry to show they are entitled to administer the estate. Probate is the process that occurs after someone has died, to administer their estate, collect debts and pay any tax due before the assets are distributed

66 **B** An agreement must be provided immediately only if the agreement was concluded using a means of distance communication, so the best answer is that it should be provided before the client is bound by any agreement

67 **A** Appropriateness rules will apply to executing a deal in derivatives in response to a direct offer promotion. The appropriateness obligation does not apply to a client for non-complex financial instruments. A non-complex financial instrument is one that is not a derivative, which can be traded easily, where information on its value is readily available, where it does not involve an obligation that exceeds the cost of acquiring the instrument, and where understandable information on the nature of the instrument is publicly available

68 **D** Every taxpayer, including additional rate taxpayers, has a dividend allowance of £2,000 on which 0% income tax is paid

69 **B** Even if these are the only two cases, the clients have lost money and further action should be taken. It appears unlikely that the product provider could be held liable

70 **C** The UK Listing Authority (UKLA) is responsible for allowing firms onto the official list, and hence becoming 'listed' companies. The UKLA is a part of the FCA

71 **A** Tax avoidance is the legitimate structuring of a person's tax affairs, to ensure the lowest possible tax liability. Minimising your tax liability through 'tax avoidance' is not a criminal activity. However, HMRC may challenge tax avoidance schemes that go beyond efficient tax planning and may seek to defeat it through the Courts

72 **A** A European directive requires that a government either amends existing legislation or imposes new legislation in their own state to cover the regulations laid out in the directive. EU Regulations have the force of law in every EU state without the need for national legislation

73 **D** The CFA Code and Standards require that trade allocation is carried out on a fair basis. The pro rata allocation is the only fair allocation method described

74 **A** Structured capital at risk products (SCARPs) are included in the definition of retail investment products (RIPs), but not packaged products. RIPs are wider than packaged products, as this includes structured investment products, all investment trusts, and unregulated collective investment schemes (UCIS). Packaged products include collective investment schemes (unit trusts and OEICs), life policies, personal pensions and stakeholder personal pensions

75 **A** A suitability report is not required in the case of the 'basic' level of advice on stakeholder products

76 **D** A basic written agreement is only required by the regulator for a retail client

77 **D** All three – bonds, shares and options on shares - are types of specified investments

78   B   The FCA has set out the Certification Functions in the SYSC sourcebook and an employee performing one of these roles must have a certificate confirming that they are 'fit and proper' to carry it out which must be confirmed (ie certified) at least once a year. Employees carrying out Certification Functions will not be approved by the FCA to do so. It is unlikely that the past performance is relevant to the individuals current 'fitness and proprietary'

79   B   CFA Standard ID – Misconduct – states that members shall not engage in any professional conduct involving dishonesty, fraud, deceit, or misrepresentation or commit any act that reflects adversely on their honesty, trustworthiness or professional competence. Faulkner should insist that the most recent, less favourable projections be included in the report

80   B   Journalists are not carrying out the activity 'in the course of investment business'. Members of DPBs are not necessarily investment professionals and promotions to them will not be exempt

81   C   Arranging the receipt and transmission of orders, operating a MTF, and managing investments are all core activities. Safekeeping or custody services are classified as ancillary (non-core) services

82   D   The firm undertakes an adequate assessment of the expertise, experience and knowledge of the client that gives reasonable assurance, in light of the nature of the transactions or services envisaged, that the client is capable of making their own investment decisions and understanding the risks involved. This is a requirement when treating a retail client as an elective professional client, and is known as the 'qualitative test'

83   B   Insolvency is a financial state in which a company can no longer pay its bills and other obligations on time. It occurs when liabilities or debts exceed assets and cash flow. When a company becomes insolvent, it must take immediate action to generate cash and settle or renegotiate current debts, in an attempt to rescue the business and/or consider the creditors of the company. In a limited liability company, as the name implies, shareholders' liability is limited to the usually relatively small amount subscribed for the shares

84   A   Insider dealing, unlawful disclosure of inside information, and market manipulation are the three types of market abuse under the MAR. Conducting market soundings is not considered to be market abuse. Market manipulation includes manipulating transactions and manipulating devices. Dissemination is another type of market abuse and is the dissemination of information which gives a false or misleading impression

85   B   Requesting information and documentation, asking employees to attend a meeting for questioning purposes, as well as extending an investigation are all within the power of the FCA when exercising and carrying out their information gathering and investigatory powers. Where access to a firm's premises is refused, a warrant would need to be issued by a Justice of the Peace

Practice Examination 3

(85 questions in 1 hour and 40 minutes)

Questions

1 **In Stock Exchange guidance on the release of price-sensitive information, where a release is lengthy, prominence must be given to:**

A Changes in directors

B Details of directors' executive share option schemes

C Current and future trading prospects

D Material interest disclosure

2 **The category of retail investment products most closely defines the range of products on which advice will be available through:**

A A retail investment adviser offering independent advice

B A retail investment adviser offering restricted advice

C An adviser offering basic advice using pre-scripted questions

D A product provider

3 **The Bank of England has responsibility for the prudential regulation of all of the following, except which one?**

A Recognised Investment Exchanges

B Securities settlement systems

C Recognised Clearing Houses

D Recognised payment systems

4 **What is the main area of responsibility of the Financial Policy Committee (FPC)?**

A Prudential regulation of systemically important financial institutions (SIFIs)

B Macro-prudential policy

C Monetary policy

D Regulation of firms' conduct

5 **Which principle would a firm mainly be breaching if it practised churning?**

A Customers' interests

B Financial prudence

C Client assets

D Skill, care and diligence

6   **When may a firm make cold (unsolicited) calls?**

A   Between 08:30 and 20:30 Monday to Friday

B   When the recipient has an established client relationship with the firm such that the recipient envisages receiving such calls

C   Between 09:00 and 20:00 Monday to Saturday

D   When the recipient has requested the call

---

7   **A firm does not have adequate systems for compliance oversight. With which of the FCA Principles for Businesses is it failing to comply?**

A   Customers' interests

B   Financial prudence

C   Management and control

D   Skill, care and diligence

---

8   **Which of the following promotions is/are permissible, based on the information provided?**

I   A phone call to a retail client who has asked you to call about a particular product

II   A call to promote the business of the firm to an individual whom the firm has certified is a sophisticated investor

III   An unsolicited call to market an investment to an investment professional

A   I only

B   I and III

C   I, II and III

D   III only

---

9   **A parent wishes to make the maximum Junior ISA (JISA) contribution for their child in the current tax year. How much of the contribution can be invested in a cash JISA?**

A   10%

B   25%

C   50%

D   100%

---

10   **Which of the following is not correct in respect of unwritten financial promotions outside the firm's premises?**

A   They may be conducted at any time of day

B   The person communicating it must identify themself and their firm

C   The person communicating it must clarify if the client wants to continue or terminate the communication

D   If an appointment is made, then a contact point must be given to the client

---

11   **An investment fund wishes to make a financial promotion. Given that the fund has been available for seven years, which of the following is/are required for any past performance information that is presented?**

       I   It must quote performance for at least the last five years

      II   It must attach a statement saying that past performance is no guarantee of future performance

     III   It must provide a comparison of performance by similar funds

A I only

B I and II

C II and III

D I, II and III

12   **Which of the following is not a requirement of SYSC?**

A Apportionment of responsibilities so that they can be monitored and controlled by directors

B Allocation of one or more individuals in the functions of dealing with the apportionment and overseeing the establishment of systems and controls

C Maintaining appropriate systems and controls

D A firm must maintain a separate compliance function

13   **When assessing suitability in the course of giving advice to a professional client, the firm needs, as a minimum, to take account of:**

A Investment objectives only

B Investment objectives and financial position only

C Investment objectives and knowledge and experience only

D Investment objectives, financial position and knowledge and experience

14   **Which of the following is true of member firms of the London Stock Exchange?**

A They must quote firm prices in those securities in which they deal as principal

B They are obliged to register as market makers

C They may only act as principal for some securities and agent for others

D They can act as either agent or principal in different transactions

15   **Which of the following does not amount to market abuse?**

A Communicating information before a transaction is announced to gauge the interest of specific potential investors

B Collaborating to secure a dominant position over the supply or demand for a financial instrument

C Creating unfair trading conditions through high-frequency trading

D Use of fictitious devices to affect the price of financial instruments

16 **Erica has recently passed an appropriate examination and is employed as an adviser by Deancourt Financial Advisers. Erica's friend Azin studied the same exam with Erica and is an adviser with Beardown Advisers. During a social event, Azin tells Erica that one of her clients, Colin, has been repeatedly critical of the service he receives from Beardown. Azin does not know that Colin also has an account with Deancourt, and Erica does not mention this. After checking with her supervisor what are the best terms she can offer but without disclosing her conversation with Azin, Erica offers Colin lower fees if he uses Deancourt for all his financial planning needs. Erica's supervisor learns of the situation and intends to raise the matter with Deancourt's Compliance Department. Which of the following is correct?**

A   Erica should be commended for taking into account Beardown's weak position

B   Deancourt should tell Colin that the confidentiality of information was breached

C   Deancourt should write to Colin and ask whether he is dissatisfied with the service provided by Beardown

D   Deancourt should ask the Financial Ombudsman Service (FOS) whether any complaint has been made by Colin

17 **Someone would be guilty only of secondary insider dealing if:**

      I   They are in possession of insider information

      II   They know it to be from an inside source

      III   They have the information through their office, vocation or profession

A   I only

B   I and II

C   I and III

D   I, II and III

18 **The normal settlement period for UK equities is:**

A   T + 5

B   T + 3

C   T + 2

D   T + 1

19 **What is the most significant regulatory change arising from the uncovering of manipulation of the multi-trillion dollar currency markets within banks?**

A   Establishment of Payment Systems Regulator

B   AIFMD

C   Changes to financial promotion rules

D   Individual accountability regime

20 **A firm must provide to the regulator, twice yearly, a report containing (for the reporting period) information about:**

    I   The total number of complaints received

    II   The total number of complaints closed

    III   The total number of complaints known to have been referred to and accepted by the FOS

    IV   The names of any complainants who have made two or more complaints against the firm in the reporting period

A I and II

B I, II and III

C I, II and IV

D I, II, III and IV

21 **By which of the following could inside information be supplied?**

    I   A director of the company

    II   A secretary employed by the company

    III   A shareholder of the company

A I and II

B I and III

C II and III

D I, II and III

22 **How frequently must an open uncovered derivative position be reported to a retail client?**

A Every week

B Every two weeks

C Every month

D Every six months

23 **Which of the following statements is incorrect regarding whistleblowing procedures?**

A Rules and guidance are set out in SYSC

B The rules relate to the Public Interest Disclosure Act 1998

C Whistleblowing would cover making disclosures relating to criminal offences or damage to the environment

D A firm may exclude the employees' whistleblowing rights in their contract of employment

24 **Which of the following is not one of the FCA Principles for Businesses?**

A Financial prudence

B Best execution

C Management and control

D Clients' assets

25 **The Mental Capacity Act 2005 enabled the creation of the:**

A   Established power of attorney

B   Enduring power of attorney

C   Principal power of attorney

D   Lasting power of attorney

26 **For unregulated markets, the FCA has created a process for recognising industry codes for unregulated financial markets and activities, known as 'FCA recognition'. Which of the following are codes that have been recognised by the FCA?**

      I   FX Global Code

      II   UK Money Market Code

      III   Commodities Benchmark Code

      IV   Standards for Lending Practice Code

A   I only

B   I and II

C   I, II and IV

D   II, III and IV

27 **The LSE is able to conduct investment business. It is correct to state that the LSE is:**

A   Authorised by the FCA

B   Authorised by the PRA

C   Given special powers by the Department for Business, Energy & Industrial Strategy

D   Exempt from authorisation

28 **Edgar Hughes-Willard has been studying the ethical requirements of the regulatory regime in the retail financial services sector. He has discovered that, as a retail investment adviser, he will need to hold a Statement of Professional Standing (SPS) if he wants to give independent or restricted advice.**

The SPS will be issued by:

A   The Prudential Regulation Authority

B   The Financial Conduct Authority

C   The Financial Skills Partnership

D   A body accredited by the Financial Conduct Authority

29 **Which of the following is not a specified investment under FSMA 2000?**

A   Gilt repos

B   Spot FX

C   Emission allowances

D   Spread betting

30 **A firm pays money of its own into a client bank account and subsequently retains that money in the account, in order to prevent a shortfall in client money. This is known as:**

A Prudent segregation

B Net negative add-back

C Rolling stock method

D Internal custody reconciliation

31 **Which of the following is incorrect regarding a firm's responsibilities and liability under anti-money laundering legislation?**

A The firm must establish internal reporting procedures

B The firm must establish identification procedures for customers, except for one-off transactions of a value less than €50,000

C The firm must establish appropriate educational programmes for all relevant employees

D Where a firm has not established the required internal systems, then the firm will be committing a criminal offence if money laundering takes place. The penalty is a maximum of two years' imprisonment and an unlimited fine

32 **In order to encourage institutional shareholders to become more active and engaged in corporate governance, the Financial Reporting Council has issued:**

A The City Code

B The Stewardship Code

C The UK Corporate Governance Code

D The Shareholders' Charter

33 **The UK Corporate Governance Code is best described as:**

A A statutory requirement

B A regulatory requirement

C Having a 'comply or explain' approach

D Voluntary

34 **In relation to identifying per se professional clients for MiFID business, which of the following is not a 'large undertaking'?**

A A company with: €15m balance sheet, €35m net turnover, €3m own funds
B A company with: €35m balance sheet, €45m net turnover, €1.5m own funds
C A company with: €25m balance sheet, €25m net turnover, €2.5m own funds
D A company with: €45m balance sheet, €15m net turnover, €4m own funds

35 **Which of the following is covered by the scope of MiFID?**

A A multilateral trading facility

B A commodity trading firm

C A philanthropic foundation

D A reinsurance firm

36 **What distinguishes the requirement to assess 'suitability' and the requirement to assess 'appropriateness' in respect of investment advice?**

A   There is no difference as they are both required protections for retail clients

B   'Suitability' involves making a personal recommendation and this is not necessarily the case with 'appropriateness'

C   'Appropriateness' applies only to professional clients

D   'Suitability' only applies to dealing in derivatives or warrants for a retail client

37 **Which are correct in relation to SETS?**

I   Orders are matched electronically
II   It is order-driven
III   It is quote-driven

A   I and III

B   I and II

C   II only

D   III only

38 **Price discovery and transparency are most closely associated with:**

A   Gathering evidence in the regulatory enforcement process

B   Revealing of equilibrium prices in financial markets

C   Stripping out of transaction costs to reveal true prices

D   Abolition of adviser charging

39 **What is the rate of stamp duty reserve tax (SDRT) on UK share transfers?**

A   ½% of the consideration

B   1% of the consideration

C   2% of the consideration

D   ¼% of the consideration

40 **Which of the following are true of the market abuse regime?**

I   The offences cover various insider dealing activities and distorting the market
II   Only regulated firms and their employees are subject to the regime
III   The FCA can penalise anyone for abusive behaviour
IV   The FCA can oblige authorised firms who have behaved abusively to make good losses to customers

A   I, II and IV

B   I and IV

C   I, III and IV

D   III and IV

41   A non-taxpayer receives a dividend of 10p per share on 500 shares. How much tax, in pounds and pence, can the investor reclaim?

Important! You should enter the answer only in numbers strictly using this format: 0.00

Do not include spaces, letters or symbols (but decimal points and commas should be used if indicated).

42   What is the rate of corporation tax for Spenser Watts plc, a company that earned total profits of £3,650,000 in the current financial year?

A   30%

B   20%

C   19%

D   It is not possible to answer based on the information given

43   An alternative route to admission to the Official List in the UK is to seek a listing on the Aquis Stock Exchange (AQSE) Main Market. AQSE also operates the AQSE Growth Market. Which one of the following is the correct admission criteria for a listing on the Growth Market?

A   To have at least 10% free float of shares in the hands of the public

B   To have at least 12 months audited accounts

C   To have at least two independent non-executive directors

D   To have at least £200,000 market value of equity shares listed

44   All of the following are costs that can arise from the principal–agent problem, except which one?

A   Round-trip costs

B   Misuse of company resources

C   Expropriation

D   Perquisites

45   Which of the following statements are true?

    I   Defined benefit schemes promise a pension related to the final salary of the participant
    II   The individual plan member bears the main risk with a defined contribution schemes
    III   Defined contribution schemes are sometimes referred to as money purchase schemes

A   I and II
B   I and III
C   II and III
D   I, II and III

46   **Which type of market depends upon market makers maintaining prices at which they are willing to trade?**

    A   A price-driven market

    B   An order-driven market

    C   A quote-driven market

    D   A dark liquidity pool

47   **A house situated in Derbyshire, England is bought for £287,000 in November of the current fiscal year. What will be the stamp duty land tax payable by the buyer?**

    A   £4,350

    B   £3,240

    C   £5,740

    D   £14,350

48   **An individual dies leaving an estate of £353,000 to their children. How much inheritance tax is payable?**

    A   £141,200

    B   £28,000

    C   £11,200

    D   £0

49   **Lifetime transfers are subject to inheritance tax:**

    A   If made within three years of death

    B   If made within five years of death

    C   If made within seven years of death

    D   If made within nine years of death

50   **Consider a firm of retail investment advisers. Which of the following would you not expect to be included in a 'terms of business' letter sent to clients?**

    A   The regulator of the firm

    B   The charges involved

    C   Details of to whom any complaint should be addressed and where to contact them

    D   The FCA Principles for Businesses

51   **Which of the following is not normally one of the objectives of a fact find?**

    A   To determine personal information

    B   To determine ethical preferences

    C   To determine the level of diversification

    D   To determine hard facts

52 **What is the purpose of an investment policy statement?**

    I   To detail the stocks that the fund will hold

    II   To specify the asset allocation the fund will use

    III   To specify market timing options

A   I and II

B   I and III

C   II and III

D   I, II and III

53 **Which of the following most closely describes a real liability?**

A   A payment that is due to be paid within the next twelve months

B   A liability that changes in monetary terms as we experience inflation

C   A liability that remains static in monetary terms as we experience positive inflation

D   A liability pay a loan that is secured on real property (land and buildings)

54 **Which of the following are parts of the FCA Handbook?**

    I   Decision Procedure and Penalties Manual

    II   Supervision

    III   Regulation of Professionals

    IV   Principles for Businesses

A   I, II and IV

B   II and IV

C   III and IV

D   I and III

55 **Within how many weeks after receiving a complaint should a complainant be informed of their right to use the Financial Ombudsman Service (FOS)?**

A   Four weeks

B   Six weeks

C   Eight weeks

D   Ten weeks

56 **Which of the following asset classes is not permitted under the UCITS III Product Directive?**

A   Derivatives

B   Gold

C   Money market

D   Warrants

57 **Rory Matthews dies in July 2020. He had made no lifetime transfers within the previous seven years. Inheritance was charged at 36% on the chargeable estate. This is because:**

A At least 10% of the net estate was left to charity

B Rory was not UK-domiciled

C HMRC has charged a penalty in addition to the usual amount that would be due

D It was possible to utilise unused nil-rate band from a spouse or civil partner who predeceased Rory

58 **Which of the following is true of an ordinary power of attorney?**

A The ordinary power of attorney applies on the incapacity of the donor

B The power may not be revoked by the donee

C The power will cease on the death of the donee

D The ordinary power of attorney may not be given as a trustee

59 **What effect will a shorter timescale have on the risk attitude of an investor?**

A No change

B Increased risk tolerance

C Reduced risk tolerance

D Reduced risk implications

60 **The Competition and Markets Authority (CMA) is carrying out a Phase II review of the merger of two retail groups, Coatville plc and Hatts plc. This indicates that the CMA believes that the merger involves**

A A breach of the City Code

B National security issues

C Public interest issues

D Substantial lessening of competition

The following information relates to Questions 61 to 66.

Milburn plc are a medium-sized manufacturing company which has established an occupational pension scheme for their workers. Employees pay 7% of their wages to the scheme, and the scheme promises to pay a pension on retirement which is based on the number of years worked and the salary of the worker in their last three years of employment.

61 **Which of the following best describes the style of scheme being operated by the company?**

A Defined contribution

B Money purchase

C Stakeholder pension

D Defined benefit

62   **Which UK regulator is responsible under the Pensions Act 2004 for regulating work-based pensions such as this one?**

A   The OPRA

B   The Pensions Regulator

C   The Financial Conduct Authority

D   The Information Commissioner's Office

63   **Members of the pension scheme will be given specific information regarding the investment of money held within the scheme. What name is given to this document?**

A   Statement of investment principles

B   Deed of title

C   Trust deed

D   Mandate

64   **How often is the Statement of Investment Principles (SIP) required to be published and sent to fund members?**

A   Monthly

B   Semi-annually

C   Annually

D   As required

65   **If the company were to be unable to meet their obligations, what scheme established under the Pensions Act 2004 could offer protection to members?**

A   Financial Services Compensation Scheme

B   Financial Ombudsman Service

C   Pension Protection Fund

D   Pension Compensation Scheme

66   **Under the Pension Protection Fund, what would be the maximum compensation offered to the employees who are not yet retired, as a percentage (%) of their pension payments due?**

Important! You should enter the answer only in numbers strictly using this format: 00

Do not include spaces, letters or symbols (but decimal points and commas should be used if indicated).

67 When residential property is sold, stamp duty land tax is payable by

A   The buyer and the seller

B   The buyer or the seller

C   The buyer

D   The seller

68 What is the current nil rate band for inheritance tax?

A   £175,000

B   £12,300

C   £355,000

D   £325,000

69 An individual dies leaving an estate on £866,000, half of which is paid to their children, with the remainder being paid to their spouse. How much inheritance tax is payable?

A   £216,400

B   £48,000

C   £43,200

D   £0

70 Which of the following are real liabilities?

I   Mortgage loan (as a liability of the homebuyer)
II   Index-linked pension (as a liability of the pension scheme)
III   School fees (as a liability of the parent)

A   I and II

B   I and III

C   II and III

D   I, II and III

71 Which of the following will comprise soft facts in a fact find?

A   Details of credit card liabilities

B   Details of risk tolerance

C   Details of outstanding mortgages

D   Details of children's ages

72 Which of the following classes of asset carries the lowest level of capital risk?

A   Cash deposits

B   Corporate bonds

C   Gilts

D   Domestic equities

73   **Who would normally prosecute a firm for conducting unauthorised regulated activities?**

A   The Department for Business, Energy & Industrial Strategy

B   The London Stock Exchange

C   The Financial Conduct Authority

D   The Treasury

74   **Nedra Alexander is a financial analyst with ABC Brokerage Company. She is preparing a purchase recommendation on F & H Corporation. Which one of the following situations would least likely represent a conflict of interest that should be disclosed?**

A   Alexander is on retainer as a consultant to F & H Corporation

B   Alexander's brother-in-law is a supplier to F & H Corporation

C   ABC holds a substantial common stock position of F & H Corporation for its own account

D   Through a family trust Alexander has material beneficial ownership of F & H Corporation

75   **Which of the following is not one of the main money laundering offences?**

A   Assistance

B   Tipping off

C   Theft

D   Failure to report

76   **Where a person knowingly participates in money laundering, what is the maximum prison term they may face in a criminal court?**

A   2 years

B   5 years

C   7 years

D   14 years

77   **Where an employee of an authorised firm suspects that money laundering is being carried out by a client, to whom should they normally report this?**

A   Their firm's Money Laundering Reporting Office

B   Their firm's Chief Executive Officer

C   Their firm's Human Resources Officer

D   The National Crime Agency

78   Which of the following is/are set out as an offence under the Terrorism Act 2000?

      I   Use and possession of funds for terrorism

      II   Fund raising

      III   Funding arrangements

  A   I only

  B   II and III

  C   I and III

  D   I, II and III

79   Which of the following is not a possible penalty for the civil offence of market abuse?

  A   Unlimited fine

  B   Six months prison sentence

  C   Restitution order

  D   Public statement

80   Which of the following could be used to settle Eurobonds?

  A   Euroclear

  B   The SETS system

  C   LCH Clearnet

  D   The London Stock Exchange

81   Which of the following instruments is/are covered by the insider dealing legislation in the Criminal Justice Act (CJA) 1993?

      I   FTSE Index futures

      II   Warrants

      III   Contracts for difference

  A   I and III

  B   II and III

  C   I and II

  D   I, II and III

82   The maximum penalty for insider dealing is:

  A   Seven years' imprisonment or an unlimited statutory fine

  B   Seven years' imprisonment and an unlimited statutory fine

  C   Six months' imprisonment and a £5,000 statutory fine

  D   Two years' imprisonment and an unlimited statutory fine

83   An investment bank GDS plc carries out a number of activities relating to its client Bella plc. GDS acts as Bella's corporate broker. It expects to give advice on a possible merger of Bella with Colleen Baker plc, a listed company which is not a client of GDS. GDS Bank has a market making business unit which makes a market in the stock of Bella plc.

In the context of its relationships with Bella plc, what is the main purpose of information barriers that GDS plc may have in place?

A   To restrict the flow of confidential information to the press

B   To enable disclosure of conflicts of interest

C   To prevent personal account dealing by employees

D   To enable GDS to carry on its various types of business

84   Suspected money laundering transactions should usually be reported by firms to:

A   The Bank of England

B   The Serious Fraud Office

C   The Stock Exchange

D   The National Crime Agency

85   The FCA has published rules that require authorised fund managers (AFM) to assess the value for money of each of their funds. A senior manager must take 'reasonable steps' to ensure that the AFM carries out this assessment of value for money and acts in the best interests of fund investors. Within what time period must the report be published?

A   Reports must be published within four months of the fund's annual accounting period end date

B   Reports must be published within three months of the fund's annual accounting period end date

C   Reports must be published within six months of the fund's annual accounting period end date

D   Reports must be published within 30 days of the fund's annual accounting period end date

Answers

1   **C**   The listing rules encourage companies to release new information to the market on a regular basis. Companies should have a consistent procedure for both determining what information is price-sensitive and for releasing it. Where an announcement is lengthy, LSE guidance is that prominence should be given to current and future trading prospects

2   **A**   An RIA offering independent advice will need to provide unbiased, unrestricted advice based on a comprehensive and fair analysis of the relevant market. To reflect the range of products that a consumer would expect such an adviser to have knowledge of, the regulator has introduced the term 'retail investment product'. A relevant market should 'comprise all retail investment products which are capable of meeting the investment needs and objectives of a retail client'

3   **A**   The Financial Services Act 2012 makes the Bank of England (BoE) responsible for regulating settlement systems and Recognised Clearing Houses (RCHs). The BoE is also responsible for the regulation of recognised payments systems under the Banking Act 2009. Recognised Investment Exchanges (RIEs) are regulated by the FCA. The other options available (settlement systems, recognised clearing houses (RCHs) and payment systems) are referred to as financial market infrastructures

4   **B**   The Financial Policy Committee (FPC) addresses issues of financial stability and resilience at the 'macro' level – that is, at the level of the economy and the financial services sector and sub-sectors

5   **A**   The firm would be in breach of the customers' interests principle (PRIN 6). Churning (and switching) relate to the deliberate overtrading of client accounts for the purpose of generating commission. Churning relates to investments in general, for example where a firm may buy/sell shares frequently in a way that is not in the best interests of the client. Switching refers to overtrading within and between packaged products

6   **B**   A call cannot be described as a 'cold call' if the recipient requested the call. The FCA rule states that a firm must not make a cold call, unless the recipient has an existing client relationship with the firm and the relationship is such that the recipient envisages receiving cold calls. There are no set time limits in COBS for when cold calls can be made, as long as the call is made at 'an appropriate time of day'

7   **C**   The management and control principle (PRIN 3) requires firms to have adequate risk management systems, and must take reasonable care to organise and control its affairs responsibly and effectively, that would include adequate systems for compliance oversight

8   **B**   Under COBS, where a retail customer has requested the call, it is allowable. Certified sophisticated investors are exempted from s21 FSMA 2000, but the certification must not come from the firm whose business is being promoted. An unsolicited call to market an investment to an investment professional would be allowable because the investment professional is exempt from protection provided by s21 and COBS

9   **D**   There are cash Junior ISAs, and stocks and shares Junior ISAs, with a single overall limit for each child per tax year which can be allocated in any proportions between the two types of Junior ISA. The overall maximum investment in a Junior ISA is £9,000 in the current tax year

10 **A** Such communications may only be conducted at an 'appropriate' time of day. The FCA rule states that where a firm communicates a non-written financial promotion it should only do so at an appropriate time of day; the purpose of the communication, and the firm represented, should be stated at the outset; it should clarify whether the client would like to continue or terminate the communication, and should terminate the communication at any time the client requests.; and a point of contact should be given, so that any further appointment can be cancelled

11 **B** There is no requirement to show performance against that of similar funds. In addition, past performance cannot be the most prominent feature of the communication, and the reference period and source of information must be clearly stated

12 **D** The Senior Management Arrangements, Systems and Controls (SYSC) focuses on the responsibilities of directors and senior management to ensure the firm has appropriate control, supervision and accountability systems in place. It may or may not be appropriate for the firm to have a separate compliance function

13 **B** The suitability rules require firms to take account of the client's knowledge and experience, financial position and investment objectives. However, when advising a professional client the firm is entitled to assume that the client has the necessary experience and knowledge in that particular area. Therefore, the firm would only need to take account of the client's investment objectives and financial position

14 **D** LSE member firms are not obliged to quote firm prices unless they have registered as market makers. Nor are they obliged to register as market makers. They have dual capacity which gives the ability to act as principal or agent in different transactions

15 **A** Communicating information before a transaction is announced to gauge the interest of specific potential investors is known as a 'market sounding'. Market soundings are part of the normal functioning of financial markets and are not considered to be market abuse

16 **B** This is an ethical matter. Azin has acted unethically by confiding in Erica about her client's affairs, and Erica has acted unethically in acting on that information. Deancourt is free to offer competitive terms to clients in an effort to bring in more business, but in this case it did so based on information it had received following a breach of confidentiality. An ethical approach could involve disclosing this breach to the client

17 **B** For the purposes of the legislation, a person has information, as an insider, if he knows it is from an inside source and knows that it is inside information (ie price-sensitive). These suggest being guilty of 'secondary' insider dealing. If they have information from their own office or employment, that is described as 'primary' insider dealing

18 **C** The current standard settlement of London Stock Exchange equity transactions is T+2, being trade date plus two business days. Settlement is made through CREST, which is a computerised system that allows investors to hold shares in an electronic rather than paper form. The settlement of UK Government gilts is also carried out through CREST, which operates a computerised settlement system for its members, with settlement being T+1 (trade date plus one business day)

19 **D** Part 4 of the Financial Services (Banking Reform) Act 2013 set out new regimes to be applied by the financial regulators (the FCA and PRA) in order to provide for the assessment and accountability of individuals in the banking sector. The new regime includes the Senior Managers Regime (SMR), the Certification Regime (CR), and the conduct rules

20   **B**   Although B is the best answer, firms must in fact only report any complaints that have not been resolved by close of business on the business day following receipt of the complaint. The main aspects being reported to the FCA in the biannual report (twice a year – ie every 6 months) are the number of complaints, completions of complaints within four weeks, eight weeks and over eight weeks from receipt, and the number of complaints accepted as valid by the firm

21   **D**   All employees are, by virtue of their office, potential holders of inside information. Shareholders are also a potential inside source. Insider dealing is the dealing in a public company's shares by individuals with access to material non-public information about that company

22   **C**   Via a periodic statement, which must be sent out at least monthly. Normally, the firm must provide a periodic statement once every six months, however where the portfolio is a leveraged portfolio, the periodic statement must be provided at least once a month

23   **D**   A firm cannot exclude an employee's whistle blowing rights. The Public Interest Disclosure Act 1998 (PIDA) establishes a framework for the protection of employees making a 'protected disclosure' in cases of whistle-blowing. These rules are contained with SYSC 18. Firms must also include a provision in employment contracts clarifying that nothing in that agreement prevents an employee, or ex-employee, from making a 'protected disclosure'

24   **B**   Best execution is an FCA conduct of business rule rather than one of the Principles for Businesses. Financial prudence (PRIN 4), management and control (PRIN 3) and clients' assets (PRIN 10) are all principles for businesses

25   **D**   The Lasting Power of Attorney (LPA) created by the Mental Capacity Act 2005 is similar to the previous Enduring Power of Attorney (EPA), except that the Mental Capacity Act also allows people to appoint an attorney to make health and welfare decisions, known as a 'personal welfare LPA'. The other LPA is known as a 'property and affairs LPA'

26   **C**   The FCA has created a process for recognising industry codes for unregulated financial markets and activities, known as 'FCA recognition'. The FX Global Code is maintained and updated by the Global Foreign Exchange Committee; this Code sets global principles of good practice standards in the foreign exchange market, promoting the integrity and effective functioning of the wholesale foreign exchange market. The UK Money Markets Code (MM) is maintained and updated by the Money Markets Committee, and sets standards and best practice expected from participants in the deposit, repo and securities lending markets in the UK. The Standards of Lending Practice for business customers is maintained and updated by Lending Standards Board, and these standards set the benchmark for good lending practice in the UK, outlining the way registered firms are expected to deal with their business customers throughout the entire product life cycle

27   **D**   The LSE is exempt from the need to be authorised by the regulator: it is instead 'recognised' – as a recognised investment exchange (RIE). The most important exempt persons are appointed representatives, RIEs and Recognised Clearing Houses (RCHs), members of the professions, and members of Lloyd's

28   **D**   Professional bodies will be able to obtain FCA accreditation and issue the Statement of Professional Standing (SPS) to their adviser members. Accredited bodies will inform the FCA of any advisers who do not meet the standards required to obtain the SPS

29   **B**   Foreign exchange is not a specified investment under FSMA 2000. Specified investments include all investment instruments and rights to those instruments, but exclude physical assets, such as land and commodities). The provision of credit, as well as regulated mortgages, are also deemed specified investments, as are structured deposits and emission allowances, as a result of MiFID II

30   **A**   Firms must have a written policy, approved by its governing body, detailing why prudent segregation is being used to address specific risks, and how the amounts so paid are calculated

31   **B**   One-off transactions may be excluded when below €15,000, not €50,000. In order for the procedures and recommendations to be effective, it is important that employees are made aware of their obligations and are trained to provide a prompt report of any suspicious transactions. Internal reporting procedures must be established by the firm, and failure to comply with these requirements, such as a failure to implement satisfactory identification procedures, constitutes an offence punishable by a maximum of two years' imprisonment, or an unlimited fine, or both

32   **B**   The Stewardship Code applies to fund managers, but institutional investors are also 'strongly encouraged' to disclose their level of compliance with the principles of the Stewardship Code. The Stewardship Code was updated in 2020. It now comprises a set of 'apply and explain' Principles. Twelve Principles aimed at asset managers and asset owners (institutional investors); and Six Principles aimed at service providers

33   **C**   The 'comply or explain' approach has been retained from the earlier Combined Code. The way this operates is widely supported by companies and investors as allowing flexibility while ensuring sufficient information for investors to come to their own conclusions

34   **A**   A 'large undertaking' meets at least two out of three of: at least €20 million balance sheet; at least €40 million net turnover; at least €2 million own funds. Company A meets only the 'own funds' criterion, and so would not be categorised as a per se professional client

35   **A**   Commodity traders and reinsurers are excluded. A philanthropic foundation is administering its own assets and, as such, is excluded. MTFs are covered by MiFID rules

36   **B**   Suitability requirements apply when making a personal recommendation and this is not so with appropriateness, which is relevant for 'non-advised' sales, which is otherwise described as 'execution-only'

37   **B**   The London Stock Exchange trading platform SETS offers electronic trading and is an automatic order matching system. It is known as the 'order-book'. It is not quotation-driven as it has no market maker involvement. SEAQ is the quote-display system used as the price reference point for telephone-based (quotation-based) execution between market participants and market makers

38   **B**   Effective securities markets have price discovery (the process through which an equilibrium price for a financial instrument is revealed continuously through bid and offer prices, and trading) and transparency (through knowing the price before, during and after a deal)

39   **A**   The amount of stamp duty reserve tax (SDRT), payable on paperless transactions, and paid by an investor who buys shares, is worked out at a flat rate of ½%, rounded to the nearest 1p. Stamp duty is ½% of the consideration, rounded up to the next £5

40   **B**   I is true – the offence of market abuse does cover various insider dealing activities as well as activities that distort the market. II is false: the regime applies to the behaviour, regardless of whom is involved. III is false: the FCA would need to apply to a court to penalise a person who is outside the regulated sector. IV is true – the FCA can oblige firms to make good losses

41   **0.00**   No tax can be reclaimed. The dividend is paid gross, before the deduction of tax, and so there is no tax that can be reclaimed by a non-taxpayer on the distribution of a dividend

42   **C**   A UK-resident company is liable to corporation tax on its worldwide profits and chargeable gains arising in an accounting period. For the financial year 2022 (1 April 2022 to 31 March 2023), companies must pay a single rate of corporation tax at 19% of their profits

43   **A**   An alternative route to admission to the Official List in the UK is to seek a listing on the AQSE Main Market. The eligibility for such a listing is the same as for the Official List and companies can choose either a premium or standard listing. AQSE also operates the AQSE Growth Market. The admission criteria for a listing on the Growth Market includes the appointment and retention an AQSE corporate adviser at all times; to have at least twenty-four months' audited accounts; to have at least 10% free float (shares in public hands); and to demonstrate appropriate levels of corporate governance, including having at least one independent nonexecutive director

44   **A**   'Round trip' costs refer to the transaction costs of buying and selling a financial instrument or investment. In the principal-agency problem, managers may use the discretion they have for self-dealing, and divert corporate wealth to themselves. They may expropriate owners' funds by embezzling funds, misuse corporate resources or transfer ownership of assets to themselves. A more common form of agency cost is the allocation of owners' funds for managers' personal consumption or perquisites, such as bigger expense accounts or corporate jets

45   **D**   All of these statements are true. There are two main types of pension fund, being defined benefit (DB), also known as 'final salary' schemes; and defined contribution (DC), also known as 'money purchase' schemes

46   **C**   A quote-driven market, such as SEAQ, requires certain market participants (market makers) to take responsibility for acting as buyers and sellers to the rest of the market so that there will always be a price at which a trade can be conducted. For such a market to operate efficiently, up-to-date prices at which market makers are willing to trade need to be made available to other market participants

47   **A**   Stamp duty land tax (SDLT) is payable on that part of the £287,000 purchase price falling within each band. (0% × £125,000) + (2% x next £125,000) + (5% × £37,000) = (£0 + £2,500 + £1,850) = £4,350.

        Residential SDLT rates

        £0 to £125,000 at 0%; £125,001 to £250,000 at 2%; £250,001 to £925,000 at 5%;

        £925,001 to £1,500,000 at 10%; Over £1,500,000 at 12%

48   **C**   Inheritance tax is payable at 40% on the value of the estate above the nil rate band – currently £325,000. Therefore, £353,000 - £325,000 = £28,000 x 40% IHT = £11,200 inheritance tax

49 **C**   Chargeable lifetime transfers (CLTs) made within seven years of death are liable to inheritance tax. A CLT will not be subject to further IHT charge provided the donor survives for seven years after making the gift

50 **D**   The FCA's Principles for Businesses (PRINs) would not normally be included in the terms of business letter sent to a client

51 **C**   In a fact find, the adviser will be looking to determine facts about the client. The fact find should establish the type and nature of the client and their attitude to risk, investment objectives in terms of risk and return, investment constraints, such as liquidity, legal requirements, time horizon, tax position and unique circumstances, and performance measurement benchmarks. The level of diversification would only be considered as part of the investment strategy to achieve the objectives of the client

52 **C**   The investment policy statement concentrates on strategic asset allocation and tactical asset allocation. The client's risk profile has a major role in agreeing an appropriate asset allocation for each financial objective. Asset allocation is a major factor in investment performance, so this is a critical stage in the financial-planning process. A number of academic studies have shown that asset allocation is the single most important factor in determining the returns of an investment portfolio

53 **B**   A real liability – for example, the liability of a pension fund to pay an index-linked pension – rises with inflation. A nominal liability is one that is fixed

54 **A**   There is no sourcebook called Regulation of Professionals. The Decision Procedure and Penalties Manual (DEPP) sets out the FCA's decision-making procedures that involve the giving of statutory notices, the penalties, and the conduct of interviews. Supervision (SUP) deals with supervisory issues and requirements concerning the regulators' relationship with firms. These are both within the Regulatory Processes block of the Handbook. The Principles for Businesses (within the High Level Standards) sets out the obligations of all FCA regulated firms, and has the FCA's eleven principles (PRINs)

55 **C**   Within eight weeks, the complainant must be given the Financial Ombudsman Service (FOS) leaflet and told of their right to use the service, a right they have a maximum of six months to take up

56 **B**   Tangible assets, such as gold, are not covered. The UCITS III Product Directive expands the range and type of financial instruments that are permitted within UCITS funds. In particular, it allows the use of derivatives for both investment and for risk reduction purposes

57 **A**   The inheritance tax rate is reduced to 36% if at least 10% of the net estate is left to charity. For individuals who are not domiciled in the UK, only transfers of UK assets are liable to IHT, but this will not change the rate on the chargeable estate. 36% is lower than the standard 40% rate, so an HMRC penalty could not be the reason. Use of a spouse's unused nil rate band could reduce the chargeable estate, but not the rate of tax charged on it

58 **C**   The ordinary power of attorney will cease at the end of a specified time, when a specific act has occurred or when the donee dies or becomes incapacitated. To extend decision making beyond this a lasting power of attorney may be needed

59 **C**   Shorter timescales lead to a reduced risk tolerance as the potential impact of risks increases. Risk tolerance is the willingness to take risk and is related to the investor's psychology, which may be assessed using the fact find process. The longer the investment time horizon is, the more risk the investor is likely to be willing to take on

60   **D**   If the CMA believes the merger will lead to a 'substantial lessening of competition', then it will normally move to a phase two investigation. If the phase two investigation finds that the merger will substantially reduce competition, the CMA has the power to either prohibit the merger or impose remedies if the merger has taken place. National security is the only defined public interest issue currently, and concern about such an issue could lead to intervention by the Secretary of State for Business, Energy & Industrial Strategy

61   **D**   In a defined benefit (DB) scheme, also known as 'final salary', the employer agrees to pay the member benefits equal to a pre-determined percentage of their salary at retirement, depending upon the number of years worked. The other alternatives all refer to types of pension scheme where no guaranteed return is paid but rather it is the value of the fund at retirement which decides the returns paid

62   **B**   The Pensions Regulator (TPR) replaced the Occupational Pensions Regulatory Authority (OPRA) in 2005. The objectives of the Pensions Regulator (TPR) include protecting the benefits of members of occupational schemes and personal pension schemes

63   **A**   Statement of Investment Principles – known as the SIPs. The Statement of Investment Principles (SIP) sets out the principles governing how decisions about investments are made, and must include the pension scheme's policy on choosing investments, the kinds of investments to be held, and the balance between different kinds; the risk, including how risk is to be measured and managed, and the expected return on investments; and the extent the scheme takes account, if at all, of social, environmental or ethical considerations when taking investment decisions

64   **C**   The Statement of Investment Principles (SIP) must be sent to members annually. The SIP has to be reviewed every three years or whenever there is a significant change in investment policy.

65   **C**   The Pension Protection Fund (PPF) offers compensation if the sponsoring employer becomes insolvent and is unable to pay its liabilities. The PPF provides compensation where an employer of a defined benefit (DB) pension scheme becomes insolvent and the scheme is unable to pay its liabilities. The PPF covers up to 100% of benefits for existing pensioners and up to 90% of benefits to those who have not yet retired. The PPF is funded by a levy on all DB pension schemes

66   **90**   Where a sponsoring employer becomes insolvent and unable to pay its liabilities, the Pension Protection Fund (PPF) will provide compensation up to 100% of benefits to existing pensioners and up to 90% of benefits to those who have not yet retired

67   **C**   Stamp duty land tax (SDLT) is payable by the buyer of a property. It is based upon the purchase price of the property

68   **D**   The nil rate band for inheritance tax is £325,000. The residence nil rate band is £175,000

69   **C**   Inheritance tax is not payable on that part of the estate which passes to a spouse or civil partner. The half of the estate transferred to the children is taxable to the extent that it exceeds the tax-free band. [(£866,000 ÷ 2) – £325,000] = £108,000 × 40% = £43,200 IHT payable

70   **C**   A mortgage loan is a nominal liability, as the amount that is outstanding will not increase with the effects of inflation

71   **B**   Risk tolerance is a matter of soft fact, while the other areas, such as credit card liabilities, outstanding mortgage amount and the children's ages are regarded as hard facts

72   **A**   Capital risk is the risk that an investment may be worth less in future than it is today. This will include the value of corporate bonds, government bonds and equities, but not cash deposits. With cash deposits, capital is normally only at risk if the deposit-taking institution fails, although inflation will erode the value of the capital. For the other classes of asset, the capital will vary with the markets

73   **C**   The FCA will prosecute for breaches of Section 19 FSMA, related to unauthorised regulated activities

74   **B**   According to Standard VIA – Disclosure of Conflicts – all potential conflicts of interest must be disclosed. The more obvious conflicts of interest are special relationships between a member and the member's firm or an issuer, underwriter or others with financial relationships, such as broker-dealer market-making activities, and positions involving material beneficial ownership of stock

75   **C**   The offence of money laundering refers to the proceeds of crime rather than the underlying crime itself. Therefore, the original crime, such as theft, is not an actual money laundering offence, however disguising the source of these criminal proceeds is

76   **D**   The maximum penalties for any offence of assisting a money launderer are 14 years' imprisonment and/or an unlimited fine, when found guilty in a Crown Court

77   **A**   The money laundering reporting officer (MLRO) would be the appropriate reporting point. The MLRO has the responsibility for reporting suspicious transactions to the National Crime Agency (NCA)

78   **D**   The Terrorism Act 2000 sets out the offences of: fund raising for terrorism; use and possession of money or property for the purpose of terrorism; funding arrangements; and also money laundering

79   **B**   A civil offence will not carry a prison sentence. Market abuse is a civil offence, and does not replace or change any existing criminal legislation

80   **A**   Eurobonds are settled through Euroclear and Clearstream. Both Euroclear and Clearstream provide securities clearance and settlement services. ICMA rules currently require settlement within 2 business days (T+2). Euroclear and Clearstream are linked electronically with each other, which allows member organisations to use either system

81   **D**   Insider dealing legislation covers equity, debt and related products, such as depository receipts, warrants, derivatives, contracts for differences and all tradable debt instruments, but not collective investment schemes, life insurance policies or commodities such as currency or gold

82   **B**   An individual found guilty of insider dealing shall be liable to an unlimited fine or seven years' imprisonment, or both when found guilty in a Crown court, also known as an 'indictable offence'. However, when found guilty in a Magistrates' court, known as a 'summary offence', there is a statutory maximum fine of £5,000 or six months in jail, or both

83 **D** Information barriers, or 'Chinese walls', can serve to insulate different business units from each other, thus managing potential conflicts of interest that might otherwise lead to GDS having to restrict or to withdraw from certain types of business

84 **D** The Money Laundering Reporting Officer (MLRO) would report to the National Crime Agency (NCA), if the offence was related to money laundering

85 **A** Under the Senior Manager and Certification Regime (SM&CR) there is prescribed responsibility for a senior individual to take 'reasonable steps' to ensure that the AFM carries out the FCA assessment of value and acts in the best interests of fund investors. The public reports must be published within four months of the fund's annual accounting period end date

BPP LEARNING MEDIA

Practice Examination 4

(85 questions in 1 hour and 40 minutes)

Questions

The following information relates to Questions 1 and 2.

George Hague has run up a number of personal debts, including an unsecured debt of £4,500 to Happy House Casino. He also owns 100% of GH Ltd, a small private consultancy in the form of a private limited company which has carried out only minor business recently. For the past six months, George has only a small income and has found himself unable to pay his debts when they have been demanded.

1   Which of the following is/are correct in respect of a petition for a bankruptcy order?

       I   Happy House Casino could be the petitioner

      II   A bankruptcy order cannot be made unless GH Ltd is insolvent

      III   George Hague could be the petitioner

   A   III only

   B   I and II

   C   II and III

   D   I, II and III

2   When the bankruptcy order is made, the official receiver takes control of George's assets. Which of the following statements is incorrect?

   A   The official receiver is an official of the Department of Business, Energy & Industrial Strategy

   B   The official receiver is an officer of the court

   C   The trustee in bankruptcy protects the bankrupt's property until the official receiver takes over

   D   The bankruptcy of George will begin on the day that the order is made

3   An adult individual decides to make use of the full ISA allowance of £20,000 in the current tax year. What is the maximum amount from the total allowance that can be invested in stocks and shares?

   A   £7,620

   B   £15,000

   C   £10,600

   D   £20,000

4   Under the General Data Protection Regulations (GDPR) which one of the following is the most correct statement regarding fines for breaches of certain important provisions?

A Fines for breaches of certain important provisions can be up to €50m or 5% of global annual turnover, whichever is the greater

B Fines for breaches of certain important provisions can be up to €20m or 4% of global annual turnover, whichever is the greater

C Fines for breaches of certain important provisions can be up to €5m or 1% of global annual turnover, whichever is the greater

D Fines for breaches of certain important provisions can be up to €40m or 2% of global annual turnover, whichever is the greater

5   Which one of the following GDPR conditions does not necessarily apply to a firm processing personal data?

A Data must be handled by those that are accountable, who must take responsibility and have appropriate measures and records in place to demonstrate compliance

B Data must be accurate and must be updated regularly

C Consent from the data subject must be specific, and once obtained, it will only be valid for the stated purpose; therefore, the data subject does have not the right to withdraw their consent at any time

D Data must not be held longer than is necessary for its lawful purpose

6   What is the minimum number of shareholders required as a quorum for a listed company to hold an Annual General Meeting (AGM)?

A Two

B Five

C Ten

D One

7   A medium-sized firm of retail investment advisers is the subsidiary of a UK-listed parent company. The firm is reviewing its procedures in the light of the Bribery Act 2010. The directors have noted that Ministry of Justice guidance sets out the principle that a commercial organisation's procedures to prevent bribery should be 'proportionate'.

The requirement of being proportionate is best described as meaning that the company's procedures should:

A Focus on the possibility of instances of bribery that could be material to the financial statements

B Be in proportion to the bribery risks it faces and to the nature and scale of the company's activities

C Focus anti-bribery efforts on markets and sectors in which bribery is least tolerated

D Be proportionate to the levels of bribery that have been experienced in the past by the company and to the complexity of the company's activities

8   Where will details of directors' transactions in the shares of a listed UK company appear?

      I   In the company's Annual Report

      II   On a Regulatory Information Service

      III   In the company's Register of Interests in Shares

A   I only

B   I and II

C   II and III

D   I, II and III

9   Ignacio sells all of his shares in Tesco plc for less than the original cost. He had owned the shares for eighteen months. Ignacio makes no other disposals of shares in the current tax year. How long can he carry forward the loss?

A   Two years

B   Three years

C   Ten years

D   Indefinitely

10   Willard is a securities dealer who has been instructed by private client managers within his firm to buy shares in a particular listed company for a number of clients of the firm. The order is partially filled. The CFA Institute Standards of Professional Conduct indicate that Willard should allocate the stock:

A   Randomly

B   In proportion to the amount of commission paid by each client

C   Giving priority to higher-performing accounts

D   In proportion to the order size relating to each client account

11   Steve, an IT consultant, is working for a firm and comes across some price-sensitive information. He is also a shareholder of the company and has already placed a personal sell order on the company's shares. Under which of the following circumstances is he not guilty of market abuse?

A   He leaves the sell order in place

B   He phones a friend and tells them to buy the shares on NASDAQ

C   He places an order to buy more of the shares

D   He buys more of the shares, having informed the firm's compliance officer

12   **Which of the following is/are true of a proxy vote?**

        I   Able to vote in a poll
        II   Able to vote on a show of hands
        III   Must be appointed in writing

A III only

B I and II

C II and III

D I, II and III

---

13   **Mrs Okiro buys some shares in X plc for £50,000 and some shares in Y plc for £40,000. In the same tax year, she sells the shares in X plc for £70,400 and the shares in Y plc for £35,300. Mrs Okiro's rate of tax on gains is 20% and the CGT annual exempt amount is £12,300. Calculate the capital gains tax payable.**

A £340

B £680

C £3,080

D £3,400

---

14   **A firm is the manager of a fund and, following a review of the Alternative Investment Fund Managers Directive (AIFMD) changes, the firm concludes that the AIFMD provisions do not apply to its fund. This could be because the fund is:**

A An infrastructure fund

B A real estate fund

C A hedge fund

D Covered by the UCITS Directive

---

15   **Within what time frame is a listed public company required to hold an annual general meeting (AGM)?**

A Within three months of the financial year-end

B Within six months of the financial year-end

C Within nine months of the financial year-end

D Not more than fourteen months after the previous AGM

---

16   **Insider dealing is an offence under the:**

A Bribery Act 2010

B Companies Securities (Insider Dealing) Act 1985

C Financial Services and Markets Act 2000

D Criminal Justice Act 1993

---

17   One of the conditions for a merger to be subject to investigation by the Competition and Markets Authority (CMA) is where the merged company has a market share of more than:

A   25%

B   30%

C   40%

D   50%

18   What is the largest gift that a parent can make on the event of their child's civil partnership that will be fully exempt from inheritance tax?

A   £0

B   £1,000

C   £3,000

D   £5,000

19   Where a parent pays money into a child's building society savings accounts, what is the maximum gross sum that can be earned before the income becomes treated as income from the parent and taxed as such? Assume that the accounts are not Junior ISAs, cash ISAs, or a Child Trust Fund.

Important! You should enter the answer only in numbers strictly using this format: 000

Do not include spaces, letters or symbols (but decimal points and commas should be used if indicated).

20   The normal method of issuance for UK government bonds is:

A   By Dutch auction

B   By variable price auction

C   A 'tap' into the secondary market

D   A tender offer

21   Where the FCA has refused to grant a Part 4A permission to a firm, then the firm can take their complaint:

A   To the FCA

B   To the Financial Ombudsman Service

C   To HM Treasury

D   To the Upper Tribunal

22 **Which of the following is/are classified as a specified investment under the Financial Services and Markets Act 2000?**

    I   Shares in a US company

    II   Exchange-traded futures

    III   Residential property

  A I only

  B I and II

  C II and III

  D I, II and III

23 **A non-taxpayer receives a dividend of £100 from a UK company. What tax repayment can the investor claim from HMRC?**

  A £0

  B £10.00

  C £12.50

  D £20.00

24 **Which of the following is the main piece of legislation which endows the Financial Conduct Authority (FCA) with its statutory powers?**

  A Financial Services Act 2010

  B Criminal Justice Act 1993

  C Financial Services and Markets Act 2000

  D Financial Services Act 1986

25 **In December of the current tax year, a house is sold for £562,000. What will be the stamp duty land tax (SDLT) payable by the seller?**

  A £0

  B £8,610

  C £18,100

  D £3,100

26 **What is the normal settlement convention for Eurobonds?**

  A T + 1

  B T + 2

  C T + 3

  D T + 7

27   One of the categories into which clients may be allocated is 'eligible counterparty'. Which of the following rules will apply to the firm's relationships with eligible counterparties?

A   Client agreements

B   Appropriateness

C   Best execution

D   Client categorisation

28   Which of the following are examples of packaged products?

    I   Units in a regulated collective investment scheme
    II   Execution-only dealing services
    III   Investment trust savings scheme

A   I and II

B   I and III

C   II and III

D   I, II and III

29   With respect to company meetings, a company is permitted to communicate with the shareholders electronically, such as by email. For the purposes of electronic communication, a notice is deemed to be sent when the electronic notice is first transmitted and delivered within what time period?

A   A notice is deemed to be sent when the electronic notice is first transmitted and delivered 24 hours after being sent

B   A notice is deemed to be sent when the electronic notice is first transmitted and delivered 48 hours after being sent

C   A notice is deemed to be sent when the electronic notice is first transmitted and delivered 7 calendar days after being sent

D   A notice is deemed to be sent when the electronic notice is first transmitted and delivered 21 calendar days after being sent

30   You have been asked to prepare a briefing document for staff on the requirements on competence for individuals carrying out retail activities, and on the standards of ethical behaviour.

Which of the following is it most correct for your briefing to state?

The regulator seeks to ensure that retail investment advisers adhere to ethical standards mainly through:

A   A requirement to hold a Statement of Professional Standing that is issued by the regulator

B   A requirement to hold a Statement of Professional Standing that is issued by an accredited body

C   A requirement that advisers follow a Code of Ethics for Investment Advisers that is published by the regulator

D   A requirement that advisers follow a Code of Ethics for Investment Advisers that is published by the Financial Skills Partnership

31 **A four-level approach was used to create a single market in financial services in Europe. What was the process called for introducing a wide range of new legislation?**

A   EMU

B   Financial Services Action Plan

C   Lamfalussy Plan

D   ESMA

32 **Who creates a power of attorney?**

A   The attorney

B   The donee

C   The settlor

D   The donor

33 **Where is a lasting power of attorney (LPA) registered?**

A   The Attorney General

B   Magistrates Court

C   Office of the Public Guardian

D   HM Treasury

34 **Which of the following circumstances is not one which a firm is required to notify to the regulator?**

A   An adviser has failed to meet agreed persistency levels for contracts arranged with clients

B   An adviser who has been assessed as competent is no longer considered competent

C   An adviser has failed to attain an appropriate qualification within the prescribed time limit

D   An adviser has failed to comply with a Statement of Principle

35 **When an individual's financial affairs are taken over by the court, under the Insolvency Act 1986 this is known as:**

A   An individual voluntary arrangement

B   Bankruptcy

C   Insolvency

D   Liquidation

36 **One of the categories into which clients may be allocated is 'professional client'.**

In order to be treated as a professional client, a retail client must be all of the following, except:

A   Experienced and knowledgeable

B   In receipt of a warning

C   Of high net worth, if an individual

D   Willing to provide a written statement that they are aware of consequences

37   With regard to the FCA's Principles for Businesses, to whom does the term 'customer' refer?

A   Retail clients only

B   Eligible counterparties only

C   Professional clients and eligible counterparties only

D   Retail clients and professional clients only

38   Who is empowered to assess the competence and capability of a person performing a significant management function for an incoming French firm providing MiFID investment services in their Edinburgh branch?

A   Scottish regulator

B   Financial Conduct Authority

C   French regulator (AMF)

D   FCA and French regulator

39   Under the Conduct Rules (COCON), which of the following requirements is a 'second tier' rule applying specifically to senior managers?

A   Disclose information of which the regulator would reasonably expect notice

B   Be open and co-operative with the regulators

C   Observe proper standard of market conduct

D   Pay due regard to the interests of customers and treat them fairly

40   Which of the following investments, when available, provide tax-free income for UK residents?

A   NS&I Guaranteed Income Bonds

B   NS&I Investment Accounts

C   NS&I Savings Certificates

D   Traded endowment policies

41   Ken Wong is preparing to give independent investment advice, and is reviewing his knowledge of the range of retail investment products. Which of the following does not fall within the definition of retail investment products?

A   100 shares in an open-ended investment company

B   100 shares in a FTSE 100 company

C   100 units in an unregulated collective investment scheme

D   100 shares in an investment trust company

42 **Which of the following are requirements of a trustee under the Trustee Act 2000?**

    I   A trustee must have regard to the suitability of the investment to the trust

    II   A trustee has a general duty to exercise reasonable care in investments

    III   A trustee must review the investments of the trust regularly

A I and II

B II and III

C I and III

D I, II and III

43 **Arthur has been saving in a personal pension plan. At what age will he normally be able to start taking an income from the plan?**

A Age 55

B Age 60

C Age 67

D State Pension Age

44 **Which of the following is/are required for an individual to attain threshold competence as a retail investment adviser?**

    I   Passing an appropriate examination

    II   Working unsupervised for three months

    III   Obtain sponsorship from a senior manager

A I only

B I and II

C II and III

D I and III

45 **Which of the following is/are true regarding the disclosure of directors' interests in shares?**

    I   All dealings must be disclosed to the company

    II   Shareholdings must be disclosed when they pass 1%

    III   Disclosure to the company must be within four business days

A I only

B II only

C I and III

D II and III

46 **Which one of the following is not covered by the UK's criminal legislation on insider dealing?**

A Debentures

B Foreign exchange transactions

C Shares

D Bonds

47 **If a firm fails to send out a confirmation notice, which of the following FCA Principles for Businesses has been breached?**

A Integrity

B Client assets

C Management and control

D Communications with clients

48 **If a firm is involved in 'churning' a customer's portfolio, which one of the following FCA Principles for Businesses has most significantly been breached?**

A Management and control

B Financial prudence

C Customers' interests

D Client assets

49 **How often should the Statements of Investment Principles (SIPs) be received by an occupational pension scheme?**

A Every six months

B Every year

C Every three years

D Every five years

50 **Which of the following will not generally be eligible complainants for the purposes of the Financial Ombudsman Service (FOS)?**

A Private individuals

B Small businesses

C Small charities

D Eligible counterparties

51 **For a transaction that is undertaken for a retail client on Tuesday 3 April:**

A It must be confirmed by telephone by the end of the business day

B A confirmation must be sent by 4 April

C A confirmation must be sent when the customer requests it

D The compliance officer will retain all confirmation notes

52 **The Statement of Investment Principles (SIPs) for a pension fund should be written by the:**

A Pension regulator

B Trustees of the pension fund

C Sponsor of the pension fund

D Company secretary

53 **Which one of the following best describes one of the FCA recognised industry codes?**

A The Standards of Lending Practice sets standards and best practice expected from participants when lending to retail clients

B The UK Money Markets Code sets standards and best practice expected from participants in the deposit, repo and securities lending markets in the UK

C The FX Global Code sets standards and best practice expected from participants in the international settlement markets

D The Custody Code sets standards and best practice expected from participants in the international global custodian markets

54 **Which one of the following statements about the Financial Policy Committee (FPC) is most correct?**

A The FPC is a legal entity within the Bank of England and is the prudential regulator for large firms including banks, insurers and larger investment firms

B The FPC publishes and provides the FCA with a biannual report on areas of integrity, protection of consumers and competition in the financial services market

C The FPC publishes two financial stability reports each year and meets at least quarterly

D The FPC meet approximately 8 times a year, and decide upon interest rate movements in the markets

55 **An investor sells £20,000 worth of shares. Which of the following must be paid by the seller?**

I Broker's commission
II Stamp Duty Reserve Tax
III Takeover Panel levy

A I, II, and III

B I only

C I and II

D I and III

56 **A UK company that is authorised by the FCA to advise on investments wishes to offer custodial services. The company should:**

A Apply to the Regulatory Decisions Committee

B Notify the Prudential Regulation Authority by letter

C Do nothing, as authorisation covers all regulated activities

D Apply to the FCA for Part 4A permission to provide custodial services

57 **An investor buys some shares in Company A for £39,700 and Company B for £30,000. These are then sold within the same fiscal year for £52,900 (Company A) and £29,400 (Company B). If the annual capital gains tax exemption is £12,300, and the investor is a basic rate taxpayer with taxable income of £15,000, what is the capital gains tax payable, in pounds to the nearest £1?**

Important! You should enter the answer only in numbers strictly using this format: 00

Do not include spaces, letters or symbols (but decimal points and commas should be used if indicated).

```

```

58 **For the purposes of exemption of promotions from the Financial Promotions Order, a high net worth individual is defined as someone with:**

A   Net income of £100,000 or more, or net assets of £250,000 or more

B   Net income of £200,000 or more, or net assets of £300,000 or more

C   Net assets of £400,000 or more

D   Net assets of £500,000 or more

59 **Which of the following statements about the various European Directives is/are correct?**

I   European Directives require each Member State to amend their own law, through the implementation of primary legislation, in order to comply

II   European Directives must be implemented by the Member State by the specified date

III   Each Member State is free to decide whether to implement a European Directive, or to retain their existing legislation

A   I only

B   I and II

C   II only

D   III only

60 **Client money can best be defined as:**

A   Money which the firm receives or holds on behalf of clients

B   Safe custody assets held by a firm

C   Money which the client deposits with the firm for payment of its fees

D   Interest payable to all customers

61 **Philip, a financial adviser, discovers that his firm has charged some of its clients a fee that is 0.3% higher than that specified in client agreements. The discrepancy has affected approximately 100 of the firm's clients. Philip has spoken with a Senior Manager in his firm. The Senior Manager said that he would ensure that the Accounts Department charges the correct amount for all future work. He does not propose to take any action to correct the past over-charging. From an ethical viewpoint, what action should Philip take?**

A   Do nothing, as the Senior Manager has higher authority within the firm

B   Contact anonymously the clients who have been over-charged

C   Prioritise the financial and competitive position of the firm by accepting and keeping confidential the Senior Manager's decision

D   Make a disclosure to the regulator under the 'whistle blowing' procedures

62   An investor wants to purchase 1,200 shares in Home Delivery plc. The current bid-offer prices being quoted are £11.62 - £11.73. Commission per trade is £3.25. What is the total round trip cost?

A   £208.88

B   £573.70

C   £571.70

D   £210.88

63   Which of the following is exempt from authorisation?

A   Broker dealing in government bonds

B   Third-party custodian

C   Depositary of an OEIC

D   Appointed representative

64   What is the age limit for obtaining tax relief on contributions to a registered pension scheme?

A   Up to 55 years

B   Up to 65 years

C   Up to 70 years

D   Up to 75 years

65   The FCA CASS classification criteria determine which CASS rules will apply to the firm. Which one of the following will be the most accurate definition of a medium sized client money firm?

A   A CASS medium sized firm is one that holds client money that is less than £10m

B   A CASS medium sized firm is one that holds client money that is equal to or greater than £1m and less than or equal to £1bn

C   A CASS medium sized firm is one that holds client money that is equal or greater than £10m and less than or equal to £100m

D   A CASS medium sized firm is one that holds client money that is equal to or greater than £10m and less than or equal to £100bn

66   What obligation is imposed on a firm by the best execution rule?

A   To obtain the best possible result for their clients

B   To base commission rates on the current best available price

C   To advise clients if the price is likely to rise or fall significantly subsequent to a transaction

D   To give best advice on a transaction

67   An individual dies leaving an estate of £5 million to a UK charity. How much inheritance tax is payable on the estate?

A   £0

B   £200,000

C   £1,683,000

D   £1,870,000

68   Mr and Mrs Kumar have assets of £455,000 and £555,000 respectively. How much inheritance tax will be payable in total, in pounds to the nearest £1), if each of them dies when the nil rate band is £325,000 on the dates of each death?

Important! You should enter the answer only in numbers strictly using this format: 000,000

Do not include spaces, letters or symbols (but decimal points and commas should be used if indicated).

```
┌─────────────────────────────┐
│                             │
│                             │
└─────────────────────────────┘
```

69   The FCA personal account dealing rules does not apply in several circumstances. Which one of the following is not one of these circumstances?

A   Personal transactions in designated investments

B   Personal transactions in units or shares in collective investment schemes

C   Personal transactions using a discretionary portfolio management service

D   Personal transactions in life policies

70   Which of the following are objectives of a regular investment performance review?

I   To determine whether and how client circumstances have altered
II   To review achieved performance
III   To consider potential portfolio rebalancing

A   I and II

B   I and III

C   II and III

D   I, II and III

71   A firm publishes a quarterly newsletter for their clients. When they make a recommendation about a particular company's shares in the newsletter, the firm is prohibited from:

A   Including any investment advice in the recommendation

B   Dealing on their own account until a reasonable time after publication

C   Giving advice to any client who is affected by a topic covered in the newsletter

D   Discretionary dealing with any client's assets without specific client instructions

72   The regulated activities of dealing and managing do not cover:

A   Shares

B   Bonds

C   Warrants

D   Motor insurance

73   The economic regulator of the payment systems BACS and CHAPS is the:

A   Financial Conduct Authority

B   British Bankers Association

C   Payment Systems Regulator

D   Competition and Markets Authority

74   Under the Takeover Code, at what percentage of holding must an offer be made?

A   20%

B   30%

C   50%

D   90%

75   Which of the following is a legal entity within the Bank of England?

A   The Financial Ombudsman Service

B   The United Kingdom Listing Authority

C   The Financial Conduct Authority

D   The Prudential Regulation Authority

76   What percentage of shareholders' voting rights is required to back a demand for a poll vote, under Companies Act rules?

A   15%

B   10%

C   5%

D   1%

77   If the FCA wishes to ban a financial promotion that it considers to be misleading then it is empowered to do so:

A   Immediately

B   Only after hearing representations from the firm

C   Only after referring the matter to the Tribunal

D   Only after allowing the firm 14 days to remove the promotion voluntarily

78 **How long does the power of a proxy last?**

A The day of the AGM

B The day of the AGM and any adjournment

C The day of the AGM plus any extension allowed by the Chairman

D Until the next AGM

79 **The Code of Conduct (COCON) sets out conduct rules for staff subject to the Senior Manager and Certification Regime, and includes various examples of behaviour which would be considered a breach of these conduct rules. Which one of the following is least likely to constitute an example of such behaviour?**

A Providing false or inaccurate information to the regulator

B Deliberately aiming to achieve maximum appropriate profits

C Deliberately failing to disclose the existence of a conflict of interest

D Misleading others in the firm about the nature of risks being accepted

80 **The FCA has a duty to aim to achieve statutory objectives as laid out by the Financial Services and Markets Act (FSMA), as amended. It has been suggested that businesses in the financial services sector might aim for the highest ethical standards and in doing so would support these statutory objectives. Which of the following would least well support this suggestion?**

A High standards of personal and business behaviour might reduce transparency which would have the effect of reducing public awareness but increasing confidence

B Higher ethical standards would improve the relationship between firm and consumer and thus improve consumer protection

C High ethical practices might discourage those who might attempt to launder money from this attempt due to the strong reputation of the financial services industry in that country

D High ethical standards would help to differentiate the UK financial services sector as a place of ethical good practice and thus would support market confidence

81 **What is the central purpose of the principles-based regulatory approach?**

A To encourage firms to adopt a more ethical frame of mind

B To shift regulatory focus towards outcomes rather than compliance with detailed rules

C To limit the scope for fraud and abuse of power

D To secure an appropriate degree of protection for consumers

82 **A UK individual is said to have died intestate if the person:**

I Dies with liabilities that exceed their assets

II Dies without making a valid will

III Dies without having made a will

A I only

B II and III

C III only

D I, II and II

83 **While performing the first client interview, your prospective client asks, 'Why does an adviser undertake a fact find?' You respond as follows.**

A   To decide whether an investment should be purchased or sold

B   To enable investment performance to be measured

C   To enable suitable advice to be given to a client

D   To enable the facts to be established when a customer has a complaint

84 **Capital risk is best described as:**

A   Potential variability of inflation rates

B   Potential variability of interest rates

C   Potential variability of current fund values

D   Potential variability of future fund values

85 **A number of client actions are being considered as suspicious with respect to money laundering regulations.**

John places £30,000 in bank notes into a joint bank account which he has established in the names of himself and his wife.

Brian sells half of his Sainsbury's holding and places it into an investment trust company.

George sells his BP shares and places the funds into a legitimate bank account. He then uses the account to fund legitimate spending.

If the suspicions are true, and these clients are involved in money laundering, which of the following statements is correct?

A   John and Brian are both involved in the placement stage

B   George is involved in the integration phase

C   All are engaging in layering

D   Only George is involved in layering

Answers

1   **A**   Anyone can apply to the court to become bankrupt, including individuals, sole traders and members of a partnership. There are different bankruptcy procedures for companies and partnerships. A person's creditors can usually petition the court to use a bankruptcy order if the person owes more than £5,000. Once a bankruptcy order has been made against a person, the official receiver administers the bankrupt person's financial affairs

2   **C**   This answer is in reverse order: the official receiver hands over to the trustee in bankruptcy. Once a bankruptcy order has been made against a person, the official receiver administers the bankrupt person's financial affairs. In the case of a bankrupt person with significant assets, the official receiver will appoint an insolvency practitioner as a trustee. The Official Receiver is a civil servant working on behalf of the Insolvency Service, but is also an officer of the court. The Official Receiver is an executive agency of the Department for Business, Energy and Industrial Strategy

3   **D**   Under the ISA rules. the investor can allocate money between cash and stocks and shares however they wish. ISAs generally have an annual investment limit in the current tax year of £20,000. This limit is flexible and can be split between the various types of ISA as desired, such as £11,000 in a cash ISA and £9,000 in a stocks and shares ISA

4   **B**   Under the General Data Protection Regulation (GDPR), fines for breaches of certain important provisions can be up to €20m or 4% of global annual turnover, whichever is the greater. Fines for breaches of other provisions can be up to €10m or 2% of global annual turnover, whichever is greater

5   **C**   Data must be handled by those that are accountable. That is, to take responsibility for what they do with personal data and how they comply with the other principles. They must also have appropriate measures and records in place to be able to demonstrate their compliance. Personal data must be processed lawfully, fairly and in a transparent manner in relation to individuals. It must be accurate and kept up to date; every reasonable step must be taken to ensure that personal data that are inaccurate, having regard to the purposes for which they are processed, are erased or rectified without delay. It must be kept in a form which permits identification of data subjects for no longer than is necessary for the purposes for which the personal data are processed. The GDPR includes new limitations on the use of consent as a justification for processing personal data. It requires that consent be specific, and once obtained, it will only be valid for the stated purpose for which it was collected and not for any other purpose. Furthermore, the data subject will have the right to withdraw their consent at any time

6   **A**   A quorum is achieved when two members (or their proxies) are present. Every public company is required to hold an AGM within six months of the end of their financial year, and the interval between AGMs must not be more than 15 months. The directors of the company must call the meeting, and it must be called by giving not less than 21 calendar days' written notice

7   **B**   The government has published illustrative guidance on what amounts to 'adequate procedures'. This requires procedures to be tailored to the individual circumstances of each business based on an assessment of where the risks lie. Small organisations may face significant bribery risks, although they are unlikely to need procedures that are as extensive as those of a multi-national organisation

8   B   The annual report will detail the shareholdings in the company that the directors may have, but not each transaction. There is no longer a requirement for a public company to keep a register of interests in shares (as s211 CA 1985 was repealed when the EU Transparency Directive was implemented in 2007)

9   D   Any capital loss which cannot be set off is carried forward indefinitely to set against future capital gains

10   D   Section III: Duties to clients – B of the Standards on Fair Dealing – states that members and candidates must deal fairly and objectively with all clients when providing investment analysis, making investment recommendations, taking investment action or engaging in other professional activities

11   A   If he takes no further action, once he has seen the price-sensitive information, then he has not committed the offence of market abuse, as the sell order was placed prior to him becoming aware of the price-sensitive information

12   D   A shareholder is allowed to attend and vote at a company meeting, however, where the shareholder cannot attend in person, they may appoint a proxy (a third party) to attend in their place. Following CA 2006 changes, proxies may exercise all the powers the member would have if they were present in person, and thus a proxy can vote on a show of hands and on a poll. The proxy granted is valid for that meeting and any subsequent adjournment

13   B

	£
Gains in the year (on X plc) (£70,400 - £50,000)	20,400
Losses in the year (on Y plc) (£35,300 - £40,000)	(4,700)
Net gain/loss	15,700
Less annual exemption	(12,300)
Amount chargeable to CGT	3,400
CGT at 20%	680

14   D   The Alternative Investment Fund Managers Directive (AIFMD) regulatory framework applies to managers of any collective investment undertaking other than those covered by the UCITS Directive, if the manager is domiciled in the EU, or if the fund is domiciled or marketed within the EU. The AIFMD covers hedge funds, retail investment funds, private equity funds, investment trust companies, and real estate investment trusts

15   B   CA 2006 requires the AGM to be held within six months of the financial year-end. The interval between AGMs must not be more than 15 months, and when the directors call the AGM, and it must be called by giving at least 21 calendar days' written notice to shareholders

16   D   Insider dealing is an offence within Part V of the Criminal Justice Act 1993 (CJA). The Companies Securities (Insider Dealing) Act 1985 was repealed by the CJA

17   A   The 'share of supply' test is met where the combined companies would control at least a 25% market share in the market sector. The CMA will also investigate all mergers that meet the 'turnover test', where the target company has a UK turnover of £70m or more

18   D   Gifts to children of up to £5,000 are permitted on their marriage or civil partnership. This is an example of an exemption which allow a person to pass on amounts, during their lifetime or upon their death, without any IHT being due

19   **100**   Note that this only applies to parents and not grandparents. This rule restricts parents from making gifts to use the personal allowances of children under 18. If the income generated from capital gifted by a parent exceeds £100 a year, then it will be taxed in the same way as the parent's own income. This rule does not apply to capital gifted by grandparents, aunts and uncles

20   **B**   A variable price auction is otherwise known as a 'competitive auction', where the bidder, if successful, will pay the price he bid. A Dutch auction is another description for a tender method of issuance. The Dutch auction method of issuing government bonds is the approach favoured by the US government when issuing US T-bonds

21   **D**   Part 4A permission is granted by the regulator where the firm satisfies the threshold conditions, and is granted for a particular regulated activity. The level of permission (authorisation) will specify the activities and investments that the firm is authorised in. Permission may be varied by the regulator, or even cancelled, where the regulator has serious concerns about the firm. If the firm wishes to appeal against a decision made by the regulator, then they may appeal to the Upper Tribunal

22   **B**   Property is not a classification of specified investment under FSMA 2000. Shares in any worldwide company are specified investments, as are exchange-traded futures. Other investments that are not covered as regulated investments include antiques and various commodities

23   **A**   Company dividends are paid gross, and so there can be no tax repayment

24   **C**   The Financial Services and Markets Act (FSMA) 2000 is the main framework for the regulation of investment business, and was amended by the Financial Services Act 2012

25   **A**   Stamp duty land tax (SDLT) is payable by the buyer, and not the seller. If you had bought the house for £562,000, then the SDLT payable would have been (£0 - £125,000 x 0%) + (next £125,000 x 2%) + (next £312,000 x 5%) = £18,100

26   **B**   Eurobonds settle two business days after the trade (T + 2). There are currently two systems available to investors for settling Eurobond transactions, being Euroclear and Clearstream. The International Capital Market Association (ICMA) rules currently specify that settlement is T+2, but all trades should be confirmed on T+1

27   **D**   Client categorisation rules apply to all three types of client, including eligible counterparties. All other rules, being client agreements, appropriateness and best execution apply to retail and professional clients only

28   **B**   The definition of a packaged product includes units in regulated collective investment schemes, investment trust saving schemes, life policies and personal pensions and stakeholder pension schemes. Dealing services are not an example of a packaged product

29   **B**   For the purposes of electronic communication, a notice is deemed to be sent when the electronic notice is first transmitted and delivered 48 hours after being sent. Any notice period therefore runs from the delivery date, being 48 hours after the electronic notice was sent

30   **B**   The Statement of Professional Standing (SPS) will be issued by accredited professional bodies. The regulator abandoned an earlier plan to issue its own Code of Ethics for retail investment advisers, however retail investment advisers must subscribe to a code of ethics.

The FCA has amended APER to emphasise personal accountability. These statements of principle apply to all approved persons, not just those subject to the retail distribution review. To obtain an SPS, advisers are required to make an annual declaration to their accredited body that they have complied with APER

31 **B** The question asks for the process of legislation which was the Financial Services Action Plan (FSAP). This process used the Lamfalussy Committee's recommendation to use a four-level approach to introduce new legislation. The FSAP has three specific objectives, that are to create a single EU wholesale market, to achieve open and secure retail markets, and to create state-of-the-art prudential rules and structures of supervision. ESMA is the European Securities and Markets Authority

32 **D** Under a power of attorney, the 'donee' (or attorney) acts for the donor. A power of attorney is a legal document that allows a person (the donor) to give another person (the donee) the power to make decisions about their financial affairs and/or their health and personal welfare

33 **C** A Lasting Power of Attorney (LPA) must be registered at the Office of the Public Guardian (OPG) to be effective

34 **A** The notification requirements do not cover persistency levels, which are a measure of the proportion of contracts that remain in force (ie have not been cancelled) after a specified time period. For employees performing certain specified activities that affect retail customers, the firm must ensure that the employee has been assessed as competent in that activity. The firm must also ensure that the employee has passed the appropriate qualification, and ensure that all of the advisers are acting in a manner that is consistent with the statements of principle for approved persons

35 **B** The question refers to individuals, and so bankruptcy rules apply. Anyone can apply to the court to become bankrupt, including individuals, sole traders and members of a partnership

36 **C** There is not a requirement that the client should have a high net worth. The firm will undertake an adequate assessment of the expertise, experience and knowledge of the client in order to give a reasonable assurance that the client is capable of making their own investment decisions and understanding the risks involved. The firm must give the client a clear written warning of the protections they may lose, and the client must state in writing that they are aware of the consequences of losing such protection

37 **D** 'Customers' excludes eligible counterparty clients, but includes retail clients and also professional clients

38 **C** Competence and capability are a home state responsibility not a host state, and as the firm is a French firm, coming into the UK, the home state regulator has this responsibility to assess competence and capability

39 **A** The Senior Management Conduct Rule SM4 is: 'You must disclose appropriately any information of which the FCA or PRA would reasonably expect notice'. The other options (B, C and D) are first-tier individual conduct rules that apply to certified staff and others.

The five individual conduct rules are as follow:

You must act with integrity; You must act with due care, skill and diligence; You must be open and co-operative with the FCA, the PRA and other regulators; You must pay due regard to the interests of customers and treat them fairly; and you must observe proper standards of market conduct

40   **C**   National Savings and Investment (NS&I) Savings Certificates and NS&I Children's Bonds are tax-free. ISA products are also tax-free investment wrappers

41   **B**   Collective investments can be viewed as a packaged form of investment, while a direct holding in company shares is not and does not count as a retail investment product (RIP). Unauthorised (unregulated) collective investment schemes count as RIPs, although they will not often be marketed to retail clients

42   **D**   The main elements of the Trustee Act 2000 are that the trustee exercises a duty of care, reviews the investments on a regular basis, and exercises their investment powers. The Act allows a trustee to make any kind of investment, including land and UK property, subject to the trust deed, having obtained and considered proper advice, and having regard to the investment criteria of the fund

43   **A**   An income, and a tax-free lump sum of 25% of the fund, can normally be taken from age 55

44   **A**   There is no requirement to obtain sponsorship or to work unsupervised. The main requirement is that the individual has passed an appropriate examination

45   **C**   Persons discharging managerial responsibilities (PDMRs), including directors, must notify the company within four business days of a transaction, both a sale and a purchase of any value. Other investors must notify a company within two business days when they acquire 3% or more of that company's shares

46   **B**   The insider dealing legislation in the Criminal Justice Act 1993 (CJA) relates to the securities of companies (ie bonds and shares) as well as options and warrants, however excludes foreign currencies. Debentures are a form of secured bonds

47   **D**   Principle for Businesses 7, Communication with Clients – applying to authorised firms – states that the firm must pay due regard to the information requirements of clients (customers and market counterparties), and communicate with them in a way that is clear, fair and not misleading

48   **C**   Principle for Businesses 6, Customers' Interests, states that the firm must pay due regard to the customers interests, and treat them fairly. Where the firm is churning a portfolio, ie trading too frequently under the circumstances, this principle is being breached

49   **B**   The Statement of Investment Principles (SIPs), published by the Trustees, should be sent out to members annually. The SIP sets out the principles governing how decisions about investments are made, and must include the scheme's policy on choosing investments, the kinds of investments to be held, and how risk is to be measured and managed. The SIP has to be reviewed every three years or whenever there is a significant change in investment policy

50   **D**   An eligible complainant is someone who is a consumer; an enterprise with fewer than 10 employees and turnover or annual balance sheet not exceeding €2 million (called a micro-enterprise); a charity with annual income of less than £1 million; or a trust with a net asset value of less than £1 million

51   **B**   Confirmation notes, unless declined, must be sent 'as soon as possible', and no later than the first business day following the execution (no later than T + 1)

52   **B**   The trustees have responsibility for writing the SIP. Trustees are responsible, in consultation with the sponsoring employer, to produce a Statement of Investment

Principles (SIP), that sets out the trustees attitude to several aspects, including the scheme funding requirements, the investments held by the fund, and the risks of the fund. The SIP is also reviewed every three years

53 **B** The UK Money Markets Code, is maintained and updated by the Money Markets Committee, and sets standards and best practice expected from participants in the deposit, repo and securities lending markets in the UK. The Standards of Lending Practice is for business customers (not retail clients), and these standards set the benchmark for good lending practice with business customers. The FX Global Code is maintained and updated by the Global Foreign Exchange Committee, and sets global principles of good practice standards in the foreign exchange (FX) market. There is also the Global Precious Metals Market Code, prepared by the London Bullion Market Association (LBMA), that sets out the standards and best practice expected from market participants in the global OTC wholesale precious metals market

54 **C** The Financial Policy Committee (FPC) aims to be a transparent and accountable body by publishing two financial stability reports each year. The FPC meets at least quarterly and, where it identifies risks, can offer advice and recommendations to the FCA and PRA in relation to oversight of the financial system

55 **D** Stamp Duty Reserve Tax (SDRT) is only paid by the buyer of a UK share that are in an electronic format, ie uncertificated. If an investor bought a certificated share, then they would pay stamp duty rather than stamp duty reserve tax. Therefore, in this question, the seller would only pay broker's commission and also the levy to the Takeover Panel, as this transaction is for more than £10,000

56 **D** The permission granted initially will specify the regulated activities and investments to which it relates – any variation will require the firm to apply again to the regulator

57 **30** Company A: Capital Gain = £52,900 – £39,700 = £13,200

Company B: Capital Loss = £29,400 – £30,000 = (£600)

Net capital gain   £12,600

Less   £(12,300) (Annual exemption)

Taxable gain: £300

Gain taxed £300 @ 10%: Tax payable = 0.10 × £300 = £30

58 **A** A certified high net worth investor is a person with an annual income of £100,000 or more, or net investable assets of £250,000 or more. The main exemptions under Part VI of the Financial Promotions Order (FPO) are with regard to certified high net worth individuals, and also sophisticated investors

59 **B** The various European Directives, such as the MiFID or the Capital Requirements Directive, seek to 'harmonise' regulations in order to create a fair market place. Each Member State is required to amend their own law to comply, either through the introduction of new legislation or through amendments to existing statute

60 **A** This is the best definition of client money. The client money rules apply to a firm that receives or holds money from, or on behalf of, a client in the course of MiFID or designated investment business. The main purpose of these client money rules is to protect investors' money in the event of the firm's insolvency. This is achieved by requiring the firm to keep clients' money separate from its own

61   **D**   The disclosure under the whistle-blowing procedure will be protected under the Public Interest Disclosure Act 1998 (PIDA). The PIDA establishes a framework for the protection of employees in cases of whistle-blowing. The FCA requires firms to adopt internal procedures to encourage employees with concerns to 'blow the whistle' internally about matters that are relevant to the FCA

62   **D**   The round trip costs are calculated as follows:

	£
Buy 1,200 shares at £11.73	14,076
Sell 1,200 shares at £11.62	(13,944)
Commission on both trades (2 x £3.25)	6.50
SDRT (0.005 x £14,076)	70.38
PTM levy for both trades (2 x £1)	2
Net cost	210.88

63   **D**   Appointed representatives are exempt persons. The other exempt persons are RIEs and RCHs, members of the professions, and members of Lloyd's

64   **D**   With regard to pension contributions, an individual under the age of 75 may receive tax relief on contributions into a registered pension scheme in a tax year. The maximum limit is the higher of relevant annual earnings is subject to an annual cap of £40,000 in the current tax year or £3,600

65   **B**   A CASS medium sized firm is one that hold client money that is equal to or greater than £1m and less than or equal to £1bn

66   **A**   The firm must take all reasonable steps to obtain the best possible result for their clients when executing orders

67   **A**   Gifts to charities are tax-exempt, therefore no inheritance tax is payable. This is one of a number of exemptions which allow a person to pass on amounts, known as a 'lifetime or upon their death transfer', without any IHT being payable

68 **144,000** Total value of estates (£455,000 + £555,000):   £1,010,000

Total nil rate bands (transferable between spouses): £650,000

Total estate subject to IHT: £360,000

Total IHT payable (£360,000 @40%): **£144,000**

69   **A**   These personal account dealing rules do not apply to personal transactions effected under a discretionary portfolio management service, personal transactions in units or shares in collective undertakings, and personal transactions in life policies

70 D They are all objectives of a performance review. Reviews are a vital part of the financial planning process. The frequency of reviews should be at least annually, and some advisers may agree to more regular reviews with certain clients. Reviews are essential to keep the client's portfolio in line with the client's objectives and changing investment perspectives

71 B They should not deal as the effect of the letter could be to increase the share price. If the company holds the stock, there could be a conflict of interest. Anyone having knowledge of the timing or content of investment research is not permitted to deal ahead, also known as 'front running' of the publication of the research in the shares to which the research relates until the recipients of the research have had a reasonable opportunity to act upon it

72 D Motor insurance is not covered by the 'dealing' or 'managing' categories. It is covered by 'effecting or carrying out contracts for insurance'. The regulated activity includes dealing in, arranging deals in or managing investments, such as shares, bonds and warrants

73 C The Payment Systems Regulator (PSR) is the economic regulator of the UK payment systems industry. The PSR is a subsidiary of the Financial Conduct Authority (FCA), but has its own objectives. The PSR regulates systems designated by HM Treasury. These systems are BACS; C&C (Cheque & Credit); CHAPS; Faster Payments Service (FPS); LINK; Northern Ireland Cheque Clearing (NICC); MasterCard; and Visa Europe

74 B 'Effective control' is achieved at 30%, requiring a mandatory offer. Any bidder who acquires 30% or more of the voting rights of a company is required to make a cash offer to all the other shareholders, at the highest price they have paid in the previous 12 months

75 D The Prudential Regulation Authority (PRA) is a legal entity within the Bank of England. The Prudential Regulation Committee (PRC) in the Bank of England is regarded as the governing body of the PRA. The UKLA is a function of the FCA, which is an independent company. The FOS is also an independent entity

76 B A poll vote may be demanded by shareholders who represent 10% of the voting rights. A poll vote may also be requested by five members, having the right to vote, or by the Chairman. It is also important to note that a proxy may demand, or assist in demanding a poll vote

77 A The regulator is able to give a direction to firms requiring them immediately to withdraw or to modify promotions which it deems to be misleading, and to publish such decisions. The firm is then able to make representations to the FCA to challenge the Authority's decision

78 B A proxy is valid for the general meeting and any adjournment, and can take one of two forms. Firstly, a general proxy, appointing a person to vote as they think fit, bearing in mind what is said at the meeting. Secondly, a special proxy, appointing a person to vote for or against a particular resolution – this is termed a 'two-way proxy'

79 B The conduct rules, which effectively replace the Statement of Principle and Approved Person code, are applicable to all staff, except for a few specific roles such as security, catering and cleaning staff. The conduct rules include acting with integrity, acting with due care, skill and diligence, being open and co-operative with the FCA, the PRA and other regulators, paying due regard to the interests of customers and to treat them fairly, and to observe proper standards of market conduct. In this question, aiming to maximise profits seems to be a normal business aim rather than a breach of integrity

80   **A**   Higher ethical standards should increase transparency rather than reducing it and as such should improve public awareness

81   **B**   The Financial Conduct Authority's (FCA) use of principles and outcomes-based regulation is used to promote ethical and fair outcomes. A more ethical frame of mind is the rationale behind the Treating Customers Fairly (TCF) initiative, which aims to deliver six outcomes for consumers. An appropriate degree of protection is one of the operational objectives of the FCA

82   **B**   Intestacy is when a person dies without having written a will, or has an invalid will. A person who dies without a will, or with an invalid will, is said to have died intestate. In these circumstances, the estate must be distributed according to the laws of intestacy, which are a statutory set of rules that leave the deceased's estate to their next of kin in a fixed order.

83   **C**   The fact find is effectively required to meet the need to 'Know your customer'. Having information about clients enables the adviser to tailor advice to the client's requirements. The fact-find should establish the type and nature of the client and their attitude to risk, their investment objectives in terms of risk and return, and also any investment constraints, such as liquidity, legal requirements, time horizon, tax considerations and any unique circumstances to the client

84   **C**   The risks described are, respectively, inflation risk, interest rate risk, capital risk, shortfall risk. Capital risk is the risk that an investment may be worth less in the future than it is today

85   **B**   George is involved in the integration phase; John is involved in the placement phase; Brian is involved in the layering phase. Placement is the physical injection into the financial system of cash proceeds obtained from some criminal activity. Layering is the separation of criminal proceeds from their source by creating complex layers of financial transactions designed to disguise the audit trail. Integration is where the laundered proceeds are put back into the economy in such a way that they appear to be legitimate investment funds

Practice Examination 5

(85 questions in 1 hour and 40 minutes)

1 An agency agreement exists between a client and their financial advisers. Given that no specific contractual arrangement exists at this stage, which of the following is least likely to be a duty of the agent as implied by law?

A   The requirement to exercise skill and care

B   The requirement to keep accounts

C   The requirement to delegate responsibilities

D   The requirement to act in good faith

2 The ISA allowance for the current tax year is £20,000. Andrea's only investment in ISAs during the current year so far is an investment of £3,000 in a cash ISA. How much can she invest in a Stocks and Shares ISA during the tax year in question?

A   £0

B   £3,000

C   £9,500

D   £17,000

3 Which of the following is not correct in respect of 'churning'?

A   It is prohibited by the best execution rule

B   It involves an unsuitable series of transactions

C   Its objective is to earn commission income

D   It is not in the best interests of the consumer

4 Which of the following is not one of the threshold conditions that the regulator will evaluate in order for a firm to obtain authorisation from the FCA?

A   Effective supervision

B   Business model

C   Issues and products

D   Appropriate resources

5 Which of the following is part of the role of the Bank of England?

A   Prudential regulation of investment exchanges

B   Setting interest rates

C   Appointing the head of the FCA

D   Setting the inflation target for the UK

6   **Under MiFID, if an investment firm sets up a branch in another EEA state, to whose local rules will the branch have to adhere?**

A   Home state

B   Host state

C   Home and host states

D   The branch can choose which rules to follow

---

7   **Xaviera believes that, two and a half years ago, she was mis-sold a retail financial product by a UK financial adviser and only recently made a complaint. The finding of the adviser firm's complaints investigators was that the case was 'without merit' and the firm declined to offer any compensation.**

12 weeks have passed since Xaviera received the firm's final response to her complaint. Xaviera now plans to refer the complaint to the Financial Ombudsman Service (FOS). Xaviera expects that the FOS's decision will award her compensation of £400,000 excluding costs.

Which one of the following statements is correct?

A   The Financial Ombudsman Service (FOS) is not the correct agency to approach in these circumstances

B   The amount that Xaviera expects to receive exceeds the maximum award available through the Financial Ombudsman Service

C   Too long a time period has passed since the event complained about for Xaviera to take her complaint to the Financial Ombudsman Service

D   Too long a time period has passed since receiving the firm's final response for Xaviera to take her complaint to the Financial Ombudsman Service

---

8   **FATCA requires all foreign financial institutions (FFIs) to provide information about their US customers to the Inland Revenue Service (IRS) in accordance with the terms of an FFI agreement entered into between the FFI and the IRS. If the firm does not enter the agreement, it is deemed to be a 'non-participating FFI' and a withholding tax charge is applied to certain payments made to it. What is the withholding tax charge applied?**

A   30%

B   20%

C   10%

D   40%

---

9   **A retail investment adviser giving independent advice is:**

A   Barred from using panels

B   Expected to review all markets when considering what is suitable for a client

C   Barred from accepting commission from a product provider

D   Required to charge hourly rates for advice given

10   What is the required delay before trading under the rules on dealing ahead of research?

A   The firm must wait until the market price has responded

B   The firm must allow a reasonable time for the clients to react before placing its own trades

C   One working day

D   There is no required delay once the information is public

11   Which of the following is not a client category under MiFID?

A   Professional clients

B   Eligible counterparties

C   Retail clients

D   Intermediate clients

12   A company director purchases shares in their company, which is listed on the London Stock Exchange. What is the company required to do?

A   Inform the market via a Primary Information Provider regardless of the directors holding

B   Inform the market via a Primary Information Provider if it takes the directors holding above 1% of the shares in the company

C   Inform the market via a Primary Information Provider if it takes the directors holding above 3% of the shares in the company

D   There is no requirement for reporting the transaction

13   If a company proposes to pay a dividend, how should this announcement normally be handled?

A   In a briefing to a group of at least two analysts

B   In a notice published in at least one national newspaper

C   By informing a Primary Information Provider

D   By sending a circular to all shareholders

14   Which of the following tests are necessary in order to treat a client as an elective professional client?

I   Qualitative test

II   Mandatory test

III   Quantitative test

A   I and II

B   II and III

C   I and III

D   I, II and III

15 **Which of the following words or phrases is not centrally related to the requirement on communication of financial promotions?**

A Clear

B Not misleading

C Reasonable

D Fair

16 **MiFID II prohibits firms that provide portfolio management services from receiving any inducements in relation to these services to clients, except for minor non-monetary benefits. Which of the following are characteristics that relate to these minor non-monetary benefits?**

    I   They are clearly disclosed

    II   They do not impair compliance with the firm's duty to act in the best interests of the client

    III   They are capable of enhancing the quality of the service provided

A II and III

B II only

C I and III

D I, II and III

17 **What is the maximum award which can be determined by the Financial Ombudsman Service (FOS), excluding costs?**

A £150,000

B £325,000

C £375,000

D Unlimited

18 **What is the minimum number of annual report and accounts that a company should have filed prior to an application for a Premium Listing?**

A One year

B Two years

C Three years

D Five years

19 **The safe custody rules are intended to achieve each of the following, except which one?**

A To prevent clients' investments earning below-market returns, by pooling firm's assets with those of clients

B To prevent clients' investments being used by the firm without the client's agreement

C To prevent clients' investments being used by the firm contrary to the client's wishes

D To prevent clients' investments being treated as the firm's assets in the event of its insolvency

20   **The FCA has the power to prosecute through the criminal courts for a number of offences, but not in respect of:**

A   Misleading the regulator

B   Insider dealing

C   Market abuse that is not insider dealing

D   Breaches of money laundering regulations

21   **A client has made a complaint to an authorised firm about advice she received from one of the firm's advisers. Two months later, the complaint has not been resolved. The next step the client may take to resolve the complaint is to:**

A   Refer the complaint to the Financial Ombudsman Service

B   Refer the complaint to the Financial Conduct Authority

C   Ask the firm to take the complaint to the Upper Tribunal

D   Refer the complaint to the Financial Services Compensation Scheme

22   **In the context of appropriateness, which of the following statements is correct?**

A   The firm must assess the client's understanding of risk

B   The rule applies when a client responds to a promotion selling non-complex instruments

C   The firm must assess the client's financial situation and investment objectives

D   The firm must not perform a transaction if they have not satisfied themselves that the instrument is appropriate

23   **Who is the primary regulator of the US equities markets?**

A   SEC

B   IRS

C   Federal Reserve

D   FCA

24   **When a firm provides performance information in relation to MiFID business, to what period must it relate?**

A   The five preceding years

B   If the product has been established for less than five years, then only three years data need be used

C   At least the five preceding years or the whole period of the life of the product if this is less than five years

D   A 12-month period only

25   **Which of the following is not a matter of hard facts?**

Details of:

A   A client's state of health

B   A client's name of address

C   A client's attitude to risk

D   A client's tax status

The following relates to Questions 26 to 30.

Martin Jameson is 80 years old and has been retired for sixteen years. He has a final salary pension. He is married with two children and one grandchild. He and his wife own their own house plus a holiday home in Northumberland belonging to Martin. They wish to prepare effectively to minimise their potential inheritance tax outgoings.

26   At the time when they visit their adviser, Martin is domiciled abroad while his wife is domiciled in the UK. They are correctly advised that the exemption available for tax-exempt transfers from his wife to Martin were she to die during the current tax year would be:

A   Zero

B   £55,000

C   £325,000

D   Unlimited

27   Assuming that Martin is UK-domiciled, which of the following would not potentially be good advice for him to follow to minimise his IHT liability?

A   Make full use of exemptions available

B   Use life assurance policies

C   Make PETs before CLTs in the tax year

D   Make lifetime gifts

28   In order to minimise IHT, Martin gives his holiday home to their children. The parents do however continue to use the house several times a year without paying rent. Which letters best describe this form of arrangement?

A   CTF

B   PET

C   CLR

D   GWR

29   The holiday house which Martin has given to their children but still continues to use rent-free has a value of £500,000 on his death four years after having given up ownership of the house. At the time of the gift, it had been worth £420,000. What sum (in pounds) would be added to Martin's death estate relating to the house on his death?

Important! You should enter the answer only in numbers strictly using this format: 000,000

Do not include spaces, letters or symbols (but decimal points and commas should be used if indicated).

[   ]

30   Martin's wife dies in June of the current tax year, leaving £162,500 to their children, with all other assets being left to Martin. Were Martin to die in the future, when the nil rate band has changed to £425,000, what available nil rate band (in pounds) would be available to use at that point?

Important! You should enter the answer only in numbers strictly using this format: 000,000

Do not include spaces, letters or symbols (but decimal points and commas should be used if indicated).

31 **In recent years, the financial services regulator has characterised its approach to supervision using the phrase:**

A 'Inspections based' approach

B 'Bank examiner' approach

C 'Outcomes focused' approach

D 'Compliance focused' approach

32 **The CFA Code of Ethics requires members to do all of the following except:**

A Use reasonable care and exercise independent professional judgement

B Promote the integrity of capital markets

C Avoid excessive remuneration

D Act with integrity, competence, diligence and respect

33 **In a merger investigation, what is the statutory time limit following a Phase II decision for remedies to be implemented?**

A 4 months

B 2 months

C 12 weeks

D 40 weeks

34 **Which of the following would be committing an offence under the Criminal Justice Act 1993 if they purchased shares in ABC plc?**

I A market maker who obtained price-sensitive information in the normal course of their business

II A director of ABC plc with price-sensitive information who undertook the transaction without intending to make a profit or to avoid a loss

III A friend of a director of ABC plc who obtained information but was unaware that it was price-sensitive

A I, II and III

B II and III

C I and II

D None of I, II and III

35 **At what rate will an additional rate taxpayer pay capital gains tax on the disposal of a non-residential asset giving rise to a gain higher than the annual exempt amount?**

A 45%

B 40%

C 20%

D 28%

36 **Which of the following is not a direct power of the FCA?**

A The right to issue principles and general rules

B The ability to compensate those who have suffered losses from the failure of regulated firms

C The right to investigate authorised firms or certain employees

D The power to recognise clearing houses and investment exchanges

37 **To which of the following do the insider dealing rules not apply?**

    I   Corporate brokers

    II   Market makers

    III   Stabilisation

A I only

B II only

C I and II

D II and III

38 **The best execution rule is designed to protect:**

A All investors

B Retail clients

C Retail and professional clients

D Retail and professional clients, but professional clients can opt out

39 **With respect to 'best execution criteria', a firm does not have to take into account:**

A The client, including categorisation as retail or professional

B The financial instruments

C The previous day's closing price

D The execution venues

40 **At firm YBG Partners, the client money requirement is calculated by taking the sum, for each client bank account, of: (1) the amount which the firm's internal records show as held on that account; and (2) an amount that offsets each negative net amount which the firm's internal records show attributed to that account for an individual client. Assume that the client money rules have been followed. We can infer from these facts that the firm YBG Partners may be:**

A Any type of FCA-authorised firm

B Any type of PRA-authorised firm

C An asset management firm

D An investment firm undertaking margined transactions in derivatives for clients

41   **Which of the following are FCA Principles for Businesses that apply to all authorised firms?**

      I   Financial prudence
      II   Relations with regulators
      III   Conflicts of interest

A   III only

B   I and III

C   I and II

D   I, II and III

42   **Which of the following is not a controlled function?**

A   Systems and controls function

B   Ancillary function

C   Significant management function

D   Money laundering reporting function

43   **Which of the following activities do the Money Laundering Regulations require a firm to do?**

      I   Perform appropriate identification checks on all new accounts
      II   Keep accurate records of transactions for five years
      III   Provide appropriate training to all staff

A   I and III

B   I only

C   II and III

D   I, II and III

44   **Which one of the following types of scheme is generally most dependent on market returns?**

A   A defined benefits pension scheme

B   A traditional '1/60th' employer-based pension scheme

C   A final salary pension scheme

D   A defined contribution pension scheme

45   **GEMMs and IDBs settle trades in UK government bonds through:**

A   Central Gilts Office

B   CREST

C   London Stock Exchange

D   Bank of England

46　De Weir plc anticipates that it will earn profits of £160,000 in its current financial year. What rate of corporation tax will the company pay?

A　5%

B　21%

C　20%

D　19%

47　In relation to the member states of the European Union, what is the consequence of the issue of a European Directive?

A　It automatically becomes law in each member state

B　It requires law in each country to be changed by their respective Parliament in accordance with the directive

C　It recommends that each state's Parliament introduces laws to implement its proposals

D　It becomes law in each member state once approved by the European Parliament

48　Lifetime transfers to an individual are chargeable to inheritance tax:

A　When paid

B　Whenever the donor dies

C　If the donor dies within seven years

D　Never

49　Under the General Data Protection Regulation (GDPR), where there is a personal data breach, an organisation must notify the Information Commissioners Office (ICO) within what time period?

A　An organisation must notify the ICO within 24 hours

B　An organisation must notify the ICO within 48 hours

C　An organisation must notify the ICO within 72 hours

D　An organisation must notify the ICO within 5 business days

50　Which of the following terms best describes the approach of the UK Corporate Governance Code and the Stewardship Code?

A　'Rules-based compliance'

B　'Self-regulatory compliance'

C　'Voluntary compliance'

D　'Comply or explain'

51   **Which of the following is true of a Multilateral Trading Facility (MTF)?**

A   It is a facility where a firm engages in multiple core investment services

B   It is a system where a firm provides services similar to those of exchanges by matching client orders

C   It is a system where a firm takes proprietary positions with a client

D   It is a facility where a firm operates in more than one location

---

52   **In December of the current tax year, a house is bought for £575,000. What will be the stamp duty land tax (SDLT) payable by the buyer?**

A   £3,750

B   £22,500

C   £9,000

D   £18,750

---

53   **An individual dies leaving an estate on £340,000, half of which is paid to their children with the remainder paid to their spouse. How much inheritance tax is payable?**

A   £6,000

B   £16,000

C   £12,300

D   £0

---

54   **A client gives specific instructions for the execution of a trade. In this case, best execution may be waived:**

A   For that trade only

B   For all subsequent trades until the client requests best execution again

C   For that category of transactions only

D   Best execution may not be waived

---

55   **A group of the clients of Brookmead Advisers have concluded contracts for different product types, have all received the contract terms and conditions on the same date – 1 April – and have all been duly informed of their cancellation rights. Distance selling was not involved. For which products had the cancellation period expired by 24 April?**

A   Personal pension plan

B   Initial income withdrawal from a stakeholder pension plan

C   Level term assurance policy

D   Cash deposit ISA

56   **Which of the following are real liabilities?**

        I   Income provision for dependents

        II   Personal pension

        III   College fees

    A   I and II

    B   I and III

    C   II and III

    D   I, II and III

57   **Which of the following are types of investment risk?**

        I   Interest rate risk

        II   Shortfall risk

        III   Capital risk

    A   I and II

    B   I and III

    C   II and III

    D   I, II and III

58   **The 'decision-specific' test for assessing whether a person has the capacity to take a particular decision at a particular time is set out in the:**

    A   Mental Health Decisions Act

    B   Mental Capacity Act

    C   Incapacity Act

    D   Financial Services and Markets Act

59   **Which of the following is a specified investment?**

    A   Premium Bonds

    B   Trade bills

    C   Real estate

    D   T-bills

60   **If the outcome of the Financial Ombudsman Service (FOS) investigation is accepted by the complainant, then it is:**

    A   At the discretion of the firm to comply

    B   Implemented by HM Treasury

    C   Binding on the firm

    D   Binding on the customer

61 Takeover Panel rules apply to:

A   All listed companies only

B   All public companies only

C   Listed companies with a market capitalisation greater than £5 million only

D   All public companies with a market capitalisation greater than £5 million only

62 Within what period of time must the Competition and Markets Authority (CMA) complete a Phase I review of a merger?

A   28 working days

B   40 working days

C   60 working days

D   80 working days

63 Martin Power heads the research department of a regional brokerage firm. The firm employs many analysts, some of whom are subject to the Code and Standards. Should Martin delegate some of his supervisory duties, which statement best describes his responsibilities under CFA Institute Code and Standards?

A   Power is released from responsibility for those duties delegated to his subordinates

B   Supervisory responsibility is retained by Power for all subordinates despite delegation of some of his duties

C   Power may not delegate supervisory duties to subordinates, because of the Code and Standards

D   Power's supervisory responsibilities would not extend to subordinates who are not subject to the Code and Standards

64 When a company attempts to take over another company, their aim is to acquire a controlling interest. Which one of the following percentages represents a controlling interest (legal control)?

A   More than 30%

B   More than 50%

C   More than 75%

D   More than 90%

65 Jerome Stanford has recently become employed by Pendleton Willard Asset management as a fund manager. When being inducted into the company, it is explained to Jerome by his supervisor that high ethical standards will be expected of him at the firm.

Jerome's supervisor explains to him the importance of acting on behalf of all stakeholders of the firm. Which of the following would be considered stakeholders?

    I   Employees
    II   Clients
    III   Shareholders

A II only

B III only

C I and II

D I, II and III

66 Macro-prudential regulation is best described as falling within the remit of:

A The Financial Conduct Authority

B The Financial Policy Committee

C The Prudential Regulation Authority

D The Money Advice Service

67 Which body has the power to commission and publish an independent review of the economy, efficiency and effectiveness of the FCA's use of resources?

A The Bank of England

B HM Treasury

C The Financial Policy Committee

D The Financial Ombudsman Service

68 Mrs Rodriguez works for an FCA authorised firm and wishes to deal in securities on her own account. Which of the following is the best description of the regulations concerning this trade?

A She must notify the stock exchange of her deals

B She should be aware of the personal dealing restrictions and inform her firm promptly of any personal transactions

C She may only deal in products offered by her own firm

D She may not deal in securities

69 Which of the following will require authorisation in all cases?

    I   Tip sheets
    II   Newspaper investment advice columns
    III   Trustees

A I only

B II and III

C I and III

D I, II and III

70   If an individual loses £40,000 in investments in the event of an authorised firm defaulting, how much compensation will be received from the Financial Services Compensation Scheme (FSCS)?

A   £10,000

B   £30,000

C   £36,000

D   £40,000

71   A company has rights as defined by law in its capacity as a legal person. Which of the following best describes its status?

A   A natural person

B   An artificial person

C   A corporate person

D   A limited person

72   Which of the following is not subject to the financial promotion rules?

A   A promotion communicated to a person in the UK

B   A cold call from someone in the UK to someone outside of the UK

C   A promotion in relation to a takeover

D   A promotion issued by an appointed representative

73   For which client types is a basic written agreement needed?

I   Retail client
II   Professional client
III   Eligible counterparty

A   I and II

B   II only

C   I and III

D   I only

74   Which of the following type of firm is outside the 'common platform' of SYSC provisions?

A   Retail investment advisers

B   Fund managers

C   Credit unions

D   Insurers

75   **Martha Reeves is preparing to give investment advice on an independent basis and is reviewing her knowledge of the range of retail investment products (RIPs).**

Which of the following does not fall within the definition of advice on RIPs?

A   Martha recommends that a single 30-year old man invests in shares of an open-ended investment company

B   Gemma, who already holds a stocks and shares ISA which includes contributions made only in previous tax years, is recommended by Martha to buy a holding of the ordinary shares of BP plc within an ISA, using contributions to be made in the current tax year

C   Martha recommends that a retired client buys ordinary shares in Foreign & Colonial Investment Trust plc

D   Martha gives advice on a Self-Invested Pension Plan that is capable of holding commercial property among its assets

76   **Which of the following is the best execution rule designed to protect?**

A   Investors generally

B   Retail clients generally

C   Retail and professional clients generally

D   Retail and professional clients, but professional clients can opt out

77   **Which of the following must be provided by a member in a six-monthly portfolio valuation?**

I   Each designated investment held and its market value or, if unavailable, its fair value
II   Total fees and charges
III   The cash balance at the beginning and end of the reporting period

A   I and II

B   I and III

C   II and III

D   I, II and III

78   **Which of the following may refer a complaint to the Financial Ombudsman Service (FOS) as an eligible complainant?**

I   A private individual
II   A small charity
III   A small business

A   I and II

B   I and III

C   II and III

D   I, II and III

79 **The Tax and Chancery Chamber of the Upper Tribunal reviews the decisions of:**

A   The FCA only

B   The FCA and the Treasury only

C   HMT only

D   The Bank of England only

80 **The conflict of interest policy of a firm is least likely to prevent:**

A   A conflict between the authorised firm and their client

B   A conflict between the authorised firm and their competitor

C   A dispute between different divisions within an authorised firm

D   A dispute between the clients of the authorised firm

81 **You are writing a brief for managers of your firm about the personal account dealing rules.**

What would be the best statement of the purpose of the rules on personal account dealing?

A   To prevent dealing when in the knowledge that the firm's research department are about to release a positive report on a security

B   To prevent dealing in shares owned by the investment company

C   To prevent dealing in shares when the company's directors have just announced the results

D   To prevent the firm taking a principal position in securities where there is a conflict of interest

82 **Which of the following statements about rules governing investment research activities is incorrect?**

A   Financial analysts can take positions in securities contrary to their current recommendations only in exceptional circumstances and with senior permission

B   Analysts must refrain from dealing on the information contained in research until the clients have been provided with time to consider it

C   Research analysts must not promise issuers favourable research coverage

D   The issuer should be permitted to review unpublished research on their company at any time

83 **Which of the following penalties may the FCA impose for all forms of market abuse?**

I   Two years' imprisonment

II   Public censure

III   Discipline of approved persons

A   I and II

B   II and III

C   I and III

D   I, II and III

84 **Which of the following is the final part of the financial planning process?**

A   Determining the client objectives

B   Formulating recommendations

C   Obtaining relevant information

D   Selecting funds

85 **Mr Singh is the holder of 4% of a company's voting shares. He is not the Chairman nor a director of the company. He wishes to demand a poll vote at the company's general meeting. Who else's support along with Mr Singh would be sufficient in order to demand the poll, under Companies Act rules?**

A   Four other shareholders

B   Two other shareholders who hold 1% of the voting shares between them

C   One other shareholder who holds 4% of the voting rights

D   No support is needed from other persons: Mr Singh alone is entitled to call for a poll

Answers

1   **C**   The duty of an agent in the absence of an agreement would require that the agent act in person rather than delegate responsibility

2   **D**   There is no separate limit for Cash ISAs. The investor can allocate their ISA investment between cash and stocks and shares however they want up to the annual limit of £20,000. Therefore, as £3,000 has already been invested in the cash ISA, the remaining £17,000 of the current tax year's annual allowance can be invested in a stocks and shares ISA

3   **A**   A series of transactions that are each suitable when viewed in isolation may be unsuitable if the recommendation or the decisions to trade are made with a frequency that is not in the best interests of the client. The practice of 'churning' is not linked to the rule on best execution

4   **C**   Threshold conditions (COND) sets out the minimum statutory conditions that a firm is required to satisfy, and continue to satisfy, in order to be given and to retain authorisation. 'Issues and products' is a description of the third pillar of the FCA's supervision model, and is not one of the threshold conditions

5   **B**   The Bank's Monetary Policy Committee (MPC) sets benchmark interest rates, as part of its monetary policy role. In the UK economy, the Government places an emphasis on controlling inflation by using interest rates. This is carried out by the Bank of England's Monetary Policy Committee (MPC)

6   **B**   If a firm has a physical presence in another EEA country, it must adhere to the local rules of that country for most of the Conduct of Business rules, hence the most appropriate answer is the host state rules. However, it is worth noting that there are a few minor exceptions, such as personal account dealing rules, that follow the home state rules

7   **B**   The maximum money award the FOS can make is £375,000 for complaints referred to it after 1 April 2022. The FOS is the correct agency, and the complaint is within time limits (six months since the firm's final response; six years since the event, or three years since becoming aware of the problem or since the person could reasonably be expected to become aware of it)

8   **A**   FATCA requires all foreign financial institutions (FFIs) to provide information about their US customers to the Inland Revenue Service (IRS) in accordance with the terms of an FFI agreement entered into between the FFI and the IRS. If the firm does not enter the agreement, it is deemed to be a 'non-participating FFI' and a 30% withholding tax charge is applied to certain payments made to it

9   **C**   Panels may be used to help review the market. The firm will not be expected to review markets for products that do not meet a client's needs and objectives. The adviser's charging structure may or may not be based on hourly rates, but commission must not be taken from product providers

10   **B**   COBS is worded such that firms must provide clients with a 'reasonable opportunity to act' – otherwise known as 'front running'

11   **D**   Intermediate clients are not a classification category used in COBS. The three client categories are eligible counterparties, professional clients and retail clients

BPP
LEARNING
MEDIA

12   **A**   All deals conducted by directors must be announced to the market. The Disclosure and Transparency Rules (DTRs) deal with reporting transactions in a company's securities, including derivatives, by 'persons discharging managerial responsibilities' (PDMRs), which includes directors. PDMRs must notify the listed company within four business days. Then, the listed company must notify the market as soon as possible thereafter, and no later than the end of the following business day. This notification must be through a primary information provider (PIP), also known as a regulatory news service provider

13   **C**   It is important for this information to be communicated to the market in a fair and transparent fashion. The company will communicate the information to a Primary Information Provider (PIP), who will then distribute the information to the market as a whole through quote vendors such as Bloomberg and Reuters

14   **C**   The qualitative test requires experience, expertise and knowledge. The quantitative test requires a certain frequency of transactions (an average frequency of ten per quarter over the previous four quarters), minimum portfolio value (exceeds €500,000) or knowledge of transactions from professional work in the financial sector (at least one year in a professional position)

15   **C**   The key words used are: fair, clear and not misleading. Principles for Businesses 7 (PRIN 7) requires firms to ensure that all communication is fair, clear and not misleading

16   **D**   MiFID II prohibits firms that provide portfolio management services from receiving any inducements in relation to these services to clients, except for minor non-monetary benefits that are capable of enhancing the quality of the service provided; do not impair compliance with the firm's duty to act in the best interests of the client; and are clearly disclosed

17   **C**   The maximum money award the FOS can make is £375,000 for complaints referred after 1 April 2022. For awards over this, the firm is invited to pay the excess, but is not compelled to do so

18   **C**   For a premium listing on the LSE, the company should have filed published accounts covering at least three years. The admission criteria for a listing on the AQSE Growth Market is to have at least 24 months of audited accounts

19   **A**   The rules aim to restrict the commingling of client's and firm's assets and minimise the risk of client's investments being used by the firm without the client's agreement or contrary to the client's wishes, or being treated as the firm's assets in the event of its insolvency

20   **C**   Market abuse is a civil offence within the Market Abuse Regime (MAR), not a criminal offence, although there is a criminal regime for insider dealing within the Criminal Justice Act 1993. The FCA is likely to start with an investigation based on breaches of the civil market abuse regime

21   **A**   A firm receiving a complaint must, within eight weeks of the receipt, send the complainant either a final response, or a written response that explains why the firm is not in a position to make a final response, and informs the complainant that they may now refer the complaint to the FOS. The complaint must normally be referred to the FOS within six months

22   **A**   The aim of the appropriateness check is to determine whether the client has the experience and knowledge to be able to understand the risks involved. The firm must ask the client to provide information about their knowledge and experience in the investment area, so as to

enable the firm to assess whether the product or services envisaged are appropriate for the client

23 **A** The Securities and Exchange Commission (SEC) is the relevant US regulator for securities exchanges. Please note that the Securities and Exchange Commission (SEC) and the Commodity Futures Trading Commission (CFTC) regulate derivatives exchanges in the USA

24 **C** Information on past performance must include appropriate information covering at least the five preceding years, or the whole period the investment service has been offered/provided, or the whole period the financial index has been established if less than five years

25 **C** The client's attitude to risk can be regarded as a 'soft' fact. Hard facts cover personal information, such as name, address, date of birth, National Insurance number, state of health, marital status, residence and domicile status, employment details and family details. Levels of current income assets and liabilities are also hard facts

26 **C** Gifts between spouses are exempt, if spouses are domiciled in the UK. Where one spouse is non-domiciled, the exemption available on transfers to the non-domiciled spouse is limited to £325,000, the same as the IHT nil rate band

27 **C** The others are all potentially correct advice. Annual exemptions are allocated chronologically during the tax year, however. CLTs are immediately chargeable to IHT so these should be done first to avoid the PETs using up the annual exemptions

28 **D** A Gift with Reservation (GWR) would best describe this arrangement. The gift with reservation rules means that it is difficult to gift wealth away and still retain any benefit, such as giving away a holiday home to the children but continuing to use the holiday home without paying full market rent

29 **500,000** As Martin continues to use the house rent-free, it would be treated as if it were still part of his estate and its full value at the time of death would be added to his estate

30 **637,500** The unused portion of Martin's wife's nil rate band would be added to his own nil rate band at his death. This would be (£162,500/£325,000) = 50% × £425,000 = £212,500 plus the nil rate band on death of £425,000, which gives a value of **£637,500**

31 **C** The Financial Conduct Authority (FCA) has used principles and outcomes-based regulation to promote ethical and fair outcomes. The regulators' philosophy has been characterised as resting not per se on principles, but rather on judging the consequences of the actions of the firms and the individuals supervised: this is what is meant by outcomes-focused regulation

32 **C** The CFA Code of Ethics does not specifically address the issue of remuneration. The CFA Code of Ethics requires a firm and its employees to:

1. Act with loyalty to their clients and act with reasonable care and exercise prudent judgment;

2. Deal fairly and objectively with all clients when providing investment analysis, making investment recommendations, taking investment action, or engaging in other professional activities;

3. Provide suitable recommendations when in an advisory relationship;

4. Provide fair, accurate and complete information when communicating investment performance information; and

5. Preserve confidentiality of client information unless the information concerns illegal activities, disclosure is required by regulation or is permitted by the client

33   **C**   The CMA has up to 40 days to undertake an initial (phase one) study of a merger. If the CMA believes the merger will lead to a 'substantial lessening of competition', then it will normally move to a phase two investigation. Phase two decisions are taken by independent panels of experts. There is a statutory time limit of 12 weeks following the Phase two decision for remedies to be implemented

34   **D**   The Criminal Justice Act 1993 (CJA) provides certain defences to insider dealing, including an individual who passes on information in the proper performance of their duties but did not expect the recipient to deal; also, where the deal was not done to make a profit or avoid a loss; also, where a market-maker had inside information in the course of their business, but acted genuinely for that business. Price stabilisation is also a valid defence. As a friend of the director, you are only an insider if you 'know' it is inside information, and therefore are not committing an offence

35   **C**   CGT for additional rate taxpayers is charged at a rate of 20% assuming the disposal is non-residential, otherwise it would be 28%

36   **B**   The ability to compensate those who have suffered losses from the failure of regulated firms rests with the Financial Services Compensation Scheme (FSCS) and not the FCA

37   **D**   Market makers and stabilised securities are special defences regarding insider dealing. The Criminal Justice Act 1993 (CJA) provides certain defences to insider dealing, including an individual who passes on information in the proper performance of their duties but did not expect the recipient to deal, and where the deal was not done to make a profit or avoid a loss

38   **C**   The best execution rule is aimed at protecting both retail and professional clients. Professional clients cannot opt out of best execution. The term 'all investors' would include eligible counterparties

39   **C**   Prices can move dramatically from one day to another so when seeking 'best execution' today, yesterday's price is not relevant. When determining what the best possible result is, firms must take into account price, costs, speed, likelihood of execution and settlement, size, nature or any other consideration that is relevant to the execution of the order

40   **C**   YBG Partners is using the net negative add-back method to perform its internal client money reconciliations. This method is only available to certain types of asset management firm and loan-based crowdfunding firms, and only if the firm does not undertake margined transactions for clients

41   **D**   All three are Principles for Businesses

42   **B**   Ancillary function is not a controlled function. There are five categories of controlled functions: a) governing functions; b) required functions; c) systems and control functions; d) significant management functions; and e) customer functions

Please note that these have effectively been replaced by the Senior Managers Regime (SMR) for individuals who are subject to regulatory approval; the Certification Regime that requires relevant firms to assess the fitness and propriety of certain employees who could pose a risk of significant harm to the firm or any of its customers; and the Conduct rules replacing the statement of principle and approved person code, which are applicable to all staff , except for a few specific roles such as security, catering and cleaning staff. (The CFA UK Official Training Manual still has some information on controlled functions)

43   **D**   The Money Laundering Regulations deal with the institutional liability and require a firm to have all of these activities in place

44   **D**   The risk with a defined contribution (DC) pension scheme is very much with the employee. The other three options are different ways of describing the same type of scheme (defined benefit, also known as a final salary scheme) where the investment risk is borne by the employer

45   **B**   The settlement of gilts is carried out through CREST, which operates a computerised (electronic, dematerialised) settlement system for its members, including GEMMS and large banks. The settlement period is T+1

46   **D**   The rate of Corporation Tax is 19%. A UK-resident company is liable to corporation tax on its worldwide profits and chargeable gains arising in an accounting period. For the financial year 2022 (1 April 2022 to 31 March 2023), companies must pay a single rate of corporation tax at 19% of their profits

47   **B**   It is not effective until the local law has been changed

48   **C**   These are also known as potentially exempt transfers (PETs). A potentially exempt transfer (PET) is a lifetime gift that is free of IHT if the person who makes the gift lives for seven years after the gift is made

49   **C**   For financial firms, it is the General Data Protection Regulation (GDPR) that will govern their data protection responsibilities, and the Information Commissioner's Office (ICO) will monitor implementation and compliance with the GDPR. Under the GDPR, if there is a personal data breach, an organisation must notify the ICO within 72 hours of the breach and, in certain high-risk circumstances, they must contact the individuals to whom the personal data relates without undue delay

50   **D**   While compliance is not strictly required, companies should explain where they do not comply with the codes. The UK Corporate Governance Code is not a rigid set of rules. It consists of principles and provisions. The Corporate Governance Code therefore adopts a 'comply or explain' basis

51   **B**   A multilateral trading facility (MTF) provides an alternative order matching system to an exchange. The client orders match with other clients so the firm operating the system does not take proprietary positions

52   **D**   Stamp duty land tax (SDLT) is payable on that part of the £575,000 purchase price falling within each band. (0% × £125,000) + (2% x next £125,000) + (5% × £325,000) = (£0 + £2,500 + £16,250) = £18,750.

Residential SDLT rates

£0 to £125,000 at 0%; £125,001 to £250,000 at 2%; £250,001 to £925,000 at 5%;

£925,001 to £1,500,000 at 10%; Over £1,500,000 at 12%

53   **D**   Inheritance tax is not payable when the estate passes to a spouse or civil partner. The half of the estate transferred to the children is covered by the nil rate band, and the remaining 50% nil rate band is transferred to the surviving spouse

54   **A**   When a firm executes an order following specific instructions from the client, it should be treated as having satisfied its best execution obligations only in respect of the part or aspect of the order to which the client instructions relate. The fact that the client has given specific

instructions which cover one part or aspect of the order should not be treated as releasing the firm from its best execution obligations in respect of any other parts or aspects of the client order that are not covered by such instructions

55   **D**   Cash deposit ISAs carry a 14 day cancellation period. A retail client has a right to cancel a packaged product within 14 calendar days – this includes cash ISAs. For life policies and pension (including personal and stakeholder pension) schemes the cancellation period is 30 calendar days. Cancellation rights apply to transactions that have been advised or that are subject to the distance selling rules.

56   **D**   All are real liabilities, rising through inflation

57   **D**   All are examples of investment risk. The risk that the investment may be worth less in future than it is today, which is known as capital risk. Interest rate risk relates to the fact that the Bank of England base rate is likely to change over time, which ultimately feeds through to the rates of interest paid on deposit accounts. Shortfall risk is the risk that the investment return will literally fall short of the amount required for the investor to meet their objectives

58   **B**   The Mental Capacity Act 2005 sets out a single 'decision-specific' test for assessing whether a person lacks capacity to take a particular decision at a particular time. The Mental Capacity Act 2005 created the Lasting Power of Attorney (LPA). There are two types of LPA. The 'property and affairs' LPA gives a person the ability to make decisions about somebody else's financial affairs. Secondly, the 'personal welfare' LPA gives a person the ability to make decisions relating to somebody else's personal healthcare and welfare, including decisions to give or refuse consent to treatment on their behalf

59   **D**   Premium bonds are National Savings and Investments (NS&I) products, and are tax-exempt. Trade bills, such as cheques/other bills of exchange, are excluded from the definition of a specified investment, as is buying real estate or land. Please note that Treasury bills of exchange are regarded as specified investments

60   **C**   The firm must comply with the ruling of the Financial Ombudsman Service (FOS). If the complainant accepts the determination, it is binding on the firm, but if the complainant rejects the determination, the firm is not bound by it. A determination can be a money award or a direction. The maximum money award the FOS can make is £375,000 for complaints referred aft er 1 April 2022

61   **B**   The City Code applies to all UK public companies, both listed and unlisted. It also applies to certain private companies where the company has been listed in the last ten years

62   **B**   The statutory period is 40 working days. The Competition and Markets Authority (CMA) has up to 40 days to undertake an initial (phase one) study of a merger. If the CMA believes the merger will lead to a 'substantial lessening of competition', then it will normally move to a phase two investigation

63   **B**   Under Standard IVC – Responsibilities of Supervisors, members may delegate supervisory duties to subordinates but delegation does not relieve them of their supervisory responsibilities. Any investment professionals with employees subject to their control or influence are considered to have supervisory responsibilities, and are required to take steps to prevent anyone under their supervision from violating the law or the Code and Standards

64 **B** A controlling interest is where a company owns more than 50% of another company. If a company owns 30% of the shares, this is known as 'effective control', rather than legal control (> 50%)

65 **D** The various groups with an interest of some kind in the business and its activities are termed stakeholders and would include all of the groups mentioned

66 **B** The Financial Policy Committee (FPC) is a Committee at the Bank of England, with responsibilities in macro-prudential ('systemic') regulation and in the monitoring of stability and resilience in the financial system. Therefore, the FPC monitors and responds to systemic risks

67 **B** This is one aspect of the accountability of the FCA to the Treasury

68 **B** As Mrs Rodriguez is an employee of a FCA authorised firm, to prevent conflicts of interest she must comply with the personal account dealing requirements in her contract of employment

69 **A** Trustees will generally only be considered to be conducting investment business if paid for their services, as trustees who do not hold themselves out to the market as providing a service are on the list of excluded activities. Secondly, a media publication is also an example of an excluded activity, that does not require authorisation. However, tip sheets are a specific example of a publication that would require authorisation. The Perimeter Guidance Manual (PERG) contains guidance about circumstances in which authorisation is required, or exempt person status is available, including guidance on the activities regulated under the FSMA 2000 and the exclusions that are available, known as 'excluded activities'

70 **D** The maximum award per claim, in relation to protected investment business, would be 100% of the first £85,000, which would result in an award of the full £40,000

71 **B** The law recognises 'artificial persons' in the form of corporations. A legal person has rights, protections, privileges, responsibilities and liabilities under law, just as natural persons do. Common examples of legal persons include companies, sovereign states and co-operatives. A natural person is a human person, ie an individual

72 **C** A financial promotion is an invitation or inducement that aims to persuade the recipient to engage in investment activity. However, communications related to takeovers are subject to the Takeover Code, and not the financial promotion rules

73 **A** MiFID II requires firms to enter into a basic written agreement with professional clients as well as retail clients, and this must be done for each investment service or ancillary service, not just for new clients

74 **D** The only types of regulated firms outside the common platform are insurers, managing agents, and the Society of Lloyd's. Very few firms are outside the scope of the common platform organisational requirements

75 **B** Directly held shares are not in a packaged form and so are not included within the definition of RIPs. OEIC shares, investment trust shares and SIPPs are all within the definition of RIPs, whether or not the investments are held in an ISA or child trust fund. SIPPs are capable of holding commercial property, subject to the SIPP provider's own rules

76 **C** The best execution rule is aimed at protecting both retail and professional clients. Professional clients cannot opt out of best execution. The term 'investors generally' would include eligible counterparties

77 **D** All of these are required. The periodic statement will include a statement of the contents and the valuation of the portfolio, including details of each financial instrument held, its market value, or fair value if market value is unavailable and the cash balance at the beginning and at the end of the reporting period, and the performance of the portfolio during the reporting period. It will also include the total amount of fees and charges incurred during the reporting period, itemising at least total management fees and total costs associated with execution, and including, a statement that a more detailed breakdown will be provided on request

78 **D** A complaint may be dealt with under the Financial Ombudsman Service (FOS) only if it is brought by, or on behalf of, an eligible complainant. An eligible complainant could be a private individual or a small business, charity or trust (within specified limits)

79 **A** Where a party has concerns over a decision made by the FCA, it may appeal to the Tax and Chancery Chamber of the Upper Tribunal, known as the Upper Tribunal. The Upper Tribunal will conduct a complete rehearing of FCA enforcement and authorisation cases where the firm or individual and the FCA have not been able to agree the outcome

80 **B** Regulatory requirements on conflicts of interest aim to protect the interests of the client. Potential conflicts of interest occur between the firm (including individual employees) and clients, and between different clients of the same firm

81 **A** This is the best available answer. This is because the personal account dealing rules apply to employee trading where a conflict of interest arises. These rules apply to any relevant person who is involved in activities that may give rise to a conflict of interest, or who has access to inside information as defined in the Market Abuse Regulation (MAR), or to other confidential information relating to clients or transactions with or for clients by virtue of an activity carried out by the person on behalf of the firm

82 **D** Pre-publication drafts can be previewed by the issuer only for the purpose of verifying compliance

83 **B** The market abuse regime is a civil offence regime, and so no jail sentence is available, although insider dealing is a criminal offence within the Criminal Justice Act 1993. An approved person could face FCA disciplinary action

84 **D** The other activities must be carried out before selecting the funds in which to invest. The financial planning process should ideally adopt the following sequence:

1. Establish and define the client–personal financial planner relationship;

2. Gather client data and determine goals and expectations;

3. Analyse and evaluate the client's financial status;

4. Develop and present the plan;

5. Implement the financial planning recommendations; and

6. Monitor the financial plan and the financial planning relationship

85 **A** A poll vote may be called by shareholders having 10% of the total voting rights, or by five members who are entitled to vote, or by the Chairman. A proxy may demand, or join in demanding, a poll